Ecumenism in Retreat

How the United Reformed Church
Failed to Break the Mould

MARTIN CAMROUX
Foreword by David Cornick

WIPF & STOCK · Eugene, Oregon

Wipf & Stock
An Imprint of Wipf and Stock Publishers
199 W. 8th Ave., Suite 3
Eugene, OR 97401

www.wipfandstock.com

PAPERBACK ISBN 13: 978-1-4982-3400-9
HARDCOVER ISBN 13: 978-1-4982-3402-3

Manufactured in the U.S.A.   05/16/2016

Contents

Foreword

ECUMENISM WAS A DOMINANT narrative in twentieth-century church life in Western Europe. It was the hope of those generations who knew too well the legacies of religious hatred (particularly between Catholic and Protestant) and the nationalisms that were potent factors in two world wars. Lest we forget, its achievements were considerable. In England in particular it played no small part in defusing the culture wars between Protestant and Catholic, and Nonconformist and Anglican, which had been established in the long years of the English reformations. On the global stage in 1964 it led to the first meeting between a Pope and an Ecumenical Patriarch since the Council of Florence in 1439. Institutionally, it established a series of national and international meeting places (for that is what a "council" is) between Christians across the world that were the ecclesiastical equivalent of the League of Nations and the United Nations. In doing so it brought North and South and East and West into conversation. All the raw pain of colonialism and living under totalitarianism found its way to the surface in the deliberations of the World Council of Churches. What is surprising is not that there was so little agreement, but that there was so much, as Christians with profoundly different backgrounds and experiences recognised that despite their differences being "in Christ" was somehow a greater reality.

In England, as in many parts of the world, the heady enthusiasm of the 1950s and early 1960s led to the hope that "full visible unity" might be made manifest in (at least) a united Protestant church that would include the Church of England, the churches of the Reformation, and the Methodist Church. It was a dream that floundered by the narrowest of margins. The story of the formation of the United Reformed Church in 1972 cannot be divorced from that context—it was, indeed, the first union of churches of different traditions in England since the Reformation. It was intended as a short-lived catalyst on the way to wider union. This book explains why that was not to be, and as it does so it reveals the shortcomings of a particular interpretation of the ecumenical imperative.

Some books are costly to write because they reach to the roots of who we are and what we believe. This is such a book, written by a United Reformed Church minister who was himself caught up in that dream, working generously and wholeheartedly in ecumenical contexts. What was felt on the pulses in pastorates is here balanced with careful archival research and innovative use of oral history. The result is a case study in ecumenism that is all the more valuable and timely as ecumenists acknowledge the shortcomings of some paradigms that were formative half a century ago, and search for those which can express today the unity of Christ's ever more diverse people.

David Cornick
Churches Together in England and Robinson College, Cambridge

Acknowledgments

THIS BOOK IS BASED on my PhD thesis at Anglia Ruskin University, which provided me with a delightful oasis of quiet and peace in the midst of what was then a busy life. I am grateful to my family, my wife Margaret and my wonderful children, Eleanor and Michael, both for the practical help they have offered by checking my manuscript for the seemingly endless grammatical errors and for their willingness to forego our normal discussions at dinner over the relevance of Kant's critique of the ontological proof for the existence of God (or the like) for rather more arcane discussions such as the distinction between qualitative and quantitative research. I am especially grateful to my son, Michael, the historian in the family, for his willingness to share his dissertation on Seebohm Rowntree with me.

Anglia Ruskin University's system of external supervision has enabled me to benefit from the endless encouragement and encyclopaedic understanding of the Revd. Dr. David Cornick, General Secretary of Churches Together in England, and before that Principal of Westminster College Cambridge and General Secretary of the United Reformed Church. Without David's gentle support this thesis would not even have been conceivable. It has been a pleasure too to confirm that behind the façade of David's Barthian exterior lies a genuinely liberal spirit. My supervisors at Anglia Ruskin, first Dr. Mary Abbot and then, for most of the degree, Professor Sarah Brown, were both hugely helpful.

Beyond that a number of friends gave me invaluable support. Dr. David Peel, formerly Principal of Northern College, Manchester, read some of my chapters with a rigour which reflected the sharpness of his mind and his great personal kindness. The Rev. David Lawrence gave me huge encouragement to take a critical view of the United Reformed Church. Professor Malcolm Payne also kindly looked at my manuscript in the midst of a busy life. I am grateful to Margaret Thompson at the Reformed Studies Library at Westminster College and the staff of Dr Williams's Library and Lambeth Palace Library, at all of which I spent many happy hours. At Dr Williams's Library it was good to meet on occasions with Dr. Alan Argent, whose spirited advocacy of independency helped confirm my commitment to the United Reformed Church. I am grateful also to the Rev. John Proctor of Westminster College, who first put me in touch with Anglia Ruskin when I began enquiring about the possibility of a PhD. I am also very grateful to Nathan Rhoads, my copy editor, for his patience in attempting to sort out my grammatical infelicities.

Vital to this research has been the interviewing of many of those involved in the United Reformed Church and the wider ecumenical movement. Apart from some of those mentioned I am therefore grateful to the Rev. Dr. Brian Beck, Professor Clyde Binfield, the Rev. Ronald Bocking, John Bradley, Dr. Stephen Brain, the Rev. Tony Burnham, the Rev. Graham Cook, the Rev. Christine Craven, the Rev. Martin Cressey, the Rev. Michael Dales, the Rev. Michael Davies, the Rev. Michael Dunford, Bob Fyffe, the Rev. George Gibson, Dr. David Gooch, the Rev. Dr. Kenneth Greet, the Rev. Donald Hilton, the Rev. Michael Hopkins, Dr. Diana Jones, the Rev. Ernest Marvin, the Rev. Sheila Maxey, the Rev. Dr. Stephen Orchard, the Rev. Alan Paterson, the Rev. Dr. Roger Paul, Norman Pooler, the Rev. John Reardon, the Rev. John Richardson, the Rev. Dr. Alan Sell, the Rev. Dr. John Sutcliffe, the Rev. Dr. Colin Thompson, the Rev. Dr. David Thompson, the Rev. Tony Tucker, the Rev. Ernesto Lozada-Uzuriaga Steele, and Mrs. Margaret Williams. Not the least of the pleasure in talking with them were the lunches some of them provided and in other cases the shared meals in restaurants. In the light of the history of the ecumenical movement the fact that some of the best of these meals were at the Athenaeum Hotel seemed linguistically appropriate.

I am grateful to the Coward Trust, the United Reformed Church Ministerial Education programme, and Trinity United Reformed and Methodist Church Sutton, for entirely funding my research between them.

Abbreviations

ACTS	Action of Churches Together in Scotland
AEE	Areas of Ecumenical Experiment
BCC	British Council of Churches
CCBI	Council of Churches in Britain and Ireland
CCLEPE	Consultative Committee for Local Ecumenical Projects in England
CICCU	Cambridge Inter-Collegiate Christian Union
C of E	Church of England
CTBI	Churches Together in Britain and Ireland
CTE	Churches Together in England
CUS	Congregational Union in Scotland
CYTUN	Churches Together in Wales
EFCC	Evangelical Federation of Congregational Churches
FIEC	Fellowship of Independent Evangelical Churches
GEAR	Group for Evangelism and Renewal
IVF	Inter-Varsity Fellowship
LEP	Local Ecumenical Project or Local Ecumenical Partnership
PCE	Presbyterian Church of England
SCM	Student Christian Movement
URC	United Reformed Church
WCC	World Council of Churches
WSCF	World Student Christian Federation
YMCA	Young Men's Christian Association

1

Ecumenical Renewal

IN HIS ENTHRONEMENT SERMON in 1942 William Temple famously declared the ecumenical movement to be "the great new fact of our era,"[1] and for much of the twentieth century it was the major metanarrative for church renewal. By the end of the century, however, the enthusiasm had largely dissipated, the organizations which represented it were in decline, and the hoped for organic unity looked further away than ever. In this book I want to study this ecumenical failure through the prism of the United Reformed Church, which was formed in 1972 by a union of the Congregational and Presbyterian Churches, and saw its formation as a catalyst for ecumenical renewal. As the only church union across denominational boundaries in England (with the minor exception of its own union with the Churches of Christ in 1981) it offers a unique perspective on the ecumenical movement. It has been almost entirely neglected as a subject for academic research and offers considerable opportunities for original research.

It was Plato who said that "the unexamined life is not worth living"[2] and this story is part of my life. The mid-1960s was an exciting time to be a Christian. John Robinson's *Honest to God* (1963) had fired me with the conviction that the church could change and be renewed and that you could bring a total honesty to the religious search. Nothing was off limits. Everything was possible. Then, while a student at the University of Hull from 1966 to 1969, I met ecumenism. I joined the Congregational-Baptist

1. Temple, *Church Looks Forward*, 2.
2. Plato, *Plato in Twelve Volumes*, 1:38a.

Society, the Methodist Society, and the Student Christian Movement. I enjoyed bread-and-cheese lunches at the Anglican and Catholic chaplaincies and in the Quaker chaplain office. I became Chairman of the ecumenical Christian Association (which united the different denominational student societies) and led ecumenical meetings and conferences. Like John Robinson it seemed to me that that the existence of so many churches was "an abomination . . . surely now on its way out . . . and the prayers and actions of all Christians must be engaged in furthering the movements towards organic unity at every level."[3] But this was only the beginning. A great renewal of the church was imminent. From the perspective of the Roman Catholic Church, but with wider application, Michael Novak could conclude:

> Old patterns are dissolving. In such a time, The Spirit's activity is almost tangible. . . . The jesters of the fountains smile and say "This too shall pass," but meanwhile an age of creativity has begun.[4]

In retrospect it is clear that much of this was not thought through. I assumed organic unity was right because it was the prevailing zeitgeist of the circles in which I moved. It never occurred to me to compare it with other models of unity, or ask whether I would want to belong to an established church, or indeed if church unity was really a matter of concern to anyone outside the church. I hardly noticed that the evangelical Christian Union did not share our enthusiasm and had little contact with the rest of us, or we with them. Everywhere barriers were coming down, the spirit moving. As John Robinson put it, "Faith has been let loose."[5]

Meanwhile my own Congregational Church, under the strong guidance of its General Secretary, John Huxtable, was moving to a union with the Presbyterians, which would break the ecumenical logjam and be the first step towards the wider union we all looked for. It became for me a life commitment. Ordained as a United Reformed Church minister in 1975, of the four churches I have served three were in local ecumenical partnerships, including two joint URC-Methodist churches. This book is an attempt to reflect historically, theologically, and sociologically upon my experience and the ecumenical hope I have cherished.

I make no claim to be a detached observer. I am a twenty-first-century, white, male, British Christian from a liberal Reformed tradition

---

3. Robinson, *New Reformation?*, 25.

4. Novak, *Open Church*, 362.

5. Ibid., 18.

whose working life has been committed to the ecumenical movement. It is impossible for me to be a value-neutral observer. Inevitably my beliefs will influence my judgement and the point in history from which I observe will affect what I see. As the theologian Rudolf Bultmann has insisted, the "demand that the interpreter must silence his subjectivity and extinguish his individuality . . . is . . . the most absurd one that can be imagined."[6]

This does not mean that the attempt to write" objective history should be set aside. Historians and theologians will have views but should seek not to allow them to dictate their conclusions. Richard Evans puts the historian's task powerfully: "I will look humbly at the past and say . . . it really happened, and we really can, if we are very scrupulous and careful and self-critical . . . find out how it happened and reach some tenable though always less than final conclusions about what it all meant."[7] That is what has been attempted in this book. We may choose our research area and questions according to our preferences, but not our conclusions.

SECULARIZATION THEORY

The sociological context both for ecumenism in general and for the history of the United Reformed Church in particular is a secularizing society. Secularization theory is one of the classic metanarratives of the sociology of religion and originates with one of the founding fathers of sociology, Max Weber, and his interpretation of modernity. Its meaning was well expressed by Bryan Wilson in his *Religion in a Secular Society*, where he defined secularization as a process by which "Religion—seen as a way of thinking, as the performance of particular practices, and the institutionalisation and organization of these patterns of thought and action—has lost influence . . . in western societies."[8] Today it is a sharply contested concept with options ranging from Steve Bruce's conviction that *God Is Dead* (2002) to John Micklethwait and Adrian Wooldridge's belief that *God Is Back* (2010). The suggestion is sometimes made that secularization is an ideological anti-religious concept. It is certainly true that to Marxists, and to positivists like Comte, the decline of religion was an inevitable part of progress. Weber, while not welcoming the "disenchantment of the world," nonetheless saw the rationalization of society as inexorable and Wilson, deeply influenced

6. Bultmann, "Problem of Hermeneutics," 255.

7. Evans, *In Defence of History*, 253.

8. Wilson, *Religion in Secular Society*, 11.

3

by Weber, expected that as traditional societies modernized they too would secularize.

The recent history of religions has not entirely supported this expectation. In the most technologically advanced society in the world, the United States, religion still plays a vital part in cultural and political life as it does in new emergent economies like South Korea. Secularization is not an obvious feature of African societies and in the Islamic world there appears to be desecularization with increasing Islamic influence on government and society and the growth of Salafist Islam. In Europe immigration has led to multi-faith diversity and Pentecostalism is making rapid progress in South America and Africa and, to some extent, Europe as well. This is very far from the situation that Comte, Marx, or Weber expected.

Although some like Bruce still maintain a largely unchanged view of secularization there has been a great deal of revisionism. Some would see it as merely a European phenomenon not replicated elsewhere. Some former exponents of secularization have recanted. Peter Berger, for example, is now offering a critique of the idea that religion is on the decline at all.[9] Harvey Cox, who in the 1960s became famous by announcing the arrival of *The Secular City* (1965), came to believe that secularization was *The Myth of the Twentieth Century* (2000). Even in Britain some commentators are now arguing that what is taking place is not secularization but the resacralization of society and Heelas and Woodhead claim to see a spiritual revolution taking place.[10] In this scenario we are witnessing a tectonic shift in the sacred landscape in which Christianity is replaced by spirituality. In what may be an important clarification Grace Davie argues that far from the undoubted secularization of Europe being typical, it is in fact exceptional. There is, she argues, scant evidence for secularization not only in the United States but also in Latin America, Sub-Saharan Africa, and parts of Asia. Thus Davie concludes, "Secularisation is essentially a European phenomenon and is extrinsic rather than intrinsic to the modernising process per se."[11] A counterargument offered by Bruce is that the societal impact of the new spiritualities is small, that the decline of religious institutions in Europe is continuing and that there is considerable evidence of growing secularization in the United States and in the new economies of Asia.

9. Berger, "Secularism in Retreat."

10. Heelas and Woodhead, *Spiritual Revolution*.

11. Davie, *Europe*, 161.

A major attempted revision of secularization theory has been that of Callum Brown, who argues that, far from secularization being a long-term trend in British society, "quite suddenly in 1963, something very profound ruptured the character of the nation, and its people, sending organised Christianity on a downward spiral to the margins of social significance."[12] Changing attitudes expressed in, for example, pop music destroyed the concept of the traditional woman committed to a home-based culture and so led to the death of pious femininity. Since religious life centred upon a feminine culture this was disastrous for the church. This perspective has been vigorously contested by Green, who, drawing heavily on Rowntree, argues that the long-held link between the English people and the Protestant faith was lost in the period from 1920 to 1960.[13] He charts the decline of church attendance, the collapse of the Sunday schools, the abandoning of Sunday observance, and the widening gulf between the churches and the general culture.

Another major challenge to secularization theory is what is known as rational choice theory, which draws upon economics and stresses supply-side factors in religious growth. Rodney Stark, Roger Finke, and Laurence Iannaccone argue that a free and competitive religious market creates greater religious diversity and choice and more vital religion. By contrast, state monopolies lead to religious stagnation.[14] Where religion has declined therefore the problem is not secularization but insufficiently competitive religion. The ideological grounding of this in American capitalism is obvious and many of its assumptions, such as that the demand for religion is constant, are dubious. As a general explanatory model this seems to fail. In Europe homogeneous Catholic and Orthodox societies such as Spain, Ireland, and Greece have higher rates of church attendance than heterogeneous Protestant ones like Britain. Chaves and Gorski tested twenty-six articles or chapters that sought to analyze the links between religious plurality and high rates of religious attendance, noted that only 12 percent of examples given appeared to support the paradigm, and concluded: "The empirical evidence contradicts the claim that religious pluralism is positively associated with religious participation in any general sense."[15] We

---

12. Brown, *Death of Christian Britain*, 1.

13. Green, *Passing of Protestant England*.

14. See, for example, Stark, *Triumph of Christianity*.

15. Chaves and Gorski, "Religious Pluralism."

should not, however, rule out the possibility that it may have relevance in particular contexts, including the growth of new churches in England.

It is beyond the scope of this book to attempt a comprehensive theory of secularization. It is, however, my contention that Green is right in arguing that there has been a long experience of secularization in British culture. As he says, "A significant process of secularization did happen in Britain."[16] The history of the United Reformed Church and its predecessors is explicable only within that context.

ECUMENICAL ORIGINS

The ecumenical movement is about the visible unity of the church. According to its constitution the first purpose of the World Council of Churches is "to call the churches to the goal of visible unity in one faith and Eucharistic fellowship expressed in worship and common life in Christ, and to advance towards that unity in order that the world may believe."[17]

The origins of the ecumenical movement are complex. In its most fundamental sense one can trace its origins to the New Testament, but in its modern form assertions like "the World Missionary Conference, Edinburgh, 1910, was the birth place of the modern ecumenical movement"[18] are commonly made. This is an oversimplification. Edinburgh was essentially a missionary conference not an ecumenical one. Indeed it is ironic that the international committee responsible for the Conference explicitly rejected the term *ecumenical* as a self-description, on the grounds that the use of the term was not only clumsy but misleading, since a real ecumenical conference would have considered a wider range of subjects and would have included other historic churches that were not represented there. John H. Ritson, Secretary of the British and Foreign Bible Society, observed that the word ecumenical had been dropped, "as it cannot be used truthfully while great sections of the Church are in no way connected with the Conference."[19]

Even viewed as primarily a missionary conference, Edinburgh was not the originator of international cooperation. There had been earlier international missionary conferences beginning in New York and London in 1854

16. Green, *Passing of Protestant England*, 311.

17. Kinnamon and Cope, *Ecumenical Movement*, 469.

18. Latourette, "Ecumenical Bearings, 362.

19. Ritson, letter to H. Smith, 2008.

and ecumenical cooperation could be seen much earlier in, for example, the formation of the London Missionary Society in 1795 by evangelical Anglicans and Nonconformists. Nonetheless it remains true that Edinburgh did set up a Continuation Committee, which led to the International Missionary Council and gave rise to organizational patterns leading to the creation of the World Council of Churches (WCC). It is also true that, as Brian Stanley argues, it reflected an "ill-defined yet inescapable consciousness forming in the minds of the participants in June 1910 that a new dawn was breaking for Christianity."[20]

Along with the international missionary movement, the other seed-ground of ecumenism was student Christian activism and this again had begun well prior to 1910. The Young Men's Christian Association (YMCA) originated in London in 1844 and then spread to the United States, where it drew support from virtually all the main Protestant denominations. One of those influenced by the YMCA was the American layman John Mott, who was to be the leading figure in the founding of the international World Student Christian Federation (WSCF) in 1895, with its watchword, "The evangelization of the world in this generation." The British section, the Student Christian Movement (SCM), was to be of central importance in the growth of ecumenism and in 1908 when the SCM held a national conference at Liverpool, over the exit were the words *Ut omnes unum sint*, "that they all may be one" (John 17:21). In his history of the SCM Robin Boyd notes that by this date "Unity was already being added to mission."[21]

ECUMENICAL MOTIVATION

The motivation for the ecumenical movement is much disputed. Those involved naturally saw this as a reflection of God's will for the church, as New Delhi proclaimed that "Unity . . . is both God's will and his gift to the Church."[22] Many like John Huxtable saw Christian disunity as reason to be ashamed.[23] This, however, prompts the question of what motivated them at this particular point in history to come to this discovery. The cynical answer is that it was primarily a reaction to church decline. So John Kent argues, "The mounting hostility of western society to organized Christian-

20. Stanley, "World Missionary Conference," 26.

21. Boyd, *Witness of the Student Christian Movement*, 9.

22. Wainwright, *Ecumenical Movement*, 61.

23. Huxtable, *New Hope*, 15–16.

ity, the formation of anti-Christian movements—Fascism, Marxism, third world nationalism, the weakness of the individual churches as generators of the idea of God in human society—all these factors pushed institutional Christianity towards organic unity of some kind."[24] Similarly from a sociological perspective Bryan Wilson sees essentially the same process at work: "this process has in part been a growing recognition of the essential weakness of religious life in the increasingly secularized society. The spirit has descended on the waters and brought peace between churchmen of different persuasions only as those churchmen have recognized their essential marginality in modern society."[25] To Wilson ecumenism represented the willingness of churches to abandon theological belief systems in the interests of survival.

That there is a connection here is difficult to doubt. Many of the pioneers were explicit about it. As long ago as 1918 J. H. Shakespeare, then General Secretary of the Baptist Union, advocating union within Nonconformity and between it and the Anglicans, spoke of the "ugliness and folly of our divisions" and argued that the decline in church attendance "is a very serious call to set our house in order, and to arrest a decline which otherwise implies that the denominations slowly bleed to death."[26] It is clearly the case, as Morris observes, that in both Europe and America "The Protestant churches most active in the ecumenical movement in the Twentieth Century were generally those undergoing decline."[27] In Britain, as we shall see, the experience of decline was normally a motivating factor in local ecumenical partnerships and the belief that unity would contribute to evangelism was widespread. To the Methodist Geoffrey Wainwright it seemed that "As long as the communities are not reconciled with one another they can hardly bear convincing witness before the world to Christ's reconciling work, for if the horizontal corollary is not in evidence, even the vertical achievement may be called in question."[28]

In the missionary context the situation is complex but the main motivating factor of the Anglo-Saxon Protestant (often SCM-influenced) missionary leadership was a perceived sense of the weakness of the missionary enterprise. J. H. Oldham, who for a long time was the main shaping figure

24. Kent, *End of the Line*, 118.
25. Wilson, *Religion in Secular Society*, 154.
26. Shakespeare, *Churches at the Cross-Roads*, 72.
27. Morris, *Church in the Modern Age*, 177.
28. Wainwright, *Ecumenical Movement*, 61.

in international missionary work, was clear at Edinburgh about the critical problems facing the missionary church: "In many countries the problem of making Christianity indigenous, and of building up a strong, independent, self-supporting, self-propagating Church is even more pressing than that of securing more foreign missionaries."[29] It was especially in Asia that this pressure was felt and was to produce the major motivation towards ecumenism as a source of mission. As Jeremy Morris points out there was a good deal of triumphalist rhetoric at Edinburgh but there was also a real underlying anxiety. The rise of Japan, the increase of nationalism, and a concern about the growth of Islam all suggested a more difficult missionary environment, while there was a significant recognition of the decline of the church in the Christian heartlands. As one speaker put it, "men are not coming forward as ministers, not coming forward as missionaries, because they are not coming into membership of the Christian Church at all."[30]

None of this means that we can identify church decline as the sole motivating factor in ecumenism. It is certainly true that for some ecumenism was seized upon as a possible way of promoting more effective mission, but it would be quite wrong to imply that some kind of sociological determinism led to a simple motivational cause and effect. Ideology, in this case theological belief, was also important in determining whether ecumenism was seen as an appropriate response to decline. Indeed this book will demonstrate that an acceleration of church decline was to coincide with a decline in ecumenical commitment, directly contrary to the Wilson thesis. Further, as David Thompson perceptively points out, Wilson's assumption that the ecumenical movement involves the surrender or compromising of theological principles is "to take sides in the argument" as to what Christian principles are, and has "clear evaluative as well as descriptive connotations."[31]

Nathaniel Micklem, Principal of the Congregational Mansfield College, was at one time Professor of New Testament at Queen's Theological College in Kingston, Ontario, and a member of the United Church of Canada, which included Methodists, Congregationalists, and Presbyterians. He writes: "One of the considerations that made it hard to return to England later was the thought that once again I should be involved in our

---

29. Oldham, "Editor's Notes," 1.

30. Morris, *Church in the Modern Age*, xix–xx.

31. Thompson, "Motivation of the Ecumenical Movement," 472.

wretched denominational divisions."[32] On what sociological grounds can we assume that this is a surrender or compromise of principle rather than an assertion of it? When he returned to England and to Mansfield College, Micklem found himself with the task of teaching the philosophy of religion. He based his teaching on the first three books of Thomas Aquinas' *Summa Philosophica*. That Aquinas was a Roman Catholic was a matter of indifference to him. Ecumenism was never simply born of weakness but also of genuine discovery of a commonality in Christ and a wider perception of catholicity.

ECUMENISM AND LIBERAL THEOLOGY

The intellectual and theological factors in ecumenism need to be recognized, in particular the relationship between ecumenism and liberal theology. The term liberal theology requires careful definition. It can be defined narrowly in terms of a particular form of nineteenth-century theology. So Daniel Day Williams defines it as:

> the movement in modern Protestantism which during the nineteenth century tried to bring Christian thought into organic unity with the evolutionary world view, the movements for social reconstruction, and the expectations of a 'better world' which dominated the general mind. It is the form of Christian faith in which a prophetic-progressive philosophy of history culminates in the expectation of the coming of the Kingdom of God on earth.[33]

This, however, defines liberal theology by its secondary rather than its primary characteristics and covers only one form of a much wider project. By contrast Gary Dorrien, whose three-volume history, *The Making of American Liberal Theology*, is the most substantive contemporary study of liberal theology, argues that this limited definition underestimates the persistence of the liberal religious tradition and "has the effect of obscuring the liberal origin of ideas that are now taken for granted by most theologians."[34]

The alternative, more comprehensive approach to liberal theology is to see it as an Enlightenment project, with its origin in Kant, Schleiermacher, and Hegel, seeking to mediate religious faith to a skeptical world. I

---

32. Micklem, *Box and the Puppets*, 67.

33. Williams, *God's Grace and Man's Hope*, 22.

34. Dorrien, *The Making of American Liberal Theology 1805–1900*, xv.

therefore define liberal theology as "a contextual relating of the gospel to contemporary culture and knowledge which reflects intellectual criticality and the liberal values of tolerance, openness, and inclusion." This is in line with Gary Dorrien's definition: "Liberal theology seeks to reinterpret the symbols of traditional Christianity in a way that creates a progressive religious alternative to atheistic rationalism and to theologies based on external authority."[35]

None of this is without ambiguity. Not all theologians fall exclusively into one category and liberal theology shapes and interacts with many other theological traditions. Many Anglicans are liberal Catholics and the most influential liberal tradition in the Free Churches is evangelical liberalism. On the other hand those who reject liberalism may still be influenced by liberal ideas. Dorrien argues that even Barth, while asserting the priority of the word of God in a rejection of liberal theology, still "took his doctrine of revelation from Hermann, who got it from Hegel."[36]

As for evangelicalism, Roger Olson in his *A–Z of Evangelical Theology* (2005) argues the term has no precise or agreed meaning and offers seven distinct definitions which only occasionally overlap! One possible approach is to identify it by the use of what has been called the "Bebbington quadrilateral" of biblicism, conversionism, crucicentrism, and activism,[37] but any term that is the self-designation both of Billy Graham and Harry Emerson Fosdick is clearly not without ambiguity. On balance the terms *liberal* and *evangelical* may reveal more than they obscure but it is well always to remember Alfred Korzybski's dictum, "the map is not the territory it represents."[38]

Nonetheless, with whatever caution we qualify the terms, broadly ecumenism has been centered mainly on the liberal Protestant churches and has rarely been influential in conservative fundamentalist denominations. The leadership of the ecumenical movement was never exclusively liberal; at Amsterdam in 1948, for example, the influence of Karl Barth was considerable as was that of Orthodox theologians like Georges Florovsky. Tomkins observed in his journal, "They excommunicate each other and denounce each other as heretics from adjacent chairs."[39] Not surprisingly, Tomkins

35. Ibid., xxiii.

36. Dorrien, *Kantian Reason and Hegelian Spirit*, 471.

37. Bebbington, *Evangelicalism in Modern Britain*, 2–17.

38. Korzybski, "Non-Aristotelian System."

39. Hastings, *Oliver Tomkins*, 71.

commented, "there remains a hard core of disagreement between totally different ways of apprehending the Church of Christ."[40] But if ecumenism was never exclusively liberal, liberals were significantly more involved in ecumenism than any other theological grouping. In America, Gary Dorrien observes of the leaders of twentieth-century Protestantism, "Most of them were ecumenical enough in their liberalism to ascribe a merely secondary significance to historic confessional differences."[41] In England key figures like Oliver Tomkins, J. H. Oldham, and Leonard Hodgson were united by a common liberalism.

A study by Dean Bolden of churches in the United States found a clear theological element in receptiveness to ecumenism—in general, the more liberal a church's theology the more likely it was to be ecumenically committed. Bolden divided churches on a fundamentalist/non-fundamentalist spectrum based on the earlier studies of Glock and Stark, who divided denominations into four categories of liberal, moderate, conservative, and fundamentalist. In this categorization there were twenty-nine fundamentalist denominations and nineteen non-fundamentalist. No fundamentalist denominations scored high on ecumenical activity and nineteen of the twenty-nine fundamentalist bodies scored low.

Cross-Tabulation of Ecumenical Activity by Theology[42]

	Low	Medium	High
Fundamentalist	19	10	0
Non-Fundamentalist	2	7	10

While the religious culture of the USA is significantly different from that of the UK the same general pattern can be discerned here. It is no coincidence then that it was the mostly liberal URC who saw themselves as ecumenical pioneers while the Assemblies of God certainly were not. So for example the Fellowship of Independent Evangelical Churches (FIEC) includes in its statement of belief that its members should not belong to Churches Together because this includes churches that, they believe, fail to exhibit biblical truth.

The role of the SCM in Britain was vital and helps explain the centrality of liberal theology to much of the ecumenical movement. From

40. Ibid. 71.

41. Dorrien, *Making of American Liberal Theology, 1805–1900*, 398.

42. Bolden, "Organizational Characteristics."

the time of the founding of the YMCA in 1844 onwards there had been internal dissent between liberal and conservative tendencies. This intensified with the disaffiliation of the Cambridge Inter-Collegiate Christian Union (CICCU) in 1910 and the formation of the Inter-Varsity Fellowship (IVF) in 1927.[43] SCM and IVF became identified (not entirely unfairly) with liberal and conservative theologies, respectively. Steve Bruce, whose PhD thesis was a comparison between the SCM and the conservative IVF, argues that liberalism was not only associated with the ecumenical movement but "probably essential" to it.[44] This may well be right but there are important qualifications. It is certainly true that the SCM, such a key player in the development of ecumenism in Britain, came out of an evangelical milieu that was evolving in a liberal Protestant direction and was increasingly identified with liberalism. But not all the theologians associated with SCM were necessarily liberal, for example Barth, Berdyaev, and Brunner. SCM also gave a welcome to the biblical theology movement, which was in some ways a reaction against liberalism.

Nonetheless, liberalism was highly influential in the SCM and one of their central differences with the conservative evangelical IVF was the priority they gave to ecumenism. So Lesslie Newbigin, later to be one of the driving figures in the ecumenical movement, on arriving at Queens College, Cambridge, in 1928 found himself drawn into the liberal SCM:

> There was a lively branch of the Student Christian Movement. . . . They were committed to their faith and ready to talk about it, but also open to difficult questions and ready to take me as I was— interested but sceptical and basically unconvinced. I never felt that they were trying to 'get at me,' as I did about the 'evangelical group.'[45]

Newbigin was just one of a whole generation of seminal figures of the ecumenical movement in its most creative period whose SCM experience was at the core of their ecumenical vision. Its commitment to "liberal orthodoxy, biblical studies, a concern for Christian unity and social problems"[46] was to influence generations of students in this way. John Richardson, for example, who was to be Ecumenical Secretary for the Methodist Church and would later work for Churches Together in England, says:

43. Boyd, *Witness of the Student Christian Movement*, 26.
44. Bruce, "Sociological Account of Liberal Protestantism," 402.
45. Newbigin, *Unfinished Agenda*, 9–10.
46. Hastings, *History of English Christianity*, 542.

> I came from a Methodist Chapel background in Lancashire which was warm, taught me to pray and read the Bible. . . . But it was narrow. It was anti-ecumenical, even bigoted at times. Then I went to University and joined the SCM . . . I went to Swanwick. Damascus wasn't in it. Roman Catholics were Christians. It was fantastic.[47]

SCM people went on to be at the core of the ecumenical movement. Adrian Hastings offers a list of SCM staff in the 1930s, including Alan Booth, Kathleen Bliss, Francis House, Dick Milford, Lesslie Newbigin, David Paton, Ronald Preston, Ambrose Reeves, Alan Richardson, and Robin Woods, who went on to play key roles in ecumenical movement.[48] Later so many SCM people went into the World Council of Churches that it was sometimes referred to as "the SCM in long trousers." Roger Boyd offers an equally impressive list of those who worked for national SCMs and in WSCF who staffed the WCC.[49] In terms of secularization theory it is difficult to see why the 1960s was a high point in ecumenism. The influence of liberal theology may, however, offer a significant clue.

MODELS OF UNITY

Ecumenism is sometimes equated with organic unity, and indeed this model of unity was central for the birth of the United Reformed Church, but this has not been the only understanding of unity. Any meaningful understanding of ecumenism needs to recognize the variety of ecumenical models of unity. The Toronto Declaration of the World Council of Churches Central Committee in 1950 specifically affirms that

> Membership in the World Council does not imply the acceptance of a specific doctrine concerning the nature of Church unity. The Council stands for Church unity. But in its midst there are those who conceive unity wholly or largely as full consensus in the realm of doctrine, others who conceive of it primarily as sacramental communion based on common church order, others who consider both indispensable, others who would only require unity in certain fundamentals of faith and order, again others who conceive

47. Richardson, interview.
48. Hastings, *Oliver Tomkins*, 24.
49. Boyd, *Witness of the Student Christian Movement*, 157.

the one Church as a universal spiritual fellowship, or hold that visible unity is inessential or even undesirable.[50]

The predominant first conception was a form of cooperation among a fellowship of churches. This was for example the view of Wim Visser't Hooft, the first General Secretary of the World Council of Churches. "For Wim, one feels, if the WCC worked well, nothing much more was required."[51]

Along with the idea of a fellowship of churches often went models of unity that stressed unity in common action. J. H. Oldham, the other great pioneer of the World Council of Churches, responded to the rise of secularism prior to the Second World War by seeing the primary necessary response as theological, in the need to discover the distinctive nature of Christian theology and then explore it adventurously in the contemporary world. Oldham was something of an elitist. As Visser't Hooft observed: "It was said at the time that for Oldham the road to the Kingdom of God went through the dining room of the Athenaeum."[52] But Oldham's ideas were central to the missionary power of the church and he saw a key role of the ecumenical movement as to "offer an opportunity of mobilizing the best Christian thought of the world, both theological and lay, to meet the situation more effectively than has ever been attempted so far."[53] This later found expression in "the Moot," which was a meeting point he established for a small, exclusive group of Christian leaders and thinkers. It met twenty times between April 1938 and December 1944, with a membership that included Karl Mannheim, Alec Vidler, Eric Fenn, Sir Walter Moberly, T. S. Eliot, and John Baillie,[54] and had a hope of intellectually redirecting and reinvigorating British society.

It was not until the 1960s that a third model, organic unity, became the central strategy of ecumenism. A vital figure at this point was Oliver Tomkins, who was Bishop of Bristol and the key person in the Faith and Order section of the World Council of Churches. Tomkins had learned his theology from the SCM and from there moved on to the WCC. It was he who was largely responsible for formulating the Lund Principle of "doing together everything except those in which deep differences of conviction

50. Kinnamon, *Vision of the Ecumenical Movement*, 146.

51. Hastings, *Oliver Tomkins*, 166.

52. Visser't Hooft, *Memoirs*, 41.

53. Oldham, letter to Mott, 14 November 1934, quoted Clements, *Faith on the Frontier*, 284.

54. Ibid., 363–389.

compel them to act separately."[55] Then it was his Faith and Order section who at St. Andrews in 1960 adopted a report that offered a new definition of the unity that was being sought: "The unity which is God's will and his gift to the Church is one which brings all in each place . . . into a committed fellowship with one another." As Tomkins noted in his journal: "We have now succeeded . . . in getting first of all the full Faith and Order Commission and then the whole Central Committee to accept our 'Future report'—the greatest point being the inclusion of a definition of the meaning of church unity which goes beyond anything *explicitly* said before by either Faith and Order or the WCC."[56] This was then affirmed by the World Council of Churches Assembly at New Delhi in 1961, which outlined "the nature of our common goal—the vision of the one church (which) has become the inspiration of our ecumenical endeavor."[57] Tomkins wrote:

> There is no time to play with. History is not on the side of our divisions because God is not. Can we unite in the name of the freedom of love and quickly

Others were less sure and they were careful to add:

> This brief description of our objective leaves many questions unanswered. We are not yet of a common mind on the interpretation and the means of achieving the goal we have described.[58]

Organic unity was, however, never without its critics. Michael Kinnamon, who was General Secretary of the Consultation on Church Union in the USA, expressed his hesitations as:

> Legitimate gifts of the Spirit, embodied in the denominational heritages, can be lost or overlooked. The focus on structural union can detract from needed emphasis on mission. Resistance to the new united Church can lead to new divisions in the body of Christ.[59]

Further, the entrance of the Roman Catholic Church into the mainstream of the ecumenical movement inevitably pointed away from local unions, which were contrary to its ecclesiology, in favor of dialogue between

55. Third World Conference on Faith and Order, Lund, Sweden, 1952.

56. Hastings, *Oliver Tomkins*, 118.

57. Visser't Hooft, *New Delhi Report*, 117.

58. Kinnamon, *Vision of the Ecumenical Movement*, 154–55.

59. Ibid., 32.

the globally organized world communions. Concerns of this sort led to greater support for the concept of "reconciled diversity," which has been especially influential in America. In 1983 the "Cold Ash Report" from the International Anglican-Lutheran Joint Working Group defined the goal of full communion as "a relationship between two distinct churches or communions. Each maintains its own autonomy and recognizes the catholicity and apostolicity of the other,"[60] and this definition was endorsed in principle by the American report *Called to Common Mission*. In 1991 Konrad Raiser (General Secretary of the World Council of Churches, 1993–2003), in his *Ecumenism in Transition*, argued that this was the new paradigm which now had to replace the concept of organic unity. Others were more critical. Lesslie Newbigin from the first had seen reconciled diversity as little more than a justification for the status quo. "It offers an invitation to reunion without repentance and without renewal, to a unity in which we are faced with no searching challenge to our existing faith and practice, but can remain as we are."[61] More recently Jurgen Moltmann described it as "the sleeping pill of the ecumenical movement. We stay as we are and are nice to each other."[62]

THE ATTEMPT TO ACHIEVE ORGANIC UNITY IN ENGLAND

Of the various models of ecumenical renewal, the United Reformed Church was unambiguously committed to organic unity. This reached its high point in England in the 1960s. At the original suggestion of the Congregationalist Daniel Jenkins an informal body called the Inter-Church Group was formed in October 1960 seeking to bring together Anglican and Free Church leaders. It included many old SCM veterans like Kenneth Slack, David Paton, Eric Fenn, and Oliver Tomkins together with younger people like John Robinson and the Congregationalist John Weller. It became a think tank for unity. After the New Delhi Assembly the Inter-Church Group planned the way forward with a conference to be initiated by the British Council of Churches. A series of regional conferences was held and then a conference in Nottingham in 1964. This brought three key resolutions:

60. Anglican-Lutheran Joint Working Group, *Anglican-Lutheran Relations*, 25.

61. Newbigin, "All in One Place," 293.

62. Moltmann, *Broad Place*, 86.

1. A resolution, largely formulated by the Anglican theologian David Jenkins, asserted that the differences between the churches, "though important, are not sufficient to stand as barriers to unity. They do not separate us at the point of our central affirmation of our faith, and they can be better explored within a united Church."[63]

2. To invite the member churches to covenant to work and pray for a reunion by an agreed date. "We dare to hope that this date should not be later than Easter Day, 1980. We believe that we should offer obedience to God in a commitment as decisive as this."[64]

3. "To designate areas of ecumenical experiment, at the request of local congregations, or in new towns and housing areas. In such areas there should be experiments in ecumenical group ministries, in the sharing of buildings and equipment, and in the development of mission."[65]

This was an astonishingly radical set of proposals. What produced this radicalism? The increasing secularity of the 1960s was certainly a factor, as it was becoming ever clearer just how marginal and irrelevant the churches were to much of society. David Paton, the study advisor to the Conference, warned: "It is clear today that for all our much speaking, our words are not really heard outside our own circle."[66] In section 5 of its reports the Conference admitted:

> God is reminding us of our part in Christ's mission to the world, and is beginning to transform us and our institutions into more effective instruments of his reconciling will. At present much of our Church activity and organization is irrelevant to this mission, and needs to be pruned; our churchgoing is too much divorced from the realities of the world; and our division into separate denominations in each place obscures and frustrates Christ's reconciling power.[67]

But this factor alone is not sufficient to explain this dramatic commitment to unity. If the 1960s were a difficult decade for the church each subsequent decade was to get progressively worse but none produced such visionary schemes. Perhaps an agenda for change of this sort requires hope

63. Davies and Edwards, *Unity Begins at Home*, 75.

64. Ibid., 78.

65. Ibid., 79.

66. Ibid., 57.

67. Ibid., 71.

as well as desperation and it was liberal theology that was decisive. After the conservative 50s the early 60s was to be a radical time in theology, most notably with the publication of John Robinson's *Honest to God* in 1963. This was followed in 1965 by his *The New Reformation*.

> Almost overnight one is conscious of the ground moving under one's feet. There is a ferment in the Church, which even a couple of years ago I think no-one could have predicted.[68]

In January 1964 the Paul Report advocated redeployment of the clergy, and John Robinson was a key figure in the birth of the Report. In October 1963 the group Parish and People was reorganized, with a commitment to reform and renewal, and in January 1964 Eric James became its full-time secretary with a brief to "stump the country" in favor of reform. As he wrote, "There was much enthusiasm and excitement and high hopes at the time."[69] In October 1965 the first edition of *New Christian*, a fortnightly journal, was published. It was ecumenical and radical and edited by Trevor Beeson, who had been involved in both Parish and People and ecumenical renewal. The Chairman of the editorial team was the Presbyterian Kenneth Slack, who had been General Secretary of the British Council of Churches. The opening editorial declared: "At a time of ferment and reformation in the Church, there is a need for a channel of communication which is open to new thought and action coming from different quarters."[70] Anything seemed possible.

The sense of hope was deepened by unexpected developments in the Roman Catholic Church. When in 1958 Cardinal Roncalli succeeded Pope Pius XII, the candidate of a caucus of conservative Italian cardinals, little change was expected. In fact within three months of his election Pope John XXIII summoned a General Council. He talked of *aggiornamento* (bringing up to date) and astonishingly of Christian reunion. The Second Vatican Council, meeting between October 1962 and December 1965, led not only to a change of the mass from Latin to local languages, but also emphasized that the whole church is the people of God and seemed to be opening the way to a less hierarchical church. Relations between Catholics and Protestants rapidly began to change. In England Archbishop Fisher had been deeply suspicious of Catholics.

---

68. Robinson, *New Reformation?*, 17.

69. James, *Life of Bishop John Robinson*, 137.

70. *New Christian*, 7 October 1965.

> I grew up with an inbred opposition to anything that came from
> Rome. I objected to their doctrine: I objected to their methods of
> reasoning: I objected to their methods of operation in this country,
> So I grew up, and I saw no reason for differing from my opinion
> as the years went by.[71]

Now he went to Rome to see the Pope. "It was quite obvious to the
world that Pope John was a different kind of Pope."[72] As one public school
headmaster wrote to John Robinson, "This is a tremendously exciting time
to be alive in the history of the Church."[73]

Catching the mood, Roger Lloyd, a canon of Winchester Cathedral,
began his *The Ferment in the Church* with the words: "The prospect of a new
Reformation is clearly in sight. . . . The storm signals are quite unmistakable. . . . No way of halting it exists."[74] It was this which helped to set the
dramatic mood at Nottingham. As David Edwards reflected: "It may be that
our century . . . is now being given a new Reformation—a Reformation, this
time, through reunion."[75]

It did not happen. Striking as its resolutions were, and visionary as
Nottingham seemed at the time, the results fell far short of what they dared
to hope. The most radical commitment, unity by 1980, not only was not
achieved but simply never became a priority for most of the churches. The
resolution in practice had very little impact. The delegates at Nottingham
may have voted for unity but the denominations had not and showed limited commitment to the prospect.

What is more, even at Nottingham there had been dissenting voices.
No fundamental change was possible without the willingness to move of
the Church of England. But there were those in the Church of England
whose concern was not so much to unite Protestant churches as to seek
renewed unity with Rome. To them it seemed that a union between the
Church of England and the Nonconformists could only set back this wider,
greater hope. At Nottingham their main representative was John Moorman,
the Bishop of Ripon. He had been an observer at the Vatican Council and
was excited by the possibilities of Catholic-Anglican renewal. In his journal he noted how "uncomfortable" the Conference made him, particularly

71. Purcell, *Fisher of Lambeth*, 271.

72. Ibid., 273.

73. Robinson and Edwards, *Honest to God Debate*, 71.

74. Lloyd, *Ferment in the Church*, 7.

75. Davies and Edwards, *Unity Begins at Home*, 94.

disliking "a determination on the part of the young (especially Noncon-formist young)" to force through the 1980 timetable.[76] He was one of the fifty-three voting against and while the Conference discussed what should follow Nottingham he sat in his room and read *The Trial of Oscar Wilde*.

> Those of us who voted against it will be regarded, no doubt, as re-actionaries, lacking in zeal and faith. But I'm afraid many of those who voted for it will be disappointed when the time comes—un-less by then they have learned sense."[77]

Nor were the Anglo-Catholics the only ones sitting out on Notting-ham. Among evangelicals there were diverse attitudes towards ecumenism. The standard evangelical position was that organizational unity was unim-portant and the risks involved in ecumenism too great. When the World Council of Churches was formed in 1948 *The Advent Witness* linked it to the great whore of Revelation 17.[78] Attitudes did soften. From about 1955 many conservative evangelicals began to share in the week of prayer for Christian unity and in local councils of churches. The Keele Evangelical Anglican Conference of 1967 welcomed the possibility of dialogue with Catholics on the basis of Scripture. Such openness, however, was both lim-ited and relative. Among Anglican groups such as the Church Society "there remained a phalanx for whom the defense of Reformation principles was the over-riding priority."[79] Outside the Church of England outright hostility to ecumenism remained. In 1966 Martyn Lloyd-Jones fractured the evan-gelical world by calling for evangelicals to separate out from the historic churches. This reinforced the long-standing opposition to ecumenism of groups such as the Baptist Revival Fellowship, who saw ecumenism as com-promising the truth, and strengthened the anti-ecumenical Fellowship of Independent Evangelical Churches. Even for more moderate evangelicals there was often little enthusiasm for ecumenism. Look up Nottingham in the index of Timothy Dudley Smith's biography of John Stott, the revered Anglican evangelical, and you will find no reference to the Faith and Or-der Conference of 1964 but only one to the National Anglican Evangelical Congress of 1977.[80]

76. Hastings, *Oliver Tomkins*, 128.

77. Ibid.

78. *The Advent Witness*, September–October 1949, 459.

79. Bebbington, *Evangelism in Modern Britain*, 256.

80. Dudley-Smith, *John Stott*.

The significance of this opposition was to become clear with time. No new scheme for organic unity came out of Nottingham. However, conversations between the Anglican and Methodist Churches had begun as long ago as 1956. A first report in 1958 proposed a two-stage moving together, with full intercommunion and a mutual recognition of ministries, and then later organic unity at an unspecified date. Whether or not Methodist ministers would be reordained during the service of reconciliation was left deliberately vague—in the hope that everyone would find in it what they wanted. A final report was published in 1968, to which the Methodist Conference gave its approval by 76 percent. However, the Anglican Convocation gave only 68.5 percent support, less than the 75 percent agreed necessary. Those against were mostly Anglo-Catholics led by Bishop Moorman and Graham Leonard, the Bishop of Willesden. There was also opposition from some Anglican evangelicals who felt that the deliberate ambiguity of the service of reconciliation was an intentional deception. In a letter to *The Times* Lord Fisher called it "open double-dealing."[81] To John Stott the reconciliation service was equally unacceptable since it left open the possibility that the historic episcope was necessary: "I for one could not possibly subscribe to such a doctrine."[82]

To Oliver Tomkins this was "a shameful day for the Church of England. . . . We are too divided to unite with anyone."[83] For Methodists the result was shattering. As Rupert Davies, one of those most involved, wrote:

> In Methodism, the main result was a certain numbness, followed by a feverish preoccupation with denominational affairs. There was an admirable absence of bitterness among those who could have maintained that the Church of England had 'led them up the garden path.' But no one knew what the next step was, and for a time few steps of any kind were taken.[84]

This growing disillusion was widely felt. Writing in 1966, Kathleen Bliss had asked Oliver Tomkins, "How long will the present head of steam behind the drive for unity between separated churches last I wonder?"[85] By the end of the 60s it seemed that situation had been reached. In 1969, when issuing a revised edition of his 1960 book, *The British Churches Today*, Ken-

81. *The Times*, 21 January 1969.

82. Dudley-Smith, *John Stott*, 62.

83. Hastings, op.cit, 147.

84. Davies, George and Rupp, *A History of the Methodist Church*, vol.3, 379.

85. Hastings, *Oliver Tomkins*, 148.

neth Slack, the General Secretary of the British Council of Churches, sadly noted: "Passage after passage written in 1960 has seemed strangely optimistic and has had to be excised."[86] Oliver Tomkins too lamented: "So much of my efforts seem to have led nowhere at all."[87] By 1974 Visser't Hooft could publish a book with the ominous title *Has the Ecumenical Movement a Future?*

There were, however, those who thought there might be a way through. To some in the Congregational and Presbyterian Churches it seemed that if a church could demonstrate that organic unity was possible this *might* open the way to others. They would be that church.

86. Slack, *British Churches Today*, xi.
87. Hastings, *Oliver Tomkins*, 149.

2

The Formation of the United Reformed Church

CONGREGATIONALISM

THE ORIGINS OF CONGREGATIONALISM go back to sixteenth-century Puritanism, when the Independents were part of the radical wing of the Reformation, influenced both by the Reformed and Anabaptist traditions. They were not willing to wait for a godly prince to reform the church but, as Robert Browne said, sought reform "without tarrying for anie." They believed that, under Christ, it was the ordinary believers with whom authority in the church lay. "The voice of the whole people," wrote Browne, "guided by the elders and forwardest, is said to be the voice of God."[1] Under Queen Elizabeth the earliest congregations were suppressed but new congregations formed in James's reign and it was their search for the freedom to practice their religion which led to their being the core of those who in 1620 sailed on the Mayflower to establish Plymouth Colony in what became Massachusetts.

The Civil War brought the Independents into the center of English life. They played a significant role in the New Model Army and the Commonwealth and supported the abolition of the Prayer Book and of bishops. Later when the monarchy was restored nearly 1,000 clergy refused to accept the new church settlement and in all a total of 2,029 clergy, lecturers, and

---

1. Peel and Carlson, *Writings of Robert Harrison*, 404.

24

fellows were ejected from their posts.[2] Subsequently they faced a period of severe harassment and social exclusion until the passing of the Toleration Act in 1689, and after that still faced continued discrimination. The foundational myth of Congregationalism was formed by this experience. Congregationalists quoted with approval Macaulay's maxim that the true dissenter "prostrated himself in dust before his maker, but set his foot on the neck of his king."[3]

The Independents became a distinct social, intellectual, and political constituency outside the established church. Surviving persecution, their numbers rose dramatically through the influence of the Evangelical Revival. In 1715 there were 203 surviving congregations in England. By 1851 there were 2,604.[4] The later part of the nineteenth century witnessed profound changes in what was now called Congregationalism. By the mid-1850s biblical criticism began to be accepted in the denomination and Calvinism was abandoned. "Once the process began, the Calvinist doctrines of Congregationalism disappeared with unusual speed and equally unusual absence of discomfort."[5] In the place of Calvinism many Congregationalists welcomed liberal theology.

Liberal theology made its initial impact in Germany and was significantly later in its influence in Britain. Among Congregationalists the decisive moment was the Leicester Conference of 1877, which marked the increasing dominance of a new generation of more liberal-minded ministers in the leadership of the church.[6] Typical of this new liberalism was the first Principal of Mansfield College Oxford, Andrew Fairbairn, "the father of Liberal Evangelicalism among Congregationalists."[7] Ever since the Universities Tests Act of 1871 Congregationalists had wanted a college in Oxford. To achieve this Spring Hill College in Birmingham moved to Oxford in 1886, becoming Mansfield College, with fine neo-Gothic buildings designed by Basil Champneys. The chapel was described by David Cornick as "a bold fugue in stained glass, statues and wood"[8] and by the German

2. Watts, *Dissenters*, vol. 1, 219.
3. Macaulay, *Complete Works*, vol. 7, 53.
4. Watts, *Dissenters*, vol. 2, 23.
5. Chadwick, *Victorian Church*, 407.
6. Hopkins, *Nonconformity's Romantic Generation*, 85–121.
7. Jones, *Congregationalism in England*, 269.
8. Cornick, *Under God's Good Hand*, 122.

theologian Friedrich Heiler as "the most Catholic place in Oxford."[9] There was even a stained glass window of Plato. It was Congregationalism in its pomp making a claim to be at the center of Oxford life—the Free Church equivalent to the Anglicans at Christ Church. The college appointed Fairbairn as its first principal and through it he mediated German liberalism into Congregationalism. Like Mansfield he radiated the confidence of the moment. In March 1893 he published *The Place of Christ in Modern Theology*, claiming that the most distinctive feature of modern theology was "a new feeling for Christ" that could be attributed to the liberal quest for the Jesus of history. "We feel him more in our theology because we know him better in history."[10]

It was Fairbairn who in 1898, anticipating a sabbatical leave in India, asked Alfred Garvie to lecture in his place at Mansfield. Garvie had grown up a Presbyterian but had become a Congregationalist because the latter did not use creeds. Fairbairn suggested he address issues raised by the German theologian Albrecht Ritschl, who following the lead of Kant argued for Christianity as essentially a moral system, non-metaphysical in character, centering on the kingdom of God. Garvie was not himself a Ritschlian, but he believed there were positive elements in his work and his *The Ritschlian Theology* (1899) was the first work in English to make a positive case for his views.[11] There were those who alleged that Garvie, himself a liberal evangelical, made Ritschl seem more positive and better than he really was!

The twentieth century continued the liberal ascendancy in Congregationalism. R. J. Campbell's "New Theology" was a spectacular if effervescent example of this, but more substantively much Congregational theology was influenced by the liberal agenda for renewal. The first major study of Schleiermacher in England came from Fairbairn's successor at Mansfield, W. B. Selbie. "If the work of theological reconstruction is to be well-done, it must be rooted and grounded in history. For this purpose Schleiermacher is all important."[12] Later substantive contributions to liberal theology came from C. J. Cadoux and Albert Peel. Less significant was the work of what was known as the Blackheath Group, centering on Frank Lenwood and Thomas Wigley, who questioned the Trinity and the divinity of Christ. Cadoux's strictures that "some persons known to themselves and others as 'modern-

---

9. Davies, *Worship and Theology in England*, 56.

10. Jones, *Congregationalism in England*, 268.

11. Dorrien, *Kantian Reason and Hegelian Spirit*, 408–9.

12. Selbie, *Schleiermacher*, vii.

ists' have indulged in a somewhat undiscerning and cavalier treatment of the Bible and of the Church's traditional doctrines"[13] would be relevant here. At a popular level an indication of the essentially liberal nature of Congregationalism is the fact that in the mid-twentieth century the most popular preacher among Congregationalists was Leslie Weatherhead. Himself a Methodist, Weatherhead was regarded by his own denomination as too theologically dangerous for Wesley's Chapel, but ministered to the Congregational City Temple from 1936 to 1960.[14] For Donald Hilton, future Moderator of the URC's General Assembly, one of the highlights of his honeymoon was going to hear Weatherhead preach.[15]

Inevitably the Congregationalists were among the first to ordain a woman minister, Constance Coltman, in September 1917,[16] slightly before the UK gave women the right to vote. Evidence of the flexibility possible within Congregationalism is that she was accepted for ministerial training at Mansfield by Dr. Selbie and then ordained at King's Weigh House, though this was as Kirsty Thorpe has demonstrated in her *Daughters of Dissent* without any prior decision by the denomination. However, in October 1917 she was formally recognized by the Council of the Congregational Union of England and Wales. The decentralized nature of Congregationalism offered scope to radical liberal initiatives.

Historically, Congregational churches were a distinct religious subculture with their own foundational myth. Many Congregationalists believed theirs was the most faithful to the New Testament model of the church. There were deep grievances against the dominant national church and fundamental objections to its theology. In 1833 Thomas Binney could declare that the Church of England was a national evil that "destroys more souls than it saves."[17]

During the nineteenth century this distinct Congregational social identity was rapidly eroded. In 1828 the repeal of the Test and Corporation Acts allowed Dissenters to sit on borough councils and accept public office without fear of prosecution. In the same year the foundation of University College London opened higher education to male Dissenters. By the 1860s the church rate, which was a personal charge imposed on the occupier of

13. Cadoux, *Case for Evangelical Modernism*, ix.

14. Travell, *Doctor of Souls*, 93–94.

15. Hilton, interview.

16. Jones, *Congregationalism in England*, 408.

17. Ibid., 215.

land or a house in the parish even if they were not Anglicans, was effectively obsolete. What is more, as a minority of Dissenters became increasingly prosperous and upwardly mobile some felt the temptation to leave their chapels for the parish church. "It would be difficult to find a family who, for three generations, have kept their carriages and continued Dissenters," wrote a contributor to *The Monthly Magazine* in 1798.[18] Similarly once the universities were opened to the children of Dissenters they frequently came back Anglicans. There was one last flare-up of the old divisions between Dissenters and the state church when the 1902 Education Bill proposed that Anglican Church schools be subsidized out of taxes, but increasingly the iniquity of an established church seemed less pressing and the real issue was not the established nature of the Church of England but whether to belong to a church at all. By the First World War Nonconformity had gained its civil rights and all that was left was an ecclesiological motivation that seemed less compelling. As David Cornick puts it, "No one now turns a hair at the obvious injustice of all bar a tiny minority of Deans and chaplains in Oxbridge being Anglican." A nationally recognized Nonconformist culture in England died somewhere in the 1950s or 60s but it had been in decline from almost the beginning of the century.

At the same time the Congregationalists began to lose their theologically distinct ecclesiology. The traditional view could still be put. For C. J. Cadoux each local congregation was "the Universal Church in miniature." With total self-confidence he argued that Congregationalism was therefore "A truer representative of the Catholicity of the One Church than any other denomination can possibly be."[19] All of this began to look increasingly anachronistic. Progressively Congregationalists began giving increased authority to the wider councils of the church.

From the beginning of Independency there had been associations of Congregational ministers. Between 1781 and 1815 these developed into county unions of churches, which were largely but not exclusively about evangelism. The powerful Lancashire Congregational Union included in its objectives keeping in touch with the churches, collecting information about them, offering financial assistance for the building of new churches, and an annual meeting.[20] The understanding was that no authority or power would be exercised over individual churches, but secretaries of the

18. Watts, *Dissenters*, vol. 2, 602.
19. Cadoux, *Congregational Way*, 20–21.
20. Jones, *Congregationalism in England*, 175.

county unions could be influential people. In 1832 national organization began with the foundation of the Congregational Union of England and Wales. Those churches that were financially supported inevitably lost some of their independence and Congregational practice was that such churches were visited annually.

In 1919 the Congregational Union went further, creating the office of moderator, the brainchild of J. D. Jones, who believed that churches must cooperate together for mission.[21] They might argue that this was something entirely different from the office of bishop (though in fact Jones did prefer the term bishop[22]) but it was undeniably a form of personal episcopacy, and because the primary model for this was the Anglican bishop in the long run there would be an inevitable pressure to move in that direction. Significantly it was agreed at the beginning that the role was open to either ministers or laypeople, but the latter option was never chosen. In practice some of the moderators offered strong leadership.

The Congregational tradition had originated in Independency—this was now dying. Jones in particular was keen that it should. Congregationalism, he argued, must decide either "to retain its independency or to adapt some form of connexionalism" for "it cannot have the advantage of both systems."[23] Jones was Honorary Secretary to the Moderators' Meeting and as such chaired their Meetings and consistently supported centralization. "The only way to keep our Congregational witness alive . . . was . . . to turn (our) isolated fellowships into a Denomination.[24]

Theologically too there were signs of change. The theology of P. T Forsyth anticipated the Barthian reaction against liberal theology. Equally significant was the manifesto sent out to all Congregational ministers in 1939 drafted by Bernard Lord Manning, Nathaniel Micklem, and J. S. Whale. They asserted:

> The depressing and alarming thing about our churches is not their tiny congregations, their social insignificance, their political impotence. . . . If our churches are in peril, it is because they have forgotten who they are.[25]

21. Peel, *Story of the Moderators*, 11.

22. Jones, *Three Score Years and Ten*, 109.

23. Porritt, *J. D. Jones*, 79.

24. Argent, *Transformation of Congregationalism*, 167.

25. Micklem, *Box and the Puppets*, 92–99.

The three of them together became known as the New Genevans (though Whale's debt to Calvin was greater than Micklem's) and they led the charge against what seemed to them the excesses of liberalism.

> Theological liberalism had run to seed. . . . I was quite certain that the religion being taught in our churches was a form of Christianity so watered down, that it could not be called the religion of the New Testament, and that it was no proclamation of the Gospel as our fathers and all previous generations knew it.[26]

By contrast the New Genevans sought the distinctive nature of the church in Reformation tradition, emphasized the importance of the links between Congregationalism and the other Reformed churches, stressed the dignity of the ministry, and in line with Calvin saw synods as expressions of the communion of local churches with one another. As Binfield notes, they had their own dialect: "Fathers and Brethren," "God's holy Purpose," "Our most holy religion."[27] In the Congregational Lectures in 1965 the Minister-Secretary of the Congregational Union, John Huxtable, argued for a new understanding of episcopacy. Congregationalists had always seen episcopacy as exercised through the minister of the local congregation. They had now come to understand that episcopacy was exercised corporately as well as individually. It was therefore manifested not simply in the local church but through county unions, provinces, and the national union.[28]

With their stress on the close relation between Congregationalism and the other Reformed churches it was no surprise they supported the move for Congregational-Presbyterian unity in 1933. "Personally," said Manning in that year, "I have no doubt that unity with the Presbyterians is the next step. Having no sort of doubt whatever, I personally would pay almost any price to achieve that union."[29] The New Genevans took organizational form through the Church Order Group, which was formed in 1946 for mutual consultation and continued until the 1960s, and was to include a number of younger ministers such as John Huxtable, Daniel Jenkins, and John Marsh. They provided much of the intellectual leadership for the next generation of Congregationalists, and their emphasis on synodical government, a high view of ministry, and a commitment to church unity made possible the creation of the United Reformed Church and thus may justify Tony Tucker's

26. Micklem, *Religion of a Sceptic*, 53.
27. Binfield, "Learned and Gifted Minister," 115.
28. Huxtable, *Christian Unity*, 99–100.
29. Manning, *Essays in Orthodox Dissent*, 148.

judgment that "there is no doubt that Micklem's influence was decisive in preparing Congregationalists for the changes which led eventually to this union"[30]—though the influence of J. D. Jones should not be forgotten.

A major change came in 1965 when the Congregational Union in England and Wales became the Congregational Church in England and Wales. Increasingly under the influence of Micklem and the Church Order Group it seemed that Congregationalism was moving to a wider understanding of what it meant to be a church. Joseph Figures, the Lancashire Moderator, asked "what we mean by Congregationalism when we think of it in a corporate or denominational sense" and argued that "the attitude and relationship of a local church to the union should be precisely the same as the attitude and relationship of a church member to his church."[31] This was a radically new doctrine in Congregationalism. The fact that it could be put indicates what Lovell Cocks meant when he said "atomistic Independency is dead or dying."[32]

It was out of such thinking that a commission proposed a change from "Union" to "Church."

> The churches thus associated have no wish to appear as a denomination in distinction from other denominations, or to weaken their own sense of ecumenicity; but since it is not at present possible to gather all Christians into one Church order it is necessary that Congregational Churches should express in some corporate form their belonging together which is so plainly a fact of their experience.[33]

Not everyone was persuaded. A twelve-point statement was issued by a group of twenty-seven evangelicals arguing not only that "the full autonomy of the local church would be lost" but also that they could not enter into a covenant with ministers who did not hold what they regarded as sound doctrine. This would "seriously compromise witness to the Gospel."[34] At this point the influence of Martin Lloyd Jones might well be detected. Many of those who were later to join the Congregational Federation led by Reginald Cleaves were opposed and others were uneasy. Daniel Jenkins was

---

30. Tucker, "Nathaniel Micklem," 710.

31. Figures, "Corporate Congregationalism," 44.

32. Cocks, "Where Two or Three," 39.

33. Sell, *Testimony and Tradition*, 300.

34. Ibid., 304.

unhappy at the word "Church"[35] and Erik Routley indicated he preferred to think of Congregationalism as "an order within the Catholic Church."[36]

It was a decisive moment. The choice offered by J. D. Jones as to whether Congregationalism would remain in the old Independency or embrace connexionalism had been formally determined in favor of the latter. Much that was characteristic of Congregationalism remained. John Huxtable felt able to assure the doubtful that "we do not envisage that the local Church will be told what to do."[37] But Congregationalism was distancing itself from its historic beliefs and now beginning to look very different from the Baptists, whose church polity had once been its own. Adrian Hastings' comment that "Nonconformity was rendered viable in relatively large-scale modern terms but at the cost of much that was characteristic in it"[38] applies very pertinently to Congregationalism.

How lasting the New Genevan inheritance was to be is more problematic. Though there was certainly a New Genevan ascendancy for a time it was very much a top-down movement. They may have ushered in the end of Independency but it is more questionable whether their commitment to Reformation theology was ever widely adopted. Tudur Jones argues that much of their writing, especially that of Daniel Jenkins, "involved highly technical discussions of the nature of the Church" that only "touched the ordinary believer when their consequences were made manifest in the worship of the churches."[39]

It would be the case that Congregationalists and the URC would be less emphatically liberal in the second half of the twentieth century than they were in the first, and Barthian influence could be seen in significant sections of the church leadership. In the case of someone like Colin Gunton this could be extremely conservative. But liberalism was to be more resilient than some New Genevans imagined. Writing in 1954, Daniel Jenkins, a Barthian, felt able to refer to "the modernist episode" which had now given way to a renewal of the church through Catholicism and revived Reformation Protestantism.[40] He was not to know that the following decade was to see a major renewal of liberal theology and that his proclamation

35. Ibid., 300.
36. Routley, *Congregationalists and Unity*, 34.
37. Huxtable, "Covenanted Fellowship," 14.
38. Hastings, *History of English Christianity*, 115.
39. Jones, *Congregationalism in England*, 456.
40. Jenkins, *Congregationalism*, 62.

of the death of liberal theology came at the moment when Bultmann and Tillich were creating new forms of it. The New Genevans' moment passed rapidly. By the 1970s it was possible to train for the ministry at Mansfield, Micklem's old college, without meeting his name on the reading list. By now "Fathers and Brethren" sounded strangely archaic.

In any case it is far from clear that the New Genevans represented a fundamental break with liberalism at all. Alan Sell denied they were liberals on the grounds that "they weren't liberals in the sense that their theology was like that of R.J. Campbell."[41] But that would be a very narrow definition. It is certainly true that Micklem was often in antagonistic debate with Cadoux and vigorously criticized what he saw as the vapid liberalism of, for example, the Blackheath Group. His own theology, however, mediated between traditional authority systems and the modern world, as he himself acknowledged: "Through all these intellectually tempestuous years, I have been both liberal and evangelical."[42] Another New Genevan, J. S. Whale, may have said "If much of our modernism is true, then St Paul was a blockhead,"[43] but in later life he could say, "I have more in common with Morna Hooker and John Robinson than I have with the British and Foreign Bible Society."[44] Micklem explicitly drew back from his earlier rhetoric, telling John Huxtable, "I hope you will not make the same mistake I made. . . . I took it for granted that the battle against fundamentalism had been won; it hasn't and you may have to fight it again."[45] A comparison might be made with Reinhold Niebuhr in the United States, who similarly lambasted liberalism but later admitted that in fact he had never been anything else himself.[46] In the congregations liberalism remained the default theological position, and where it was challenged it was more often, and increasingly, to be by a reviving fundamentalism than by the theology of the New Genevans.

Congregationalism remained a fundamentally liberal church. Perceptively David Bebbington points out that there was never a liberal group among the Congregationalists—there was never felt to be any need of

41. Sell, interview.

42. Micklem, *Religion of a Sceptic*, 54.

43. Binfield, "Learned and Gifted Minister," 116.

44. Whale, *Christian Reunion*, 121.

45. Huxtable, *As It Seemed to Me*, 30.

46. Dorrien, *Making of American Liberal Theology, 1900–1950*, 479.

one.[47] Evidence of the influence of liberalism on Congregationalists at the time of union can be seen in the Declaration of Faith published by the Congregational Church in England and Wales in 1967, which was prepared by a commission including John Huxtable, H. Cunliffe-Jones, John Marsh, Nathaniel Micklem, Howard Stanley, and W. A. Whitehouse. On the crucial question of Scripture it was unambiguous: "The Bible must be read with fully critical attention if the Church is to discern the truth which is binding and not be in bondage to what is not binding; for the Bible is not free from human error and confusion and contradictions."[48] The breadth and openness of mind of the document is unmistakably liberal. It explicitly recognizes that truth may come from non-Christian sources[49] and from non-Christian religions.[50] Though several of the authors were New Genevans there is no compromising with Calvinist predestination: "That God should discard from this creation any creature precious to him is inconceivable."[51]

PRESBYTERIANISM

The origins of the Presbyterian Church of England were quite different. Like Congregationalism, Presbyterianism originated in the Reformation, with a more direct link to Calvin than was the case with Congregationalism. It was Calvin who advocated the rule of the church by presbyters, hence the name Presbyterian. Unlike Congregationalists, Presbyterians supported the concept of a national church, while believing it should be Presbyterian not Anglican. With the monarchical restoration in 1662 Presbyterians shared in the Great Ejectment, but most of the congregations that survived became either Unitarian or Congregational and the number of Presbyterian churches fell from 637 in 1715 to 142 in 1851.[52] Of the latter many were newly founded Scottish Presbyterian churches and when the Presbyterian Church of England was formed in 1876 it was largely composed of Scottish or sometimes Irish Presbyterian immigrants. In 1870 there were 38,000 communicants, a number that rose to over 50,000 by 1877 and to 76,071 by 1900. The peak year for communicants was 1914, when they reached

47. Bebbington, *Evangelicalism in Modern Britain*, 228.

48. Congregational Church in England and Wales, *Declaration of Faith*, 28.

49. Ibid.,11.

50. Ibid., 12.

51. Ibid., 37.

52. Watts, *Dissenters*, vol. 2, 23.

88,166.[53] Although the majority of the church reflected its mostly Scottish (or in Merseyside, Irish or Welsh) origin there were exceptions. In the Northeast there was an indigenous tradition of Presbyterianism. Michael Hopkins argues:

> Bob Andrews told me he grew up in South Shields where there were four Presbyterian churches in the town. Three of them were English and one Scottish. Berwick of course had everything twice. And of course there was Egremont which was more English than most. . . . In Stockton there was St Andrews and St Georges Churches and of course St Georges was the English Church and St Andrews the Scottish.[54]

Theologically the revived Presbyterian Church was more conservative than the Congregationalists but most Presbyterians were little concerned with the details of Calvinism and through the United Presbyterians inherited a distinctly liberal tradition. In the early decades of the twentieth century Presbyterian thinking was influenced by Westminster College, where ordinands of the Presbyterian Church of England were prepared for ministry. A classic liberal, John Oman (1860–1939), was appointed Professor of Theology in 1907 and was Principal from 1922 until his retirement in 1939. Oman was the English translator of some of the works of Friedrich Schleiermacher and sought to explore the way that God interacts with human experience. The liberal tradition continued at Westminster with H. H. Farmer and was to produce the URC's most significant philosophical theologian in John Hick.

DECLINE

Disparate as their origins were, both churches shared the experience of decline. English Congregationalist membership reached a peak in 1915. Between 1916 and 1927 nearly 10,000 members were lost in England.[55] From then on Congregational decline was continuous. These statistics obscure the real beginning and scale of the decline. If we consider church membership as a proportion of the total population then it would seem that decline began perhaps half a century earlier. Callum Brown suggests

53. Currie et al., *Churches and Church Goers*, 132–33.

54. Hopkins, interview.

55. Thompson, *Decline of Congregationalism*, 5.

Congregational attendance peaked in 1863, considerably earlier than the Church of England, which peaked in 1904,[56] though these statistics need to be treated with caution since the Congregationalists did not publish membership statistics until 1898.

Presbyterian attendances were continually boosted by immigration and did not follow such a simple curve. From its First World War peak the number of communicants fell slowly until the Second World War. Membership increased between 1947 and 1949 and again between 1955 and 1961. The relevant factor here is that the number of English residents born in Scotland increased from 366,000 in 1931 to 654,000 in 1960. After that decline set in rapidly with communicants falling from 71,100 in 1961 to 59,573 in 1970.[57] The Presbyterians never really became a fully indigenous English church, remaining dependent on Scottish immigration for membership growth—after 1946 accounting for 42 percent of new members. As decline worsened this dependence increased. English recruitment and Scottish transfers fell 20 percent and 10 percent respectively between 1920 and 1938, and 25 percent and 5 percent respectively between 1946 and 1967.[58]

If we take the broader picture in the period 1947–1972 we find that the Presbyterian Church of England lost 29 percent of its membership and the Congregationalists 36 percent.[59] In fact the reality of decline was significantly worse than these figures indicate. Prior to the First World War the number worshipping at Congregational churches was generally two or three times greater than the church membership, whereas today it is roughly equal.[60]

Congregationalism in particular found it difficult any longer to give a convincing reason for its existence. One sign of this was the number of those who grew up in Congregational churches but no longer felt the need to stay within them. Daniel Jenkins even suggests that there were more leaders of thought and action who were products of Congregational homes but had left the church than the denomination itself possessed.[61] Michael Ramsey, growing up at Emmanuel Congregational Church in Cambridge,

56. Brown, *Death of Christian Britain*, 163.

57. Currie et al., *Churches and Church Goers*, 135.

58. Cornick, *Under God's Good Hand*, 167.

59. Ibid., 167.

60. URC, *Yearbook 2012*, 16.

61. Jenkins, *Congregationalism*, 37.

was one of many who made the move into the Church of England. Others went in other directions. W. E. Orchard, originally a Presbyterian, took the unlikely step of becoming a Roman Catholic. More significant was the withdrawal from the Congregationalists of Martyn Lloyd-Jones. Jones was minister of Westminster Chapel and a leading Congregational evangelical. In October 1966 he urged his audience at the National Assembly of Evangelicals to leave their denominations and instead draw together with other evangelicals. This led to a horrified reaction from the evangelical Anglican John Stott, who was chairing the meeting.[62] The sense of being an Anglican was more important to Stott than being a Congregationalist was to Jones. What is more, Martyn Lloyd Jones could and did take Westminster Chapel out of the Congregational Union and remain its minister. Anglican evangelicals did not have that option. The decline in Congregationalism was numerical, sociological, and intellectual. The latter decline was shared in pew, pulpit, and theological college. As Adrian Hastings comments, "When the *Congregational Quarterly* ceased publication in 1958, it was saying something about the near extinction of the old sort of reading public in that tradition."[63]

By the mid-twentieth century Congregationalists and Presbyterians were in serious trouble. A biting analysis of the desperate state of the Free Churches came in 1962 with Christopher Driver's *A Future for the Free Churches?* He argued that Free Church decline had now gone so far as to be irreversible. Had he not grown up in a Congregational church he could not imagine he would ever have joined one. In the public mind the Free Churches no longer stood for anything except "Bad architecture and good works."[64] Secularization led to a general church decline. The fact that for Congregationalists, however, the decline began earlier, proceeded faster, and involved a drift not simply to secularism but, among its most educated, to the Church of England reflected the lack of self-belief within the denomination. For the Presbyterians decline was less acute and there was at least one saving grace—the old role of Scots Church in England could still be played. At St. Columba's or St. Ninian's the Scottish country dancing went on, but as secularization took its effect everywhere this could hardly be enough.

---

62. Dudley-Smith, *John Stott*, 65–71.

63. Hastings, *History of English Christianity*, 466.

64. Driver, *Future for the Free Churches?*, 18.

THE ECUMENICAL OPTION

In all this reality of decline Driver could see at least one solid gain—the ecumenical movement. That must be the way forward: "There is no future for the Free Churches, as they are, short of reunion."[65] The first responses of Congregationalists and Presbyterians to proposals for church union were skeptical. The Congregational Assembly of 1921 welcomed the Lambeth Conference's appeal for unity but had no wish to pursue it seriously. As Tony Tucker observes, the problem was not simply episcopal authority but the Congregational concept of the church as such.[66] There was the place of creeds, the established nature of the Church of England, and the autonomy of the local church. At this point Congregational self-belief was still strong enough and decline had not advanced fast enough for unity to seem necessary. Talks between the Presbyterians and Congregationalists did begin in 1932 and continued until the war but by 1935 it had been decided that full union was impossible. Moves towards unity were revived after the Second World War and a scheme of union laid before the Congregational and Presbyterian Churches in 1947. This was not proceeded with and instead it was agreed to seek "closer systematic co-operation," including in 1956 a scheme for the mutual recognition of ministries, which only passed the Presbyterian Assembly by 207 votes to 186.[67] One of the notable examples of this was to be the calling of Kenneth Slack as minister of the Congregational City Temple. By 1957 there were some thirty schemes involving joint membership or other local arrangements.

The English Presbyterians, however, were pursuing another unity option: conversations involving the Church of England and the Church of Scotland over the possibility of introducing a modified form of episcopacy into both England and Scotland. When this was rejected by the Church of Scotland the English Presbyterians were left in confusion. Out of this came new discussions with the Congregationalists. The situation now seemed to point more clearly to ecumenism in England as the way ahead.

The Joint Committee of Congregationalists and Presbyterians met for the first time on New Year's Day 1964. A few months later came the Nottingham Conference. This was the context in which the unity negotiations proceeded, but their origin long predated it. A number of questions

---

65. Ibid., 18.

66. Tucker, "Nathaniel Micklem," 27.

67. Macarthur, *Setting Up Signs*, 5.

proved difficult, such as the existence of an ordained eldership among the Presbyterians, the importance the Congregationalists placed on the Church Meeting, and Presbyterian suspicions that the Congregational moderators were a form of pseudo-episcopacy. There were also administrative and legal questions, including the preparation of a bill to deal with trust and legal matters. As the Congregational General Secretary John Huxtable admits, the negotiations were "not easy" but the union was carried through in the deep conviction on the part of many that it was part of what "obedience to the Gospel demands."[68] A scheme of union was produced in 1969 and in 1971 this received an 89-percent majority from the Congregationalists and a 79-percent majority from the Presbyterians. The new United Reformed Church was formed on 5 October 1972.

The union was not simply the product of a single cause. The dominating figure on the Congregational side was John Huxtable, who was held in huge respect by most Congregationalists. He was totally committed to the union and pursued it with passionate, strong, autocratic leadership. Huxtable was deeply influenced by Micklem and the New Genevans, with their long-held hope for uniting Congregationalists and Presbyterians, but also by the later ecumenical hope that the creation of a United Reformed Church would be the first step to a wider unity.

It would be wrong to totally dismiss Bryan Wilson's argument that ecumenism is a reaction to church decline. Stephen Orchard, later Moderator of the General Assembly and Principal of Westminster College, says he first resisted the idea of ecumenism. "It was only when I went to South Wales that I realized what ecumenism practically meant. In the village where I was minister the Baptist minister, the Methodist minister and the Church in Wales rector were in the same boat, all struggling with a declining culture."[69]

The sense that the church was failing was clearly a motivating factor but there was hope and faith as well; a sense there was a better vision for the church. This was very much in tune with the mood of the 1960s. Although today Callum Brown, for example, sees the 1960s as the point when church decline became terminal, the generally optimistic mood, at least in the earlier part of the decade, affected the churches. There was, to take the title of a popular book by John Robinson, much talk of a *New Reformation* in the church. There was a great deal of creative theology as well as some very

68. Huxtable, *New Hope*, 39.

69. Orchard, interview, 2.

ephemeral thinking. For a time, with the publication of Robinson's *Honest to God* (1963), a real debate on religion took place. As Dominic Sandbrook rightly comments, "Although the sixties are often seen as a secular, even post-religious age, in few decades of the twentieth century were religious ideas so hotly and enthusiastically debated."[70] Stephen Orchard remembers the theological mood at Cambridge where Great St. Mary's was packed out to hear theologians lecture:

> I was part of a generation being pushed to look at the church in new ways. Abandon the old. There was a theological ferment. And I found in Cambridge at that time a particularly exciting theological ferment. So although I didn't buy into Anglican ecclesiology or ritual some of the spirituality and theological thinking was so obviously rich and useful that you wanted to share it.[71]

After John Robinson left Cambridge to become Bishop of Woolwich he could say in his first confirmation address at Southwark, "You are coming into active membership of the church at a time when great things are afoot. I believe that in England we may be at a turning of the tide. Indeed at Cambridge, where I have recently come from, I am convinced the tide has already turned."[72] It was an illusion, but one widely shared.

There were exciting new liturgies and modern hymns. Women's ministry was beginning to be more recognized and there was a renewal of social commitment. New forms of community service were pioneered. The Second Vatican Council seemed to be opening the way to unimagined changes. A declaration on religious liberty emphasized the rights of conscience while the "Pastoral Constitution on the Church in the Modern World," *Gaudium et Spes*, opened up the way for cooperation with non-Catholics. Anything seemed possible. As Adrian Hastings observes,

> The mood of the Church in 1965 and 1966 remained fairly euphoric. So many new doors were opening, it was not yet clear which doors were to remain closed.[73]

Although the origin of the project for Congregational-Presbyterian unity long predated the 1960s the actual successful establishment of the

70. Sandbrook, *White Heat*, 458.

71. Orchard, interview.

72. James, *Life of Bishop John Robinson*, 111.

73. Hastings, *History of English Christianity*, 530.

United Reformed Church is firmly rooted in the context of the Nottingham Conference with its commitment to unity by 1980.

To the prime movers like John Huxtable this was not just a managerial reorganization in response to a shrinking sales market; it was a response to a belief that the divine will could be seen in this. To Huxtable organic unity was "the will of God." More than that it was, he believed, "What the Gospel demands." When a commission report was criticized Charles Haig could say, "One is naturally resigned to resent a concerted attack on what one has struggled through many long meetings to get clear, especially when one is convinced that it was the Holy Spirit who led the group into unforeseen unanimity."[74] Such comments were naturally resented by those to whom, on the contrary, it was not clear at all that the decision came from the leading of the Spirit. But they reflected the deep conviction of those committed to union that this was of God. This was religious faith motivating change. The "Basis of Union" made it explicitly clear:

> The United Reformed Church has been formed in obedience to the call to repent of what has been amiss in the past and to be reconciled. It sees its formation and growth as a part of what God is doing to make his people one, and as a united church will take, wherever possible and with all speed, further steps towards the unity of all God's people."[75]

The great hope behind this union was that it would break the ecumenical logjam and become a catalyst for a wider union. During the service Cardinal John Heenan, Archbishop Michael Ramsey, and Free Church Moderator Irvonwy Morgan each greeted the Moderator of the General Assembly and pledged, "I give thanks for this union, and share your resolve to seek that wider unity which is Christ's will."[76]

The United Reformed Church was never about just the formation of a new church—it was created in the belief that this was the solution to the churches' central dilemmas. Ecumenism was the key to successful mission. It seemed to be the churches' last best hope. It is our conviction, wrote Huxtable,

---

74. In *Christian World*, 26 October 1961.

75. "Basis of Union," A1, in URC, *Manual* (2008).

76. Huxtable, *New Hope*, 33.

that unity and mission belong together and there is a real hindrance to mission in disunity. The word of reconciliation cannot be
convincingly spoken by those who are manifestly unreconciled.[77]

Of course those who formed the United Reformed Church realized
that the merger of two small churches would not of itself lead to a fundamental change in the missionary situation in England. Only a wider union
could do that. But the creation of the URC would, it was hoped and believed, be a catalyst for such a move towards unity.

The new church, however, was not possible without a cost. There had
been considerable opposition to the union among Presbyterians, but with
the exception of two congregations in the Channel Isles who chose, not
illogically, to join the Church of Scotland, Presbyterians accepted the majority decision. Arthur Macarthur puts it very movingly:

> There was little evidence of party spirit and after the vote was tak-
> en those who had spoken against the scheme were among the first
> to commit themselves to work in and for the United Reformed
> Church. We are Presbyterians, they would say, and we abide by
> the decision of the assembly fairly reached. Many of them car-
> ried heavy responsibilities in the new Church with undoubted
> loyalty.[78]

Congregationalism, however, with a different ecclesiology, split, and
not without some rancor. 597 Congregational churches (26 percent) opted
not to join the new church. As Huxtable says, "There were those who out of
deep conviction could not be persuaded that organic unity was the will of
God. . . . It cannot be denied that harsh words were spoken and sometimes
the less pleasant features of human nature manifest."[79] From the opposite
side of the argument the President of the new Congregational Federation,
R. W. Cleaves, admits the same:

> Such is human nature that in the exchange of opinions on matters
> affecting the very life of the Churches, debates sometimes engen-
> dered more heat than the central heating systems of the buildings
> in which they were conducted. . . . There were harsh words spoken
> and written: misunderstandings led to false criticisms; there were

77. Ibid.
78. Macarthur, *Setting Up Signs*, 7.
79. Huxtable, *New Hope*, 338.

more recriminations than any of those who were involved could have foreseen.[80]

To one later President of the Congregational Federation, Alan Argent, it seemed that the hurt was not always short lived. "Congregationalists felt and were rejected as if they didn't exist and characterized as if they held extreme, almost heretical, positions when they believed their position was essentially in line with traditional congregationalism over the previous 300 years."[81] With time the hurts mellowed and relationships reopened but the break remained. A number of difficult property issues had to be resolved and in the case of the assets of Albion Church, Hull, this led to a case in the High Court. "The recourse to law proved lengthy and expensive and brought little credit, only financial, to the heirs of the former Congregationalism."[82]

Three types of Congregational churches stayed outside the United Reformed Church. Firstly, there were some who wished essentially, as they saw it, to reconstitute the Congregationalism they had lost. In October 1964 a conference was held for those unhappy with the change from a "Congregational Union" to a "Congregational Church," out of which grew the "Congregational Association for the Continuance and Extension of Congregationalism."[83] In 1969 they issued a declaration of intent to continue the old union and their belief in a "truly comprehensive commonwealth of churches living together in freedom and mutual regard," which they described as the "true goal of Federal Christian unity."[84] When the United Reformed Church was formed they therefore moved to constitute a continuing church, though the Charity Commissioners would not allow them the use of the title "Congregational Union." They therefore chose the title "Congregational Federation" and adopted as their basic principle that which established the Congregational Union in 1831:

> The Federation of continuing Congregational Churches is founded on a full recognition of their own distinctive principle, namely, the scriptural right of every separate Church to maintain perfect independence in the government and administration of its own

---

80. Cleaves, *Story of the Federation*, 10.

81. Argent, interview.

82. Argent, *Transformation of Congregationalism*, 521.

83. Travell, "Congregational Federation," 29.

84. Ibid., 30.

particular affairs; and therefore that the Federation shall not in any case assume legislative authority or become a court of appeal.[85]

In 1997 the Federation had 11,797 members and 312 churches.[86] The first two presidents of the new Federation were both women, Lady Stansgate and Elsie Chamberlain, who feared that the United Reformed Church would undermine the equal status of women ministers.[87]

Secondly, a distinctly evangelical grouping of Congregational churches emerged. Despite being predominantly a liberal church there had always been an evangelical minority within Congregationalism. In 1947 the Congregational Evangelical Revival Fellowship had been formed and then in 1967 the Evangelical Federation of Congregational Churches was formed around the statement of theological belief, "The acceptance of the Divine Inspiration and supreme authority of the Bible."[88] They were emphatic that this statement was "not a creed we seek to impose on others, but a testimony of what we ourselves believe."[89] They did, however, see the distinction between themselves and the Congregational Federation as being that the Federation gave greater centrality to the independence of the local church and had "a more flexible attitude towards theology."[90] Some in the Federation viewed this differently. "They had a doctrinal standard—which itself might have been thought an unCongregational thing to do."[91] In 1997 they had 130 churches with a total membership of 5,000–6,000 served by 107 ministers.[92]

Thirdly, a small number of churches chose complete independence and did not join any new grouping. This group was quite fluid in number. By 1997 thirty had joined the Congregational Federation, fifteen had joined the EFCC, and twenty had closed, leaving forty-four churches.[93] A number of those had adopted the practice of believer baptism and might therefore be argued to have moved outside the Congregational tradition.

85. Ibid.

86. Ibid., 33.

87. Argent, *Transformation of Congregationalism*, 158.

88. Tovey, "Evangelical Fellowship," 43.

89. EFCC, *Yearbook 1996–1997*, 27.

90. Tovey, "Evangelical Fellowship," 43.

91. Argent, interview.

92. Tovey, "Evangelical Fellowship," 44–45.

93. Argent, *Transformation of Congregationalism*, 519.

To those who chose to join the United Reformed Church this schism in Congregationalism was a cost worth paying. It had to be balanced against the desirability of a union across denominational lines, which they hoped would be the catalyst for a wider union. There was a deep and probably irreconcilable theological divergence between the different viewpoints. To those who entered the United Reformed Church unity meant organic unity. Those who stayed out saw unity wholly differently—always about the relationship between independent churches. They were never going to enter any organic union. Elsie Chamberlain might endlessly call herself an "ecumaniac" but as Alan Argent comments, "perhaps somewhere deep inside herself, she did hope that the church unity movement would lead all Christians in some way to embrace the insights of the Independents."[94] That somewhat limited the prospects. At the very beginning of Independency Robert Browne had called for "Reformation without tarrying for anie."[95] Those who joined the United Reformed Church now thought they must make the same choice. But the cost was a breaking of the old Congregational fellowship, real anguish and pain, and not a little self-righteousness. The point needs to be taken very seriously. Organic unity is intended to restore the Christ-given unity of the church, but in practice it also frequently creates new divisions and threatens the unity of organizations. That was true of the formation of the United Reformed Church and was to be demonstrated again on the two occasions when further unions took place.

94. Ibid., 208.

95. Jones, *Congregationalism in England*, 16.

3

Happy Union Once More?

THE BREECH BETWEEN CONGREGATIONALISTS and Presbyterians had been formed in the period of Commonwealth and monarchical Restoration. The first attempts to heal it belong also to that period, with the setting up of the Common Fund in 1690 and a joint statement produced by a group of Congregational and Presbyterian ministers, entitled "Heads of Agreement," signed in 1691, which led to the "Happy Union" in the same year. Sadly, as David Cornick comments, "The Happy Union was doomed from the start."[1] Now it was restored. What Congregationalists and Presbyterians had been actively pursuing for forty years was achieved in 1972.

THE UNION

On 5 October 1972 people gathered in Westminster Central Hall for a meeting that formally dissolved the Congregational and Presbyterian Churches and created a new United Reformed Church. They then moved into Westminster Abbey for a service at which John Huxtable and the leaders of the other churches committed themselves to the search for unity. Nothing could have been a clearer statement of the purpose of the new church. The generally accepted scenario for the formation of the United Reformed Church is that it hoped its creation would break the ecumenical logjam and lead to the speedy creation of a united church so that it itself

---

1. Cornick, *Under God's Good Hand*, 77.

would have only a short life. As Ronald Bocking put it, "this act of union was seen as the herald of many others."[2]

There is no question that these ecumenical hopes were for the most part genuine. No church ever came into being with a more explicit commitment to unity than did the United Reformed Church. Arthur Macarthur felt he could claim, "We are unique."[3] The United Reformed Church's stated purpose was "take wherever possible, and with all speed, further steps towards the unity of all God's people."[4] The hope for a wider union was frequently expressed. In his sermon in Westminster Abbey John Huxtable took as his text Ephesians 4:13: "until all of us come to the unity of the faith and of the knowledge of the Son of God." As Tony Tucker says, "It was a text for a grander theme than the union of two relatively small churches. The goal was nothing less than the visible unity of all God's people in one Church."[5] In the sermon Huxtable referred to his expectation that "the union of our two churches would be but the beginning of a larger coming together."

To Huxtable and Macarthur, the wider union was their primary commitment. John Marsh, who frequently put the case for union in the *Congregational Monthly*, spoke for many:

> This small act of union which we hope to achieve will, I hope, be
> a prelude to the day when a united community of local churches,
> each together in its own place, accepts the task of responding to
> Christ's commission to preach the gospel."[6]

For him and many others this wider union, not a joint Congregational-Presbyterian church, was the primary hope. "I do not think this war can be won till unity is achieved."

Of course not everyone shared this eschatological hope with equal fervor. As Martin Cressey argues, there were people in both the Congregational and Presbyterian Churches who were motivated by the fact that their churches were in decline and "were persuaded that it would be a good thing for the two churches to come together to achieve a more sustainable size."[7]

---

2. Bocking, "United Reformed Church," 14.

3. Personal letter, Macarthur Papers.

4. "Basis of Union," A1, in URC, *Manual* (2008).

5. Tucker, *Reformed Ministry*, 97.

6. *Congregational Monthly*, August 1967, 2.

7. Cressey, interview.

Donald Hilton makes clear that despite later becoming Moderator of the General Assembly of a church committed to organic union, he himself had never supported this aim. His ecumenical commitment "was a gentle growth from getting together with other Christian churches to worship and working together,"[8] never a belief in organic unity. It was "a shock" to him when he saw this was leading to episcopacy.

There was some difference of emphasis in the two uniting denominations. Among Presbyterians there was more awareness of the advantages of a joint Congregational-Presbyterian Church. When putting the case to his fellow Presbyterians Macarthur, who knew his constituency, predominantly puts the union in the context of the long relationship between Congregationalists and Presbyterians. At Presbyterian Assemblies the debate centered not so much on the possibilities of wider union as on questions such as the compatibility of the role of moderator with the Presbyterian belief in the parity of ministers and with the gain to Presbyterians of being part of a genuinely national church.

> The scheme of union asks very little major change for either of us. . . . Now that at a world level Presbyterians and Congregationalists are coming together in one great Reformed alliance, the union in England will give us the chance to be an effective "sister" church.[9]

He himself could see the supposed advantages.

> One of the things I certainly hoped in 1972 was the URC would be able to serve the unchurched Presbyterians in England in a way the PC E. could not do because of its thin spread and scattered nature. Our Bristol Presbytery had only 10 churches in it and they covered the whole of Western England and South Wales. Presbyterians moving and finding the Church of England dubious as to whether they were church members or not, became so disenchanted with the Church and with forms of worship that were strange to them that they lost all contact with the Church.[10]

Not everyone was convinced. The slightly maverick Gordon Harris could say,

8. Hilton, interview.
9. Macarthur, in *Presbyterian Outlook*.
10. Macarthur, "What Did I."

Union will certainly be achieved but not with any great enthusiasm. . . . Organic union in itself may turn out to be the marriage of two denominations on their death-bed. Instead of dying apart they now die together.[11]

For the most part, however, the belief in wider unity was strong. As Erik Routley dramatically put it, "Go home and show your people that at this Assembly God has spoken and we want to obey"[12] For the Presbyterians Arthur Macarthur declared, "The main drive of our efforts and the most distinctive note in our Basis of Union was the proclaimed intention to seek further unions and seek them quickly."[13] He could say,

> The other churches look to our union with almost frightening expectation. They expect us to see the road of ecumenical progress with a new clarity because we have united. Under God there is no reason why they should be disappointed.[14]

Reflecting on the hopes he held then, Tony Burnham remembers, "We saw ourselves as the torchbearer carrying a flame that we hoped would ignite the ecumenical passions of the other major denominations."[15]

A PROVISIONAL CHURCH

Inevitably the expectation of being a provisional church affected the actual church that was created. Ronald Bocking, who was on the Joint Committee for Conversations between the Congregational and Presbyterian Churches, suggests that the choice of the name for the new church was in part a reflection of the expected short existence of the new church. "The name was not the best name but we didn't think it would last too long."[16] Stephen Orchard makes exactly the same point:

> There was a very interesting correspondence I saw in the Joint Committee minutes leading up to union. . . . Ebenezer Cunningham, who was a former Chairman of the Union, happened to say

11. In *Presbyterian Outlook*, March 1966.

12. In *Presbyterian Outlook*, July–August 1967, 14.

13. Speech on the twenty-first anniversary of the Regent Square URC, Macarthur Papers.

14. In *Presbyterian Outlook*, October 1972, 2.

15. In *Reform*, July–August 1992, 3.

16. Bocking, interview.

that he thoroughly disapproved of the proposal we be called a Reformed church because it sounded like a group of women who misbehaved. Others didn't like the word united. So the United Reformed Church was eventually sold to us on the grounds we won't be a denomination for long so we'll put up with it.[17]

The structure adopted by the new church was also partly a reflection of its expected impermanence. The Congregational Church had been organized in county unions with a national Assembly while the Presbyterians had presbyteries and a General Assembly. The new church adopted a more complex structure than either of its predecessors with district councils, provincial synods, and a General Assembly.[18] This was the structure for a large church and in the medium term was to prove impossible to maintain. In part its adoption could simply be put down to the fact that it enabled the essentials of both pre-existing structures to be maintained. In part it may have reflected delusions of grandeur in the new church. But it also reflected the fact that if the church was not going to be in existence in the medium term then perhaps the difficult questions did not have to be faced. David Peel, who was to be Moderator of the General Assembly and Principal of Northern College, argues:

> In fairness one reason we had both district council and synod at the beginning was because we didn't think the church would last ten years. We had the district council because the Presbyterians wanted their presbyteries and the synod because the Congregationalists wanted their county unions. And we had both because we thought in the next dispensation it would all change . . . as a result lots of intelligent people agreed to fudge things and not press issues because they thought it wouldn't last.[19]

This left the United Reformed Church with an overly complex structure that put too many demands on too few people and was to prove unsustainable in the long-term. As Peel says, "At the beginning it was not a Congregational-Presbyterian Church but the wider goal that was clearly fueling my excitement."[20]

17. Orchard, interview.
18. "Basis of Union," B1–16, in URC, *Manual* (2008).
19. Peel, interview.
20. Ibid.

STRUCTURAL DECISIONS

That the church was not expected to last long did not stop the church making quite radical changes in structure in the area of ministerial deployment and finance. In classic Congregationalism the ability of a church to call a minister depended on its ability to pay a stipend, although the constraints of this were mitigated by the creation of the Church Aid and Home Missionary Society at the Leicester Assembly of 1877. Later the ministry in weaker churches was supported by the Maintenance of the Ministry Fund, from which churches who could not meet the minimum stipend could apply for help. In the Presbyterian Church of England, with its relatively large congregations and its rule that normally when a church dropped below fifty members it would close, it was found possible for all churches to be ministered to and for ministers to be centrally paid.

The URC adopted something close to the Presbyterian system, with agreed deployment of ministers and a commitment to provide ministry for all churches, though it did not adopt the Presbyterian provision for closing smaller declining churches. In the very different context of the United Reformed Church this removed from smaller churches the incentive to increase their income in the hope of being able to call their own minister, spread ministry more thinly over the churches, and imposed serious financial burdens on the larger churches (indeed gave them an incentive not to increase their membership any further). As Michael Hopkins comments, "The economic problem of the URC is that too many people are being subsidised by too few."[21] Former General Secretary Tony Burnham is equally critical:

> I thought we lost a lot by opting for the Presbyterian pattern of paying for ministry. The Congregational way encouraged the local church to be self-supporting, with the richer pastorates helping the poorer and perhaps by spreading our ministers over so many churches, we have also discouraged the development of the learned ministry.[22]

The problem accentuated with the years. In 1973 the URC had 2,080 churches with an average membership of 92. In 2012 its 1,529 churches had an average membership of 41. In such circumstances it became increasingly hard for ministry to be focused and effective.

21. Hopkins, interview.
22. Burnham, interview.

Another financial decision taken at the beginning that was, as we shall see, to prove extremely significant for the kind of church the URC was to become was the decision to place most trust funds with the synods. This was hugely consequential but no one involved saw or intended the consequences. Norman Pooler, who represented the Presbyterians and would have preferred the funds to be held nationally, as they had been with the Presbyterians, argues a number of factors were involved.

1. An accident of history had left the greater part of the funds in the trusteeship of county unions for application within restricted geographical areas of benefit.

2. Practical politics required extensive negotiation with the legal committee of the Congregational Church and the county unions.

3. The need to provide for the allocation by the Charity Commissioners of most Congregational funds—other than local church property—between the URC and non-uniting Congregational churches.[23]

One may note that none of these reasons included theological criteria or judgments as to how the decision would affect the missiological nature of the new church. Presbyterian concerns as to the role of moderator were met by sincere assurances that Congregational moderators were essentially pastoral and worked with minimal office support. No one envisaged the kind of staffing levels that the trust funds would enable synods to develop or how this would contribute to changes in the role of moderator or to the relationship between the synod and both the national and local church. In this sense the United Reformed Church went into its future blind.

There was another, even stranger blindness in the structure and ecclesiology of the new church. The United Reformed Church's overriding purpose was to facilitate an ecumenical breakthrough and become part of a wider union. Surely, therefore, the new church would be designed to ease the path into that union? Arthur Macarthur saw this clearly:

> There are two possibilities. One is that that there is a real possibility of a united church. If this is the case the United Reformed Church needs to be organised to facilitate this. The other is that there will be a continuing United Reformed Church in which case there are identity questions.[24]

23. Pooler, interview.
24. Personal letter, Macarthur Papers.

There is, however, little evidence that either of these possibilities was seriously addressed.

This is apparent from the composition of the Committee itself. The Anglican-Presbyterian Committee had logically included consultant/ observers from the Methodist and Congregational Churches. If the URC was hoping soon itself to be part of an ecumenical union one would have expected this precedent to have been followed by including observers from potential ecumenical partners. No such proposal was made. There were observers from the Churches of Christ. "The Joint Committee has already greatly profited from the 'Observations' made by the Churches of Christ observers now attending its main meetings and some of its groups; their advice was particularly helpful in the redrafting of the section on Baptism."[25] On the same principle Anglican or Methodist advice would surely have been helpful in the sections on *episcope* and lay leadership. The minutes do not record that anyone proposed this. As to the United Reformed Church being "organized to facilitate" the possibility of a united church, there is little evidence for this. The challenges that such a union would face should have been clear to all. Presbyterians had already been involved in lengthy unity negotiations with Anglicans and knew exactly what the problems were.

THE LESSONS OF ECUMENICAL HISTORY

On 23 November 1946 Geoffrey Fisher, the Archbishop of Canterbury, had issued an appeal from the pulpit of Great St. Mary's Church in Cambridge to the English Free Churches to take episcopacy into their system. Fisher saw this not as leading to organic unity but to full communion: "What I desire is that I should be freely able to enter their churches and they mine, in the sacraments of the Lord and in full fellowship of worship."[26] David Cornick comments,

> A generous interpretation would suggest that Fisher had seen enough of the difficulties to realise that there was no other way around the difficulties of reconciling episcopal and non-episcopal ministries, but it is more likely that the innately conservative Fisher

25. Joint Committee for Conversations, *Report to Assembly*, 5.

26. Hastings, *History of English Christianity*, 466.

saw no reason why the Church of England should change, but every reason why the Free Churches should alter their polities.[27]

Two main responses came from this: a search for organic unity between Anglicans and Methodists (ironically, exactly what Fisher did not want!) and a dialogue between Presbyterians and Anglicans. The English Presbyterians had been part of this. From 1954 to 1957 the Church of England and the Presbyterian Church of England were involved in quadrilateral conversations involving the Church of Scotland and the Scottish Episcopal Church, which eventually resulted in the 1957 report *Relations between Anglican and Presbyterian Churches*. Then from 1966 representatives appointed by the Church of England and the Presbyterian Church of England, with consultant observers from the Methodist and Congregational Churches, met together and in 1968 produced a report, *Relations between the Church of England and the Presbyterian Church of England*. After that they met twice a year until the Committee was dissolved in 1973.

These discussions highlighted the two main problems involved in any Reformed-Anglican union. The first is bishops. On the Presbyterian side there was a rejection of the kind of personal episcopacy to which the Church of England was committed. Presbyterians did not reject the concept of episcope as such but argued that it has always been fulfilled within the Presbyterian Church.

> We believe that in the Presbyterian Ministry and Church Order all the functions of oversight or episcope are capable of being exercised and that the experience of four centuries demonstrates that they have been exercised for the welfare of the Church and the furtherance of the Gospel at home and abroad. Presbyterian Churches have been and are unable to admit that the absence of a separate episcopal order in their ministry detracts in any essential way from its being a real ministry of Christ's word and sacraments in the universal church.[28]

This did not exclude the possibility of change.

> We are prepared to consider whether the existing Presbyteral *episcope* of the Presbyterian Church of England could in some respects be better exercised if an individual episcopate were added

27. Cornick, "Story of the British Ecumenical Endeavor," 63.

28. "Statement of Some Presbyterian Considerations," submitted to the General Assembly in 1963, in Westminster College archives.

to it, provided that it be in relation to Presbytery and General Assembly, and therefore to the whole body of the Church.

The example of the role of bishops in the Hungarian Reformed Church was alluded to here.

At first it was hoped that this matter could be settled. "Provided that an adequate concept of the bishop in presbytery can be achieved, the suggestion should not prove unacceptable to Presbyterians and deserves further exploration and discussion, particularly on the Anglican side."[29] The problem, however, was that this was not the form of episcopacy practiced by the Church of England and was never likely to be. As the third draft of the document on *Relations between the Church of England and the Presbyterian Church of England* put it:

> Presbyterians would not be prepared for the state to exercise spiritual power within the life of the Church e.g. in the appointment of Bishops—while some Presbyteries are coming to recognise the pastoral function of the Bishop, they are less likely to welcome his ruling functions.[30]

At this point there was an impasse.

There was also a problem with the idea of the eldership. On the Presbyterian side this was seen as a vital principle.

> We maintain that government and pastoral oversight in the Church should be shared by lay persons, chosen by their fellow members and set apart to their duties as a spiritual office. In the Presbyterian Church of England these are commonly called Elders: and ministers and Elders serve together in all councils of the Church.

Such a view was not acceptable to the Anglicans. Presbyterians were quite explicitly left in no doubt by their fellow Anglican Committee members that the eldership would not be acceptable to them. In 1969, when the Committee discussed the proposed URC "Basis of Union," from the Anglican side Bill Allchin observed, "The Anglican fear is not of the eldership itself but of the restriction of service in the courts of the Church to ministers and elders."[31] Similarly, "Professor Mascall replied . . . that a half-

29. Ibid., 27.

30. Ibid., 25.

31. Church of England/Presbyterian Church of England Committee Minutes, 26 June 1969.

assimilation of some laymen to the ministry tended to exclude the whole of the laity from its proper place."[32]

Anglican-Presbyterian talks ended in double failure. The wider-based Anglican-Presbyterian talks were rejected by the Church of Scotland Assembly and in the later English talks the sense of stasis was apparent to all involved. By December 1971 Peter Hinchliff of the Church of England argued for the ending of the Committee:

> I have come to feel very strongly that the Committee ought not to continue any longer in its present manner. For about five years now, since before some of the present members joined it, the pattern has been not to attempt any practical steps towards reunion since this might complicate or even hinder the draft plans for union which each partner in these conversations was in process of considering in respect of another Church. This has meant that we have had some interesting and valuable theological conversations but have always stopped short of considering their full practical implications. There has been nothing to report to our Churches. We have on several occasions asked ourselves whether we are justified in using time and money for our meetings. We have not wished to seem to quench any ecumenical flax, no matter how small the smoldering may be.[33]

The conversations between Anglicans and Methodists had, as we have seen, also failed in a way that revealed both the contentiousness of the question of episcopacy and the inherent difficulty that balancing the interests of the different parties in the Anglican Church would cause any unity scheme. Fisher was not the only one for whom unity with the Free Churches was not an overriding priority. Evangelicals might not always have organic unity as a central concern and Anglo-Catholics would be looking much more towards Rome. Getting the two groups to agree on a unity scheme was an enterprise that had to rely more on hope than experience.

A CHURCH CREATED FOR UNITY?

The difficulties facing the United Reformed Church were formidable and clear but it is surprisingly difficult to see where the possibility of ecumenical union was a significant factor in the chosen structure. A study of the

32. Ibid.
33. Hinchliff, "Future of the Church."

Committee minutes shows that the main attention of the Committee was inward-looking towards the structures of the new church, not outward-looking to a wider union. As John Huxtable puts it, "An enormous amount of time was inevitably spent on seeing in what ways the new Church might be organised as a whole."[34] Questions such as regarding synod and district boundaries, ministerial remuneration, lay presidency, and the future pattern of overseas ministry were examined in great detail. Facilitating wider union rarely influenced the discussions.

There are only two places where ecumenical considerations can be seen to have been in the minds of the Committee. The first is in relation to synod boundaries:

> Some comment has been received by the Joint Committee that in an "open-ended" union there might have been gain in giving regard to the diocesan boundaries of the Church of England. . . . The Joint Committee has considered this but is unable to find any clear guidance pointing in that direction. In any case they do not correspond, say, to Methodist Districts. At this juncture there did not seem to be significant importance in this point to give it undue weight. The Joint Committee has therefore, moved to a more sociological basis for the Provincial boundaries.[35]

The other relates to episcopacy. There is a very interesting early draft of the "Basis of Union":

> Christ's oversight of His people has in some traditions also been exercised through representative persons commonly called Bishops. The (Reformed) Church recognises that in many places, and over long periods of the Church's life, Bishops have exercised a valuable function in the pastoral care of ministers and churches, in the establishment of good order and as guardians of the fellowship.
>
> In the (Reformed) Church those men who shall be set apart to the office of Moderator/Bishop shall be given a duly recognised place in the life of the Church. Their authority shall be seen to derive from the council to whose life they are attached.[36]

This is very much the idea of bishops in presbytery which Presbyterians had considered in earlier talks; it is not the Catholic concept of bishop.

34. Huxtable, *As It Seemed to Me*, 58.
35. Joint Committee for Conversations, *Report to Assembly*, 22.
36. Draft 2, Westminster College Archives.

57

But the fact that the word is being accepted would clearly have been a major statement of the willingness to affirm personal episcope. It was not taken.

There was a good reason for this. With regard to the earlier failure in Scotland Arthur Macarthur has written:

> In 1957 the direct talks had come to a stopping point. The occasion was the strong suspicion in Scotland about the very word Bishop. Ground elder is known in Scotland as bishop weed and any gardener will tell you that it is a pestilential weed by either name. Fear of the word made headline news in the Scottish press.[37]

The tone is revealed by Ian Henderson's comment that "The tempo of ecumenicity has been set by the time-table of Anglican imperialism."[38] There is little doubt the word would have had the same effect on some in the United Reformed Church. Had the church therefore been willing to embrace it from the beginning it would have significantly facilitated discussions for union. Perhaps even Anglican bishops might have been involved in the induction of the bishops for the new church? None of this, however, made it into the final draft.

On the question of elders there was simply no recognition that adopting ordained elders would in any way be inconsistent with being a provisional church. From the Presbyterian side Norman Pooler can still say, "We saw it as something we could offer to a united church."[39] Yet none knew better than the Presbyterian leadership the problems this had caused with the Church of England. They must have known that neither the Anglicans nor for that matter the Methodists would accept it as part of a united church. If they included it within the United Reformed Church they would have to discard it as part of an open-ended union. Why therefore was it included? It is important to recognize how contentious the Presbyterian eldership was in the union negotiations. As Arthur Macarthur puts it, "The question of the ordination of elders was perhaps the issue that took us nearest to failure in the long negotiations before 1972."[40] The Presbyterians, however, were quite insistent: "Just as the responsibility of all covenanted believers within the local church to seek in fellowship the mind of Christ is the spiritual heart of Congregationalism, so the eldership has seemed to most

37. Macarthur, *Setting Up Signs*, 99.
38. Henderson, *Power without Glory*, 180.
39. Pooler, interview.
40. Macarthur, *Setting Up Signs*, 114.

Presbyterians at the heart of that tradition."[41] Reacting to a suggestion from the Congregational Assembly that the eldership should be confined to former Presbyterian churches and such Congregational churches as were led to accept it, they were adamant: "The Joint Committee cannot believe that this is the way in which one of the major treasures of the Church should be treated."[42]

The Presbyterians were emphatic that no comparison could be made between their commitment to the eldership and the Anglicans insistence on personal episcopacy. So Arthur Macarthur can write to Raul MacDonald:

> You ask whether our attitude over the eldership is any different from the Anglican attitude over episcopacy, and I think in all honesty I can claim it is very different. The Anglican/Methodist claim at this stage is, as you realize, only a means of establishing full communion between the two churches, and if in order to attain that something has to happen to make Methodist ministers acceptable, then the Church of England is taking an absolutist position in a way we have never done about the eldership. Never in recent times at any rate have we made the eldership something that would keep us separate from another church. We have certainly pressed the eldership in going forward to the Congregational Church because we believe it to be something of more value in our life and something of value to offer to another Church.[43]

No doubt this is how it seemed to Presbyterians but others might wonder whether in practice the difference was as great as Macarthur suggests. From the Congregational side of the Joint Committee Ronald Bocking says that "what we saw as the great strength of the eldership was the pastoral side" and affirms that his impression was in any case that the Presbyterians would not have come into the new church without elders.[44]

What is quite extraordinary, if the United Reformed Church was to be provisional, is that no one ever raised the question of the effect of ordained elders on a possible wider union. In the new United Reformed Church the person responsible for explaining the new eldership to the church was the Secretary for Christian Education, John Sutcliffe. He travelled around the

41. Joint Committee for Conversations, *Report to Assembly*, 4.

42. Ibid.

43. Letter to R. MacDonald, 14 July 1969, Macarthur Papers.

44. Bocking, interview.

country meeting groups of elders. According to Sutcliffe the implications were thought of by no one.

> We were very excited about the idea of a new church being born and elders were there in the Scheme of Union and we were working our way through the implications of that. Not asking the fundamental question of why on earth we were having elders. . . . We didn't ask basic questions about it. I think you can take that as gospel.[45]

In retrospect, while it was certainly hoped and believed that the United Reformed Church might have only a short life, when it came to the fundamental questions about the nature of the new church the idea that this hope might have relevance to the new church's order was never grasped by any of those involved. As Sutcliffe says, "it was the structure of a church that came into existence to be in existence. It wasn't the structure of a church we were soon to say goodbye to."[46] From the Presbyterian side Norman Pooler, responding to the question of how the hope of achieving wider unity affected the negotiations, replied,

> Well it was what we hoped. We did see if we could relate synod boundaries to ecumenical partners but it was not possible. But our concern was in creating a united church.[47]

The URC's rhetoric was that it came into existence to break the ecumenical logjam. This is indeed mostly what it believed. But the proposal to unite Congregational and Presbyterian Churches long predates this. Talks between the Presbyterians and Congregationalists began in 1932 and continued until the war, although by 1935 it had been decided that full union was impossible. Although part of the wider search for unity, this was not originally about the creation of a short-lived ecumenical church but the creation of a united Reformed church. For Nathaniel Micklem and the New Genevans it was a part of a rediscovery of a supposed Genevan heritage. Its justification, then, was the contribution a Reformed church could make to mission.

The question therefore that needs to be asked is whether, despite the genuine belief of most of its founders that they were creating a church designed to have only a temporary life, the structure of the new church

45. Sutcliffe, interview.
46. Ibid.
47. Pooler, interview.

reflected the earlier search for Congregational-Presbyterian unity rather than the needs of a church designed to seek wider unity. From the Congregational side Ronald Bocking says that in his view the internal dynamic for the two churches to merge would have happened in much the same time, in much the same way, if the Nottingham Conference and the hope of wider union had not existed:

> There had been discussions back into the 1930s. Then there was a committee in the late forties . . . then local situations began to arise, New Barnet was an outstanding one. . . . I would say that there was a general pressure that led to 1963 in many ways.[48]

Behind the rhetoric of the United Reformed Church as the originator of an ecumenical breakthrough was the reality of the long-worked-for plans for a joint Congregational-Presbyterian church. Alongside the Congregational-Presbyterian Unity Committee minutes in the Westminster College archives are the minutes of earlier proposals for a joint Congregational-Presbyterian church. Here John Marsh argues for the creation of a strong Reformed church so that it can carry on the task of evangelism alongside the Church of England. The justifications for the united church may have changed, but not the ecclesiological reality.

The inescapable conclusion is that there was a failure of strategy and leadership at the origin of the United Reformed Church. No one asked the vital questions about what actually was being done and for what purpose, or what realistic prospects of success there were. Faced by Arthur Macarthur's challenge of organizing the URC in a way that would facilitate the creation of a wider united church, or responding to the identity crisis that a lack of such wider unity would bring, they did neither. It was a major failure in intellectual discernment.

At the same time we should not perhaps be too hard on those who planned the new church. Creating a union across denominational lines had not been done before in England. Inherently it is a difficult thing to do. While in an ideal world these things might be logically planned, in any real world some matters will not be adequately reflected on, some committees will be out of their depth, and the planners must react to the pressures of their constituencies rather than always do what might be ideal. Institutions will always seek to perpetuate their life and traditions, and what could be more natural than to believe that what matters to us will always come to

---

48. Bocking, interview.

be regarded as a great gift to the whole church, if only we can properly explain it? And if the new church did not shape its structure to facilitate wider union it would face a real difficulty. If the proposals for union had been such as would have made a wider union more likely, it is improbable that either Congregationalists or Presbyterians would have voted for them.

4

The Great Disappointment

FOR THE NEW UNITED Reformed Church realizing its ecumenical dreams was its fundamental *raison d'être*. One part of this followed quickly. At the first URC General Assembly an approach for unity negotiations came from the very small Association of Churches of Christ in Great Britain and Ireland.

UNITING WITH THE CHURCHES OF CHRIST

The Churches of Christ found their origin partly in the Scotch Baptists and partly in the preaching of an Irish Presbyterian minister, Thomas Campbell, who came to believe that Christian disunity was a scandal and that the way to restore unity was for the church to model itself upon the church of the New Testament.[1] In 1842 the first Conference of the Churches of Christ in Great Britain was held in Edinburgh and in 1847 it was decided to meet annually. Distinctive beliefs included a commitment to believer's baptism, an insistence on the parity of stipendiary and non-stipendiary ministry, and the autonomy of each local congregation.[2]

However, under the influence of scholars such as William Robinson, who studied theology at Mansfield College, gradually the Churches of Christ became less certain that truth lay exclusively with their model of

1. Thompson, *Let Sects and Parties Fall*, 7–8.
2. Ibid.

the church.[3] Two Commissions, on Ordination (reporting 1941) and on the Work and Status of the Ministry (approved 1953), challenged the traditional restorationist theology of the Churches of Christ. Presbyterian or episcopal systems of church government might also be compatible with the New Testament. Perhaps believer's baptism was not essential to the church? This did not take place without dissension and between 1913 and 1948 twenty three "Old Path" churches withdrew from the Association.[4] At the same time, after rapid growth in the nineteenth century the church went into deep numerical decline. In 1930 the Association had 200 churches and 16,000 members. By the end in 1980 there were only 75 churches and 3,586 members left.[5] Like Congregationalists and Presbyterians, the Churches of Christ were now a declining church with a diminishing sense of theological distinctiveness.

The ecumenical search for unity, however, seemed to offer a new hope. The question, Norman Walters argued in 1954, was "whether we are finally going to decline into a narrow sectarian body, or whether we are going to venture in faith, grasping the countless opportunities of the ecumenical movement towards furthering the cause of Christian Unity."[6] The most obvious ecumenical partner might have been expected to be the Baptists. Indeed in 1942 the Annual Conference of the Churches of Christ approved talks with the Baptist Union to discuss closer cooperation. Little progress, however, was made and the generally conservative direction of Baptist theology in the twentieth century, after Shakespeare's influence ended, included a more cautious attitude towards ecumenism than any other major Protestant denomination. By contrast Congregationalists and Presbyterians were demonstrating their commitment to unity in such a way that to many in the Churches of Christ they now seemed credible ecumenical partners.

In 1966 the Conference of the Churches of Christ authorized approaches to be made both to the Congregational-Presbyterian Joint Committee and to the Baptist Union. They had significantly different responses. As Philip Morgan put it,

> Our conversations with the representatives of the Baptist Union were cordial but their evident lack of interest in searching for a wider organic union discouraged us. . . . In the meantime we were

3. Ibid., 130.
4. Ibid., 127.
5. Hastings, *History of English Christianity*, 626.
6. Cornick, *Under God's Good Hand*, 180.

left in no doubt of the commitment of the Congregational/ Presbyterian Joint Committee to a wider organic union.[7]

As a result Churches of Christ observers sat in on the talks between the two denominations and at the United Reformed Church's inaugural service at the Abbey. Philip Morgan was one of those for whom this was one of the great moments of his life: "Blessed was it to be alive and sharing in that day."[8]

A formal approach was made to the United Reformed Church and a Joint Committee was set up with Norman Goodall as Chairman and David Thompson as Secretary. "Two areas in particular demanded our attention—baptism and ministry."[9]

1. Historically the Churches of Christ held that only believer's baptism was valid while the Congregational and Presbyterian traditions were paedobaptist. How could these two be reconciled?

2. While the Churches of Christ had a small number of full-time ministers most of their churches were served by ordained elders and deacons and by preachers. At Communion the president was always provided by the local church and was rarely the preacher, even if there was a minister present. How could this be reconciled with the URC's commitment to a full-time ordained ministry of word and sacrament?

The mood on the Committee was positive. As Martin Cressey said, "The members of the Joint Committee believe, as did those who united to form the Church of North India, that it is not the will of the Lord of the Church that they who are one in Him should be divided over such causes as divergence of conviction about baptism."[10] As they noted, progress was helped by the fact that observers from the Churches of Christ had been present since 1967 at the Congregational-Presbyterian Joint Committee to ensure that the union contained "nothing wholly unsatisfactory."

The Joint Committee reported in 1976 proposing that both infant and believer's baptism be available in every church and that the URC should initiate a non-stipendiary ministry. This caused few problems for the URC since it had always been possible in the Congregational and Presbyterians

7. Morgan, "1972 and Churches of Christ," 25.

8. Ibid.

9. Goodall, in *Reform*, February 1974, 3.

10. In *Reform*, June 1974, 17.

Churches for adults to be baptized, while non-stipendiary ministry was being developed in other denominations and would in all likelihood have been initiated by the URC in any case. Unsurprisingly the URC overwhelmingly accepted the proposals.

For the Churches of Christ the challenge was greater. They would be only a small minority in a much larger body and would be abandoning their traditional insistence on believer's baptism. The situation was complicated by one of the groupings within their tradition in the United States, which was opposed to the modern ecumenical movement and offered financial support and ministers free of charge to congregations who did not join the URC. "It would be a gross understatement to describe the resulting tension and, in some congregations, disruption caused by this as unhappy."[11] Deeply divided, the Churches of Christ failed to reach the required majority for unity.

This was a real crisis. Rather than give up the prospect of a wider unity, the Churches of Christ chose to dissolve their Association in order to allow the majority of its churches to join the URC, with fifty-four churches supporting the union, twenty against, and one not returning a vote.[12] Those in favor joined the Re-Formed Association of the Churches of Christ, which united with the URC in 1981. Without doubt this willingness to dissolve their church showed the ecumenical commitment and belief of the majority of members in the Churches of Christ. David Thompson comments, "Ecumenical commitment goes beyond mere voluntarism, in recognising a determination to live with diversity of view. But it is perverse to use that argument of diversity to criticise those who want to make the ecumenical step, by contrast with those who prefer to stay in their own small corner."[13] It was, however, also true that in a deeply divided, fast-declining church the ecumenically minded did not have much of an alternative.

Realistically the impact of the Churches of Christ upon the United Reformed Church, never mind the wider ecumenical scene, was limited. The number of churches joining the URC was so small that in many areas of the country there was no Churches of Christ representation within the URC. The total membership of the Re-Formed Association of the Churches of Christ was less than the annual URC membership loss. But the willingness of the majority in the Churches of Christ to respond to the URC's

11. Morgan, "1972 and Churches of Christ," 28.

12. Thompson, "Dissolution of the Association of Churches of Christ," 111.

13. Ibid., 112.

initiative was exactly the response that the URC hoped its creation would lead to and was an encouragement to those who still believed wider union was possible. As Arthur Macarthur said, "If the union takes place it will be proof that the tide of which our union in 1972 was one mark, still flows. If having come together we can demonstrate that across this divide the bonds of love and charity can grow, then, that will be a very great gift to all the churches."[14] It seemed to offer hope that the URC's example might indeed make a difference.

But it also illustrated the difficulty. As Adrian Hastings comments, "Considerable as the tide was in favour of unity in most churches there was nearly always a sufficient minority opposed to block progress."[15] All churches are to some extent coalitions of different theological viewpoints and emphases. Any move to organic unity exposes those divisions and is likely to prove a cause of internal disunity and dissension. Significantly, fear of this kind of division was one of the reasons why the Baptists had been unwilling to make concessions to the Churches of Christ.[16] The negative results of it were visible not only in the splits in the Churches of Christ but in the way the creation of the United Reformed Church had already led to two breakaway churches, the Congregational Federation and the Fellowship of Evangelical Congregational Churches.

Congregationalists, Presbyterians, and Churches of Christ might feel this was a price worth paying, but would the Church of England, the most complex church of all, be willing to accept the inevitable unbalancing of its doctrinal center that any union would mean? Anglican-Methodist union had faltered on this dilemma. Would the inspiration from the creation of a United Reformed Church really be sufficient to solve it?

TOWARDS WIDER UNITY

There was no doubt that the creation of a united church did give a degree of moral authority to the United Reformed Church, at least for a time. Kenneth Greet puts it positively, "I think that the URC by coming into being opened our eyes to the possibility of quite big things happening and set us an example of what could be done."[17] From the Anglican side Horace

14. In *Reform*, May 1980.

15. Hastings, *History of English Christianity*, 626.

16. Thompson, *Let Sects and Parties Fall*, 190.

17. Greet, interview.

Dammers, who proposed the "unity by 1980" resolution at Nottingham, urged the United Reformed Church to be positive about a response to its lead. "The URC can speak with the authority of having recently moved by means of a careful timetable to a new union and unity."[18] Brian Beck was a member of an Anglican-Methodist group committed to unity and they called a conference at Christ Church, Oxford to discuss the way forward: "This was just after the URC had been formed and the Churches simply said to the URC you must take the next step."[19]

The URC's declaration in its "Basis of Union" that "The United Reformed Church declares its intention, in fellowship with all the churches, to pray and work for such visible unity in the whole church of Christ as Christ wills"[20] did not stipulate a particular model of unity. But it was axiomatic to the leaders of the new church that the goal was organic union and this was simply assumed to be the way forward.

Huxtable was convinced it was possible. His secretary, Diana Jones, is emphatic: "I think they were absolutely convinced that within five to ten years organic unity was the goal. There is no doubt at all about that."[21] For Huxtable this belief was bolstered by the enthusiasm for unity of the Archbishop of Canterbury, Michael Ramsey. Before the United Reformed Church was formed he had, Huxtable believed, made his position quite clear:

> So the goal which our churches are considering is the goal of one united church. We watch with eager interest meanwhile the steps which the Presbyterians and Congregationalists are taking together and we believe that their sharing with us in one united Church is the true goal."[22]

But when it came to it would Anglicans, or for that matter the URC, really be willing to make the changes required? About his own church's willingness Huxtable had little doubt, but there were real questions as to whether this would prove to be the case when the implications of unity became clear. The Anglican-Methodist final report, for example, had made clear that both episcopacy and their being the established church were non-negotiable aspects of unity. On episcopacy it asserted, "An essential

18. In *Reform*, January 1973, 3.
19. Beck, interview.
20. "Basis of Union," A1, in URC, *Manual* (1988).
21. Jones, interview.
22. Ramsey archives, vol. 142, 268.

part of negotiations for Anglican-Methodist unity, is that the Methodist Church should become an episcopal church at stage one," and on establishment that "the historic church relationship, modified as necessary in detail; would seem to secure for the new church its most appropriate institutional form."[23]

When Michael Ramsey made this clear to John Huxtable, Huxtable assured him that both would be acceptable to the URC. Ramsey records:

> H (Huxtable) discussed current Free Church attitudes. H said that the old-fashioned hostility to establishment . . . had largely disappeared. As for episcopacy, he foresaw more difficulty about this for ex-Presbyterians than from ex-Congregationalists who were less wedded to their old polity. He thought that for the making of a new Church the role of the episcopacy would make sense in a way that it did not make sense in relation as an internal order question.[24]

It was certainly true that objections might be expected from the Presbyterians who had concerns about even the URC office of moderator. But there were also, as the Covenant debate was to reveal, still ex-Congregationalists who rejected what they saw as the hierarchical nature of the Anglican episcopate. Establishment too would be a more difficult issue than Huxtable suggests. David Peel would not have been alone in his objection:

> What kind of Bishops might we have in mind? Surely not the established Anglican version with its state appointments and collective power, so strong that they are able to thwart the will of what ministers and so-called laity might desire through Synodical legislative processes?[25]

Even with his own church there was an element of unreality in Huxtable's enthusiasm.

Before giving his sermon in Westminster Abbey, Huxtable went to see Ramsey to discuss what he should say. Ramsey notes, "I had yesterday a very valuable talk with John Huxtable and I think that he and I have a fairly agreed view about the sort of initiative on his part which will be helpful in his sermon on 5th October."[26] "He was concerned about how far he should

23. Ibid., 78, 281.
24. Ibid., vol. 237, 38.
25. Peel, *Story of the Moderators*, 88–89.
26. Ramsey Papers, vol. 237, 36.

go in his inaugural sermon; I said I hoped he would make a plea to work for a united Church."[27] Behind this affirmative encouragement there were, however, nuances of view that Huxtable maybe did not fully grasp. Like Huxtable, Michael Ramsey was passionately committed to organic unity and had felt deeply the Anglican rejection of Methodist union. According to his biographer, Owen Chadwick, he had come to the conclusion that in rejecting the Methodists the Church of England had not behaved "with intellectual integrity" and he was no longer sure "whether he had an enthusiasm for his Church, whether he could still plead with conviction, or feel, that it was the best of all churches. It had undermined its claim to be that."[28]

No twentieth-century Anglican Archbishop had such personal links with Congregationalism as Michael Ramsey. He had grown up a Congregationalist. His father had been a deacon at Emmanuel Congregational Church at Cambridge and his paternal grandfather a Congregational minister. He was now a convinced Anglican but remained positive about the Nonconformist heritage. As Chadwick says, "It must not be thought that he was ever anything but grateful to the Congregational inheritance."[29] There seems little doubt that one reason why, despite everything, Huxtable still looked for organic union was because of the encouragement he received from Michael Ramsey. But Ramsey had gone through the experience of Anglican-Methodist failure. He understood where the Church of England now was—perhaps in a way that Huxtable did not. Writing to Peter Hinchliff, one of the Church of England representatives on the Anglican/Presbyterian talks, Ramsey wrote:

> I am a little skeptical about the kind of conversations which are designed to produce a plan or scheme. I have a suspicion that a lot of things must happen to get an altered climate in which it is worthwhile to devise a plan or scheme. This is my present mood though I do not claim that it is a thought out conviction.[30]

Some of this caution he tried to explain to Huxtable.

> He was concerned how far he should go in his inaugural sermon. I said I hoped he would make a plea to work for a united church and would present the chief issues rather than create a policy. H

27. Ibid., 38.
28. Chadwick, *Michael Ramsey*, 345–46.
29. Ibid., 345.
30. Ramsey Papers, vol. 237, 32.

seemed entirely to agree. I said it was possible either to say, (a) "this is the sort of united church we should look for" or (b) let us create conditions from which a united church may spring. My inclination is for (b) rather than (a)."[31]

The phrase "H *seemed* [italics added] entirely to agree" may be significant. Sometimes we hear what we want to hear. Certainly it is difficult to see how this note of caution shaped Huxtable's response. Huxtable does, however, send Ramsey the text of the sermon for comment and receives a supportive reply. "Thank you very much for letting me see the text of your sermon, I am sure it will help us all as we try to face the next phase and I cannot suggest any alterations which might make it more helpful."[32] What he actually thought may be open to question.

What is certain is that the need for caution was not apparent in the Abbey sermon. Huxtable is clear that God is using the United Reformed Church. "The right hand of God is upon us." And his purpose is organic union:

> From the very beginning of our nine years' work we have repeatedly stated that we hope the union of our two churches would be but the beginning of a larger coming together of the Christian communions in this country. This is still our hope.[33]

For Huxtable delay was not going to be a virtue.

> For my part I do not think we dare behave as if we had all the time in the world. One of the dangers now facing us is that we should take fright at the difficulties of achieving union or be downcast or disappointed and so be tempted to seek some lesser goal. Or even take refuge in talks about talks.[34]

The new United Reformed Church acted quickly to make its initiative. In 1973 the first General Assembly sent an invitation to all Christian churches in England to talk together to see if any way forward towards Christian unity could be found. But from the very beginning it was apparent that this was going to be extraordinarily difficult. Who, for example, should take the invitation to the Anglican General Synod? The Anglican Board of Mission and Unity, which was deeply committed to organic union,

31. Ibid., 37.
32. Ibid., 65.
33. Huxtable, sermon, Westminster College Archives.
34. Ibid.

thought perhaps the Moderator of the United Reformed Church's General Assembly, Kenneth Slack, might present the invitation. This prospect was far too alarming for some. The Bishop of Maidstone, Geoffrey Tiarks, wrote to Michael Ramsey:

> My view, for what it is worth, is that the Board of Mission and Unity's suggestion is untimely—and that it could be counter-productive. . . . There was a good deal of euphoria at the Oxford Conference in January, though I noticed there was considerable reserve on the part of the Church Union and great caution on the part of people like Eric Kemp . . . in view of the scars left after 3rd May 1972, and the weariness of the Church with such schemes, there is everything to be said now for a cautious, low-key response to the URC invitation. To introduce the Moderator of the URC, in solemn state, would heighten the tension particularly if he spoke with the kind of frantic urgency which Kenneth Greet, for example, brought to the Oxford meeting.[35]

The Secretary of the General Synod, W. D. Pattinson, was equally alarmed.

> It would be unfortunate, at the present time, and damaging to the cause of unity, if the Moderator's visit was itself the cause of division in the Synod, or if it led to a division of opinion whether we should take part at all.[36]

On behalf of the Board of Mission and Unity John Arnold met with the Archbishop to urge its case for inviting Slack. He failed, however, to convince Ramsey that such a move would be timely.

> He did not wish, at this stage, to invite the Moderator of the URC to give the invitation personally . . . an element of exhortation would be counter-productive. It is a matter of accessing the emotional state of the Synod, and he doubts whether the right kind of emotion is yet present. Frankly he would be "rather nauseated" if there was to be a great display of initial optimism. Ultimately he is qualifiedly optimistic.[37]

It may be possible that the objection to Kenneth Slack was related to his connection with the radicalism of the British Council of Churches, but

35. Ramsey Papers, vol. 261, 60.
36. Ibid.
37. Ibid. 61.

even so if the prospect of a visit from the United Reformed Church Moderator of Assembly, whoever he or she might be, can cause such concern it might be wondered how realistic the United Reformed Church's prospects of organic unity really were?

The very real difficulty, if not impossibility, of the exercise soon became apparent. A wide spectrum of churches from the Roman Catholics to the Independent Methodists responded positively to the General Assembly's invitation. It was agreed that "talks about talks" should be held and they began in 1973. At the first meeting, at the United Reformed Church House on 19 October 1973, Huxtable challenged the churches as to whether they would commit themselves to organic union. The second meeting was held at Mansfield College on 14 December 1973. It went seriously wrong. The United Reformed Church pressed the point of who would be its partners in a scheme for organic unity. One by one most churches made negative responses. Bishop Butler for the Roman Catholics explained that English Catholics "cannot envisage a local union which precedes wider level union."[38] Elsie Chamberlain, for the Congregational Federation, affirmed that Congregationalists "believed firmly in unity. The aim should be a federation of congregations" (presumably offering the Congregational Federation as a model for the unity of the whole church). For the Baptists Neville Clark challenged the whole idea of organic unity and asked for alternatives.[39] All this might have been expected. The crunch, however, came with the response of the Church of England. The report sent to Michael Ramsey records, "The Church of England was noticeably cautious and it reaffirmed that in a united church the Bishops would be the primary focus of unity." Nothing must be done to make unity with the Roman Catholic Church more difficult. Leslie Brown for the Church of England suggested that "Intercommunion might precede the achievement of full union" and stressed the need to pray for unity. Perhaps a joint statement of aims might help?"[40] Only the Methodists made a positive response. "The meeting dispersed in a mood of despair."[41] The talks faced the possibility of a complete breakdown.

For Huxtable it was a shock. He could not understand what had happened. After waiting some days for his emotions to calm he wrote a personal

38. Ibid., 194.
39. Ibid., 210.
40. Ibid., 194.
41. Ibid., 210.

letter to Ramsey. "I still have a deep feeling of disappointment about the meeting. . . . We are dismayed at what seems a change of attitude."[42] His analysis of the situation was bleak.

> On the evidence so far to hand, it looks as if the most likely out-come of the talks about talks would be a convergence between the Methodists and URC without Anglican participation. It now seems that the Methodists and ourselves are convinced that steps to further union should be taken as soon as possible. I find no such conviction elsewhere.

For a moment Huxtable's illusions had given way to reality. He had no idea what could be done. "I am at a little of a loss to know what sort of lead I should try to give at the February meeting."[43] The seeming impasse was broken by a Methodist initiative. At the third meeting at Methodist Central Hall, Westminster, on 4–5 February 1974, Donald English for the Methodists presented a paper entitled "Church Union Talks—A Possible Way Forward." Rather than immediate steps towards organic unity, it pro-posed the possibility of growing into unity with a process of consultation that would require a commission. This they decided to examine. As John Huxtable observed, "Something like unrelieved gloom prevailed over some of these sessions."[44] The failure of Anglican-Methodist union weighed heavily with them. "At the heart of this anxiety was the feeling that in those proposals the issue of episcopal ordination had been put in a form which, it was thought, was most likely to carry the Church of England: what alterna-tive could now be brought forward?"[45] It was a good question. "At times the venture seemed doomed."[46]

The Methodist proposal, however, proved productive. It was agreed that a new Churches' Unity Commission should be set up for three years to review and further the ecumenical enterprise. This new body was widely representative of most of the churches, including the Church of England, the Baptist and Methodist Churches, as well as the United Reformed Church. John Huxtable became its Executive Officer.

He would certainly not have done so unless he hoped it had a real chance of success. As Diana Jones, who moved from the United Reformed

42. Ibid., 152.
43. Ibid., 194.
44. Huxtable, *New Hope*, 25.
45. Ibid., 25–26.
46. Ibid., 26.

Church to become Huxtable's secretary at the Churches' Unity Commission, observes, "The Commission was purposely only set up for three years and that was because they really and truly believed that within three years they would have done the spadework for a united church"[47] It had apparently turned out better than the pessimists had expected. Huxtable wrote, "I hope you will think the whole thing turned out better than I had feared. There came a moment at which the whole group took a fresh turn."[48] The question that was still to be answered, however, was whether, when the group once more raised the question of organic unity, the response would be any different or would still only be the Methodists and the United Reformed Church that would actually be willing to proceed.

Meanwhile it is clear that the intellectual leadership in the process of union had not come from the United Reformed Church. Just as at the creation of the URC there had been a fundamental failure to recognize any need to design the new church in such a way as to facilitate a wider union, so now their ecumenical strategy had been revealed as illusory at the first exposure to reality. They had completely failed to recognize what should have been obvious since the failure of the Methodist Union—that the Church of England was deeply divided on organic unity with the Free Churches to an extent that made any early union difficult to imagine. They had hoped that the sight of two small churches uniting would change all this. Diana Jones remembers,

> John thought the Churches would see the URC uniting and would respond. Ever since the Reformation someone had been talking with somebody. Then an organic union actually happened. And they thought this would be an example.[49]

This was to vastly overstate the significance of two dissenting churches in the Anglican mind. After the creation of the United Reformed Church the division of opinion in the Church of England remained as serious a problem for ecumenism as before.

The reality is that:

a) The leaders of the United Reformed Church were mistaken in their analysis of the readiness of the Church of England (and others) for

47. Jones, interview.

48. Ramsey Papers, 1974, 212.

49. Jones, interview.

unity. There was a self-indulgent over-assessment of their own importance in the scheme of things.

b) Few in the United Reformed Church ever really understood Anglicanism—what episcopacy meant in its life or why to many Anglicans reunion with the Free Churches was of little significance compared to the possibility of closer links with the Roman Catholic Church. In part Huxtable came to see this: "I did not wholly realize then, though I half did, that there were influences operating which would in effect say NEVER."[50]

c) Huxtable failed to take seriously Ramsey's cautions as to the difficulties.

d) Once it became clear that the simple fact of creating a United Reformed Church had not dissolved the obstacles to unity, as they had led themselves to believe it would, it became clear that the United Reformed Church leaders had given no serious thought as to what the way ahead might be. They were fortunate the Methodists had. It is hard to avoid the conclusion that there was a strategic and political vacuum at the heart of the United Reformed Church.

> The Churches' Unity Commission, however, was to be productive. It determined that there were four essential needs: to share in one faith, to acknowledge one membership, to recognize one ministry, and to be ready to share resources. Out of this, Ten Propositions were published in January 1976, largely through the influence of the Methodist Kenneth Greet.[51] These were:
>
> 1. We reaffirm our belief that the visible unity in life and mission of all God's people is the will of God.
>
> 2. We therefore declare our willingness to join a covenant actively to seek that visible unity.
>
> 3. We believe that this search requires action both locally and nationally.
>
> 4. We agree to recognise, as from an accepted date, the communicant members in good standing of the other covenanting churches as true members of the body of Christ and welcome them to Holy Communion without condition.
>
> 5. We agree that, as from an accepted date, initiation in the Covenanting churches shall be by mutually acceptable rites.

50. Huxtable, *As It Seemed to Me*, 70.

51. Ibid., 67

6. We agree to recognise, as from an accepted date, the ordained ministries of the other Covenanting churches, as true ministries of word and sacrament in the Holy Catholic Church, and we agree that all subsequent ordinations to the ministries of the Covenanting churches shall be according to a Common Ordinal which will properly incorporate the episcopal, presbyteral and lay roles in ordination.

7. We agree, within the fellowship of the Covenanting churches, to respect the rights of conscience, and to continue to accord to all our members such freedom of thought and action as is consistent with the visible unity of the Church.

8. We agree to give every possible encouragement to local ecumenical projects and to develop methods of decision making in common.

9. We agree to explore such further steps as will be necessary to make more clearly visible the unity of all God's people.

10. We agree to remain in close fellowship and consultation with all the churches represented in the Churches' Unity Commission.[52]

The crucial proposition was the sixth, which offered mutual recognition of ministries and provided for a future recognition of new ministers by means of a new ordinal that would include episcopal, presbyter, and lay roles in ordination. This was rather less than some ecumenists had hoped for. It was not a proposal to unite the churches by 1980 or any similar date. The more modest plan was to avoid the difficulties involved in full organic unity by substituting for it an act of corporate recognition from which it was hoped a wider unity would grow. John Reardon, who was later to be General Secretary of the Council of Churches in Britain and Ireland, observes that "My wife, particularly was very enamored of the idea that we would unite by Easter Day 1980, and when later the Covenant proposals came out she said, 'Well this is no good is it? This isn't anything like as radical as we expected.'"[53] Nor was it. Adrian Hastings calls it a "sort of half-way house."[54]

Even this was to prove too ambitious. Old problems, such as episcopal ordination and the ordination of women, were to prove as fatal to this new approach to unity as they had to the old. As the originators of this new

52. Huxtable, *New Hope*, 29–30.

53. Reardon, interview.

54. Hastings, *History of English Christianity*, 62.

move towards unity, the URC had responded warmly to the Commission's proposals. In 1977 the General Assembly passed a resolution that "The United Reformed Church welcomes wholeheartedly the promise of further steps held out in the report of the Commission." As far as Proposition 6 went, it indicated that it understood by this that the United Reformed Church would accept a ministry of bishops:

> We recognise that any advance towards visible church unity in England that is to include the Church of England, the Roman Catholic Church and the Orthodox Churches must honour the convictions of those Churches concerning the ministry of bishops and must find a basis for harmony between those convictions and the doctrine of the Church as held among us.[55]

The implication was that, as the URC exercised episcope through the structures of its conciliar ecclesiology and the ministry of its moderators, there was no longer in principle an objection to bishops. This turned out not to be the case for all the URC and as ever the move to organic unity revealed divisions in the church. Historically the objection to bishops had centered on the belief in the priesthood of all believers and the equality of all ministers of word and sacrament. Was this really compatible with the Anglican historic understanding of the role of bishop? As Daniel Jenkins put it,

> Doctrines of episcopacy vary but there can be little doubt that the 'historic episcopate' as understood by most Anglicans threatens the Reformed principle of the parity of all believers and implies an attitude to tradition which we have usually rejected. Moderators have never been given the juridical or disciplinary powers, nor the teaching authority nor the kind of right to ordain and confirm which bishops have.[56]

The United Reformed Church made its definitive response to the General Assembly in 1978. Synods voted 83 percent in favor, district councils 71 percent in favor, but local churches only supported the propositions by 57 percent, with 39 percent against, revealing a deep division in the church. However, the Assembly decided to proceed on the proviso that Proposition 6 should be accorded equally to women and men and that when in the

55. URC, *Assembly Record* (1977), 111.
56. In *Reform*, July–August 1978.

future ministers were ordained this should be without any special action by the other covenanting churches.

By now a number of denominations, including the Roman Catholics and Baptists, had made clear they could not continue in this approach to unity. Five churches, including the URC, went ahead. A new body, the Churches' Council for Covenanting, was set up under the chairmanship of Bishop Kenneth Woollcombe. Its task was to draft a Covenant on the basis of the Ten Propositions. In 1980 this was set out in *Towards Visible Unity*.[57] This proposed that each church would bring forward candidates for ordination as bishops and there should be a reconciliation of ordained ministry. All the United Reformed Church representatives on the Churches' Council for Covenanting accepted these proposals. The General Secretary of the United Reformed Church, Bernard Thorogood, declared, "we cannot accept that bishops are essential to being a Christian Church . . . but I have reached the point where I believe bishops are essential for the achievement of Church unity in England."[58]

Not everyone was so convinced. Some were concerned lest the ambiguity of the service of recognition call into question the validity of Free Church ministry. Donald Hilton, Minister of Princes Street URC in Norwich, who up to this point, had been deeply committed to the ecumenical process, was "horrified"[59] to find that a Covenant was only possible if the Free Churches accepted episcopacy. In a letter to *Reform* fifteen URC ministers set out their view that "the acceptance of episcopacy by the URC as a precondition for covenanting for unity . . . will not contribute to the wellbeing and intellectual integrity of a united church and could lead to further divisions in the Church."[60] This led to the formation of an Alternative Response Group chaired by Caryl Micklem of St. Columba's Oxford, with Donald Hilton as its secretary. Over two hundred URC ministers indicated their support. Their concerns were expressed in *An Alternative Response* issued by the group in 1981. The theological heart of this was an essay by Daniel Jenkins, who was a committed ecumenist and former Professor of Ecumenical Theology, but to whom it seemed that the report demanded "our immediate capitulation, without further discussion, to Anglican claims for their conception of 'the historic episcopate.' We can

57. Churches' Council for Covenanting, *Towards Visible Unity*.

58. In *Reform*, November 1980.

59. Hilton, interview.

60. In *Reform*, January, 1981.

choose it in any colour so long as it is purple."[61] From a feminist position Kate Compston argued that if episcopacy was non-negotiable for Anglicans why was the ordination of women not equally non-negotiable to the URC?

At the 1982 General Assembly the Covenant was agreed by a vote of 434 to 196, a majority of 66.88 percent. Technically this was sufficient—fractionally over the required two-thirds majority. But in practice it put the URC in the extraordinarily difficult position of only marginally approving the results of the process it had initiated. At the level of the local church the Covenant was supported by churches representing only 52,000 of the URC's total membership of 147,000, i.e., only 35 percent of the membership. Had the United Reformed Church included in its procedure for the Covenant a reference back to local churches with a need to reach an agreed percentage of approvals, it seems probable it would have failed. Certainly acceptance of the Covenant would have led to schism. Donald Hilton and others met secretly (though somewhat unproductively) with the Congregational Federation (Hilton, interview) and some would certainly have left the URC.

In the Methodist Church, despite some weariness, there was a general welcome for the proposals. However, the Church of England once again failed to agree, the proposal obtaining a two-thirds majority among bishops and laity, but just falling short among the clergy. If the acceptance of bishops was a step too far for some in the URC, the concessions made to the Free Churches over episcopal ordination were problematic to those of Catholic persuasion. Bishop Butler, one of the Catholic members of the Churches' Unity Commission, had made clear the problems it would cause with his church.

> If the Church of England receives the already ordained ministers of non-episcopal churches as true ministers of word and sacrament this would cast doubt on the acceptance by the Church of England of the doctrine of the ordained ministry. Thus a distinct step backwards would have been taken in the prospects of revised relations between the two communions.[62]

To the more Catholic members of the Church of England a Covenant with Reformed and Methodist Churches was not worth increasing the difficulties of eventual reunion with the Roman Catholic Church. Equally unacceptable to some was acceptance of the ministry of women ministers,

61. Jenkins, "Covenant or Capitulation."

62. Coggan Papers, vol. 101, 1.

let alone women bishops. In July 1982 proposals for unity were rejected by the General Synod due to the lack of a two-thirds majority in the house of clergy. Dr. Kenneth Greet, the General Secretary of the Methodist Church, drew a bleak conclusion: "The way marked out by a whole generation of ecumenical leaders has proved to be a *cul de sac*."[63]

COMING TO TERMS WITH FAILURE

The failure of the Covenant was a shattering blow for the hope of organic unity. Kenneth Greet remembers:

> The final meeting was really a tragic occasion. Before it was over Bishop Brown of Guildford said he wasn't well and he retired from the meeting and died. I have always regarded this as part of the price that he paid for his deep commitment to the ecumenical cause. It was the only time in my life I saw a room full of church leaders all weeping, partly because of the loss of a man we had come to know and love and partly because there was a sense of shame and disgraceful failure among the Anglicans.[64]

Greet puts the blame for the failure on a lack of leadership.

> Basil Hume said "I believe in a covenant but not this Covenant." I was very frank and I said, "you two Archbishops, Runcie and Hume, killed the Covenant." With some shock he said, "why do you say that?" "Well I invited you to the Free Church Federal Congress and you gave a splendid address but you poured cold water on the Covenant. And Runcie spoke in a very half-hearted way to the Synod. So between you, you killed the Covenant."[65]

It is doubtful if the blame should be personalized in this way. Hume, as a Catholic Cardinal, could not unilaterally support a scheme that would have accepted the ordination of women URC and Methodist ministers. With Runcie the charge has more force. He was far more interested in relations with Catholics and the Orthodox than he was with the Free Churches and was equivocal at best about the Covenant. As his biographer, Adrian Hastings puts it:

---

63. Woollcombe and Capper, *Failure of the English Covenant*, 30.

64 Greet, interview.

65. Ibid.

The trouble was that, probably until the very last moment, Runcie was unable to settle in his own mind what he should do. He was unable to back with full conviction proposals about which he remained deeply uneasy, yet for the Archbishop to speak and vote against the Covenant would have branded him in ways he certainly wished to avoid.[66]

As a result, Hastings concludes, "Never did the archiepiscopal trumpet sound a more uncertain sound."[67] But Anglican-Methodist unity had failed even with the full support of Michael Ramsey and might well have done so on this occasion, whatever Runcie had said.

The problem was not just the lack of individual leadership but the deep divisions within the Church of England, which meant it was unable to move ecumenically without alienating one of its own core groupings. What Keith Robbins had observed of the post–WWI period was still true: "The questions of faith and order raised in such discussions exposed the variety of opinions which could be found within the Church of England. To tilt, too decisively in one direction or another risked its own delicate balance."[68] Or as Stephen Orchard more succinctly puts it, "The Anglicans have no capacity to get together on ecumenical questions at all."[69]

A personal note for discussion at the Lambeth staff meeting on 22 January 1981 by Christopher Hill, the Archbishop's Assistant Chaplain on Foreign Relations, illustrates the dilemma.

In any case strong support (or fervent opposition) would alienate a significant number in the Synod and beyond and jeopardise the Archbishop's leadership in sections of the Church. He has to deal with "Catholics" "open Synod men," "evangelicals," and Free Churchmen for the rest of his archiepiscopate! Whichever way he votes must not be felt to be party.[70]

In fact the same problem was illustrated by the United Reformed Church itself. The Ten Propositions had only just been accepted and the Covenant would have been deeply divisive and caused schism. Even some who had voted for them, like David Peel, were relieved when they failed, in his case because it would have led to the breaking of ties with friends. "I

66. Hastings, *Robert Runcie*, 127.

67. Ibid., 128.

68. Robbins, *England, Ireland, Scotland, Wales*, 221.

69. Orchard, interview.

70. Carpenter, *Robert Runcie*, 213.

thought afterwards, when the Anglicans had pulled the plug, I felt a good deal easier."[71] What is more the intellectual climate had turned against organic union. When Runcie described the proposal to the General Synod as likely to lead to an "energy-consuming bureaucratic quagmire"[72] he was probably voicing views increasingly widely held. Even prior to the creation of the United Reformed Church there was widespread awareness that support for organic unity was diminishing. As Bishop Woollcombe noted, the real problem was not just the minorities who opposed such union. "In the end, in all the churches, there was a general lack of the enthusiastic heart to make the Covenant happen, and so it died."[73] Lesslie Newbigin commented on "the lamentable failing of the ecumenical vision in the minds of the English church people."[74] Adrian Hastings puts it bluntly: "It all seemed to have become an irrelevance, and rather a boring one too."[75] Rather than initiating a new breakthrough towards unity, the formation of the URC and the proposal for the Covenant it led to was the last gasp of a movement that in its current form was now exhausted. As Hastings even more bluntly puts it, "It is hard at this distance of time to conclude other than that the Covenant was a too hastily constructed expression of a form of ecumenical idealism almost at its wits end to find a way forward."[76]

Perhaps for this generation of church leaders the ecumenical strategy had been their life's dream. Though the strategy had by this point failed they had nothing else to offer. Huxtable felt deeply let down, ruefully commenting that the Church of England sometimes seems to be "The bridge church over which no traffic ever flows."[77]

It is not often that religious beliefs can be proved false in a visible way. But this is essentially what happened to the belief that organic union would renew the church. It was now clear to almost everyone that no such organic union was going to happen, at least in their lifetimes. As John Reardon comments, "The internal divisions within the churches are too great."[78] The failure was made even more visible by the fact that the Nottingham

---

71. Peel, interview.

72. Hastings, *Robert Runcie*, 127.

73. Woollcombe and Capper, *Failure of the English Covenant*, 25.

74. Newbigin, *Unfinished Agenda*, 249.

75. Hastings, *History of English Christianity*, 627.

76. Hastings, *Oliver Tomkins*, 126.

77. Huxtable, *As It Seemed to Me*, 70.

78. Reardon, interview.

Conference had actually set a date, 1980, by which organic unity was to be achieved. In retrospect it should have been apparent quite quickly, and certainly with the failure of Anglican-Methodist unity, that nothing of the sort was possible. But the very setting of a date for some took on eschatological significance. God would bring it about, and soon. So John Huxtable felt the hand of God on the United Reformed Church. So Alec Davies could write in 1973,

> If we face the matter unemotionally and take Nottingham seriously, this gives the United Reformed Church a life of eight years. . . . I can only hope that ecumenism will prevail and that, in Sydney Webb's phrase about the London School of Economics . . . the United Reformed Church will be "an institution upon which the cement never sets."[79]

To write this after the failure of Anglican-Methodist unity required a suspension of disbelief and a fundamental failure of intellectual analysis. As Adrian Hastings puts it,

> It would be more than foolish to blame a long generation of committed ecumenists who put so much of themselves into realizing this model. Nevertheless by the mid-1970s the message should have been becoming clear.[80]

The question is, why could the URC leaders not see it? What exactly was going to change Anglican or Baptist minds or the sociological imperatives working against union? The then Moderator of the Congregational Western Province, Charles Haig, optimistically suggested that "A United Reformed Church which has already combined the best insights of Congregational and Presbyterian churchmanship will be in a much stronger position to talk with Baptists, Methodists and Anglicans."[81] It was indeed to be the case that its ecumenical credibility was to give the United Reformed Church, at least in its first few years, an opportunity for ecumenical initiatives. As Kenneth Greet generously puts it, "I think that the URC by coming into being opened our eyes to the possibility of quite big things happening and set us an example of what could be done."[82] There are, however, limits to the cash value of ecclesiastical good will. Good will was not going to change

79. In *Reform*, January 1973, 4.
80. Hastings, *Robert Runcie*, 125.
81. In *Congregational Monthly*, February 1968.
82. Greet, interview.

Anglican views on episcopacy, the Baptist commitment to congregational autonomy, the Methodist preference for unity with Anglicans, or induce the Roman Catholic Church to change is doctrines. Nor did other churches ever accord the United Reformed Church the significance that it did itself. None of the autobiographies or biographies of church leaders from this period make more than passing references to the United Reformed Church. The new church's General Secretaries were to discover the limits of their importance on the ecumenical scene—humiliatingly when Anglicans and Methodists simply went ahead with Covenant negotiations without them. As David Peel confesses, "I just don't think I thought it through. And I actually thought there was a charisma, a spirit about the URC that was going to move mountains."[83]

Was it possible that the structure of the URC could offer a way forward to unity? The Presbyterian members of the Presbyterian-Anglican Joint Committee did at one point suggest this. "The proposed Basis of Union creates a form of episcopal/synodical government, with safeguards for congregational initiatives, which might well serve as a blue-print for a future united church in England."[84] The vacuous nature of this hope was apparent even then.

It is important to distinguish between the project of creating a united Reformed church and the hopes that such a church could lead to wider organic union. The former had been long worked for and was achievable. Whether the problems of identity that Macarthur identified were surmountable, and whether any such church would be a more effective agent of mission than its predecessors, were open questions to which positive answers seemed possible. The idea that this new church could be the catalyst for a wider organic union, by contrast, was never a realistic possibility. This is not simply a matter of hindsight. The creators of the URC were aware of the diminishing prospects for organic unity. In 1967, at a meeting of the Congregational Council, Arthur Macarthur was blunt: "The first thing I want to say about this union is just that it is going to be too late in being achieved however fast we move from now on."

Church life had been easier in the 1950s than it now was:

> Unity was a dominant theme in the churches. But alas we failed and now it is later than we think . . . the tide of ecumenical concern

83. Peel, interview.

84. Church of England/Presbyterian Church of England Committee Minutes, 17 October 1969.

> is past the flood. A friend of mine, an Anglican who was for a time the secretary and one of the leading spirits of his local council of churches, said in my office not long ago—"I am sick of this unity business and am just going to get on with things in my own church."

He noted this negative mood was particularly strong with the young, who "did not want to spend time discussing the structures of a united church which they felt was mere institutionalism."[85]

If Methodists and Anglicans could not manage to unite, adding the United Reformed Church to the mix made the situation more complicated not less. The scale of the problem was apparent to Macarthur. In 1967, in a personal letter to his fellow Presbyterian Ernest Todd, he wrote:

> Anglican-Methodist discussions are in some trouble as you know . . . to return to a multilateral approach at this stage would be to put off all practical steps to union to the Greek Kalends. . . . To go back now with no reasonable assurance that we could make progress would be very unwise. If the High Anglicans will not wear this Methodist process of reconciliation, progress along the road of union with the C of E is out for a generation.[86]

The reason, after all, that the Presbyterians were now seeking union with the Congregationalists was not because this was their first choice but because they had discovered that the Anglican option was closed. Arthur Macarthur puts it bluntly: "Since Anglicanism pursued a policy of 'picking 'em off one at a time' and turned away from multi-lateral discussions we were forced to press ahead with our separate conversations with the Congregationalists."[87]

But to believers like Huxtable this was not about intellectual analysis—it was about belief. When in the Abbey service he declares, "God has brought us to the goal towards which we have been working,"[88] he believes what he says—God is moving them forward. If, as Erik Routley had said, "God wills it" surely it must be! When the United Reformed Church Act was brought before Parliament, the preamble declared the union to be "the will of God"—a phrase that somewhat ironically drew objections from the

85. Speech to Congregational council meeting, Southport, 14 March 1967, Macarthur Papers.

86. Letter to E. W. Todd, 18 September 1967, Macarthur Papers.

87. Ibid.

88. In *Reform*, November 1972, 9.

Rev. Ian Paisley, who argued that the House should not decide "who has the mind of the Almighty on this subject."[89] Even Arthur Macarthur for all his rational hesitations felt something of the same divine presence. Part of him either believed, or wanted to believe, that this might yet be for the renewing of the church. "So where were we going? The aim was vague as far as I was concerned. Vague yet vastly important."[90]

> It seems precious to claim that our little scheme will make enough contribution to the task to be an occasion of vision. But when two men previously estranged, put their hands and hearts together, Christ can do great things with them. How much more can he do if two bodies of Christian people who for four centuries have distrusted each other can come together for his service from Land's End to Berwick on Tweed.[91]

One may well suspect the romantic rhetoric is covering the fact that he really has no answer to his own question. But dreams motivate us in other than rational ways. Ecumenism was a life passion and a belief, not simply a rational calculation. That the possibilities were plainly narrowing did not take away the will to believe. It is well to remember that the 1960s were a time when dreams seemed possible. If peace and love were possible, why not a united church or, as John Robinson hoped, a new reformation? As Clyde Binfield comments in this context, "It is quite remarkable how intelligent men and women can delude themselves."[92]

To its believers organic unity was simply assumed to be right and coming. John Richardson was Ecumenical Officer for the Methodist Church and as such was involved in the Churches' Unity Commission and then the Churches' Council for Covenanting. He says, "During that time I think I assumed that Anglican-Methodist Unity was a done deal. I was naïve. I had no doubt at all."[93] As a young man he was influenced by the belief of more senior churchmen. "The people with whom I consorted—people like Rupert Davies, Raymond George, John Newton, then Philip Potter—they all had an ecumenical vision."[94] Out of this came his belief in a united church.

---

89. *Hansard*, 21 June 1972.

90. Macarthur, "What Did I."

91. In *Congregational Monthly*, September 1964, 1.

92. Binfield, interview.

93. Richardson, interview.

94. Ibid.

I was not precise how wide it would be. Looking back I probably lacked a strategic sense. I had a deep sense it was of God—but if you asked me to describe it organizationally I hadn't the foggiest idea. I was on the Churches' Unity Commission and was lost quite often. At the time I didn't understand the politics behind it all. I thought we could work things through. I didn't think it was doomed to failure. That was innocence and ignorance.[95]

For the United Reformed Church the influence of John Huxtable was decisive. Of the two principle movers in the creation of the United Reformed Church, Huxtable and Macarthur, there is no doubt that, despite Huxtable's greater theological achievements, Macarthur was the shrewder. With some foreboding he saw the problems and risks before Huxtable did, and with greater clarity, but he was a loyal servant of the church and tended to keep his doubts to himself. Huxtable, however, was to be the dominating figure in the creation of the new church. From the Presbyterian side, Alan Macleod, Moderator of the General Assembly in 1967, noted with surprise Huxtable's extensive influence at Congregational Church in England and Wales (CCEW) meetings, which he contrasted with the way Presbyterians handled their Assemblies.[96] Working alongside him, John Sutcliffe recognized the same degree of influence.

John Huxtable . . . had no understanding of his own power. I once challenged him about power and he said he hadn't got any, which was just nonsense. He was very, very, powerful.[97]

To Alan Argent, in his study of Congregationalism, Huxtable's use of this power and influence in the creation of the United Reformed Church was essentially manipulative, with Huxtable unwilling to accept the validity of other points of view in his determination to get his way. So when, for example, the three-hundredth anniversary of the ejection of Nonconformist clergy in 1662 was commemorated in his term of office, Huxtable made sure this was done in a muted way so that it "would not become a celebration of contemporary dissent—he made the past serve the present."[98] But in the ecumenical spirit of the 60s few would have wanted the kind of denominational assertiveness with which such events were remembered in

95. Ibid.

96. Argent, *Transformation of Congregationalism*, 478.

97. Sutcliffe, interview.

98. Argent, *Transformation of Congregationalism*, 465–66.

the past. Indeed to an ecumenical generation events such as 1662 could no longer carry the import they once had.

There is no doubt that Huxtable liked to get his way. Kenneth Greet says, "I found working with him got easier as I got to know him. But I could imagine he could be just a little bit dictatorial."[99] There is some justification in Alan Argent's assertion that "he became the churches' trusted guide."[100] But his ecumenical commitments were not simply foisted on an unwilling church; they were widely shared. No doubt there was a degree of manipulation, but there was also inspiration. When delegates leaving the CUEW Assembly of 1962 were met by students from New College with the slogan "Hux for Dux"[101] this had rather more to do with the respect and affection in which he was held than with his manipulative powers. Huxtable had real stature in the denomination and his advocacy inspired belief in the ecumenical project. It was obvious to all that he was patently sincere in his conviction that organic unity was God's will and the way God would renew the church. Such confidence inspired hope in others. As the *Daily Telegraph* said, he was "at the heart of the faction working for unity in which his presence and persuasive powers gave confidence to many wavering traditionalists."[102] As it happens, he was wrong in his assessment of what was possible. More than anyone else he was responsible for the intellectual blindness with which the church went into the union. But his influence was inspirational not just manipulative. He deluded others only after he deluded himself.

Disillusion was one of the great themes of the 1970s. As Ralf Dahrendorf sadly noted, "Gone are the high spirits, the clever ideals, the great hopes of the 1960s."[103] That was certainly true for believers in organic unity. The setting of a failed date suggests a comparison with the Millerites, the followers of William Miller, who predicted Christ's return in 1843–1844.[104] The period that followed was known as the Great Disappointment. Socially and intellectually, believers in organic unity might appear very different from the Millerites, but they too had an expectation that was born of faith, which by the end they believed despite the evidence. As Diana Jones com-

99. Greet, interview.

100. Argent, *Transformation of Congregationalism*, 462.

101. *Reformed Quarterly*, July–August 1992, 4.

102. *Daily Telegraph*, 23 November 1990.

103. Sandbrook, *Seasons in the Sun*, 297.

104. Harrison, *Second Coming*, 192–95.

ments, "they truly believed by 1980 they would have unity. It came out of belief and faith. In retrospect this had more to do with faith than reason."[105] Alan Sell comments that this was when "we had our Jehovah Witness moment and knew the date."[106] They were, however, equally wrong.

Once it became clear that 1980 was not going to bring reunion, and in fact reunion was looking increasingly less likely, ecumenists had to come to terms with its non-arrival just as Millerites had been faced with the non-arrival of their own hopes. Miller eventually admitted he had been wrong[107] and a good many committed ecumenists similarly came to realize that organic unity was simply not going to happen. David Thompson, for example, says:

> I had been deeply involved at the center of the Covenant discussions and had come to the conclusion that the Church of England would be unable to move ecumenically in relation to the Free Churches because of the question of the ordination of women and that it was reluctant to do that because it was going to mean either a split or a loss of members.[108]

A good many lost hope. John Richardson came to "a growing awareness that organizational unity was not my priority. The Churches' Unity Commission and Council on Covenanting just ground on. I think I lost heart somewhere."[109] In retrospect even Huxtable recognized the extent of his delusions: "I came to see that I had been working on a set of assumptions which I now see were too much of a pipe-dream. . . . I now see that this policy was wholly unrealistic."[110] It was a heart-rending end to a life given over to a dream of unity.

> This is perhaps a sad note on which to conclude the tale of what I tried to do in the last phase of my public life. I hope it does not seem sour. I have lived through more than half a century in which the churches have grown together in ways that are quite marvelous. . . . All that I acknowledge with much thankfulness, but I can

105. Jones, interview.

106. Sell, interview.

107. Schulz, *Being Wrong*, 216.

108. Thompson, interview.

109. Richardson, interview.

110. Huxtable, *As It Seemed to Me*, 70–71.

understand the mood of the Methodist who said to me, "They'll not lead me up the garden path a *third* time."[111]

Sheila Maxey, the United Reformed Church's first Ecumenical Officer, can now say of organic union, "I don't think anyone is looking really for that anymore."[112] That is an exaggeration. Just as some Millerites clung to their belief in an imminent Second Coming, some in the URC refused to accept anything had changed. In 2009 Graham Cook still believed it possible.

> I can't understand why not—it could happen. There's nothing to stop it anymore. The thing that stopped it was female ministry. And that's all gone.[113]

But after the failure of the Covenant few really believed this anymore. For the URC this failure was an utter disaster. As Tony Tucker says, "it now faced an uncertain future as a relatively small denomination which had been robbed of its *raison d'être*."[114] At the time of the earlier talks between Presbyterians and Anglicans Arthur Macarthur had warned that losing touch with the Anglicans would mean

> Any union between the Congregational Church and ourselves would result in a united church confused about its purpose and unable to find a role. I sometimes feel the chill of that prophecy.[115]

Why exactly should anyone join this church?

> We now have no clear platform . . . theologically that is right enough but strategically it is debilitating. . . . Our appeal now is that we are a nice group of people with warm buildings, free worship and lovely ministers. There are question marks against our future. We have declared that denominationalism is subordinate to ecumenism. So we have declared an open market. Choose any church you like—we make no claim to any important affirmation in doctrine or ecclesiology. Is that a valid stance in 1994 and the beyond?[116]

---

111. Ibid., 71.

112. Maxey, interview.

113. Cook, interview.

114. Tucker, *Reformed Ministry*, 163.

115. Macarthur *Setting Up Signs*, 89.

116. Macarthur, *Reform*, January 1994.

Indeed one might ask, if this indeed was the case, then what theologically was the justification for the URC's separate existence as a church?

For the hopes of organic unity, and indeed the ecumenical movement in England, the rejection was equally serious. Some deny this implication. In her *Method in Ecumenical Theology: The Lessons So Far*, the Anglican ecumenicist Gillian Evans does not deny that compared with the 1960s what followed was a time of ecumenical disillusion. She notes J. E. Vercruysse's description of the ecumenical mood as one of "disillusionment," "profound skepticism," and "resignation"[117] but argues it is of the nature of ecumenical progress that the first parts are always the easiest. She quotes Edward Cassidy: "The ecumenical journey is sometimes compared to the ascent of a high and difficult mountain. In the early stages of the climb, one makes rapid and easy progress; then the going gets more difficult and in the final stages every move forward is the result of great effort combined with special technical skill."[118] Evans argues that it is now more possible than it was before to identify the recurrent issues and recognize the inevitability of difficult work to be done before they can be overcome. "A large part of the answer undoubtedly lies in taking our time and a long term view. The ecumenical task is enormous and we have to adapt a timescale appropriate to the scale of the problems. On that proper scale the setbacks look like small interruptions and not major disasters."[119] She quotes Yves Congar: "In all great things delay is necessary for their maturation."[120]

It is certainly true that there was a major underestimation of the problems involved in organic unity both within the United Reformed Church and among ecumenists. They made light both of the sociological and theological problems and allowed wish fulfillment to cloud their judgments. They rarely understood churches other than their own. But the revealing of the problems did little to help overcome them. For Gillian Evans the failure of the Covenant is progress because it clarifies the issues and allows slow progress to be made towards them. It is just as likely, if not more so, that unity requires moments of extraordinary theological commitment, and that if this moment passes, even with the United Reformed Church, organizational resistance to change will mean that old church identities are reasserted. Much more likely than Gillian Evans' slow move to distant

117. Vercruysse, "Prospects for Christian Unity," 185–98.
118. Cassidy, "Uphill Ecumenical Journey," 653.
119. Evans, *Method in Ecumenical Theology*, 6.
120. Congar, *Dialogue between Christians*, 44.

objectives is the scenario that David Thompson offers: "If the churches lose interest in anything beyond co-operation, eventually even that will wither and die with a change of generation."[121] Before the Covenant vote Huxtable had assessed that if should it fail "then the movement towards Christian unity will be given perhaps the most serious setback it could receive in this land; and the consequences of that failure are hard indeed to reckon."[122] There was more realism in that than in Gillian Evans' optimism.

Earlier the Congregational theologian C. H. Dodd had asked, "do we care more about saving the face of our denomination than about the *Una Sancta*?"[123] The answer was clearly, for some, yes. At the time of the 1969 failure of the Anglican-Methodist union scheme Gordon Savage, Bishop of Southwell, observing that the Methodists were prepared to accept episcopacy and a threefold ministry, asked, "What more, in the Lord's name I ask, does the Church of England expect?"[124] He drew then the conclusion that only bitter experience taught John Huxtable and the URC.

> For the Church of England the scheme is finished. It is dead. It is no longer on the agenda. The Anglican vote has killed it and we must not allow pious thought to imagine it will somehow resurrect itself. . . . How can we seriously expect any other church ever again to enter upon discussions with us for unity if after walking together for fifteen years with the Methodists we say no without giving a theological reason, and without proposing a positive alternative?[125]

The United Reformed Church was the forlorn hope of ecumenical advance. It made its move when the moment had already passed. It hoped that somehow its mere existence would break the ecumenical logjam. In fact it left the English church scene largely unaltered.

121. Thompson, "Edinburgh 2010," 399.

122. Huxtable, *New Hope*, 83.

123. Dodd et al., *Social and Cultural Factors*, 53.

124. Coggan Papers, vol. 3, 56.

125. Ibid.

5

Local Unity

THE FAILURE OF THE national search for organic unity shifted the focus for unity from the national to the local. Until then it had often been assumed that local expressions of unity needed a wider national unity if they were to succeed. Without it, John Huxtable asserted in his Abbey sermon, "Local initiatives would end in confused impotence"[1] With the failure of the Covenant, however, the alternative possibility began to be considered. Perhaps if national unity was not a possibility local unity might instead be the way forward? By 1975 the perceptive Norman Charlton was already looking to this possibility in the ecumenical pioneer town of Swindon, as Stephen Brain records:

> I remember at one point Norman saying, towards the end of his ministry, just before he left that it was no good looking to see any coming together nationally. That was pie in the sky, and if any unity was going to come it would come from the grass roots level.[2]

LOCAL ECUMENICAL PARTNERSHIPS

By 1982 local ecumenical initiatives already had a considerable history and indeed a prehistory. The longest standing LEPs are four union Congregational-Baptist churches (the oldest, Hunstanton, formed in 1870). These

1. In *Reform*, November 1972, 3.
2. Brain, interview.

were the product not of the modern ecumenical movement but of the earlier search for closer unity between Congregationalists and Baptists. It was not, however, until the 1960s that local initiatives began in any number. By 1964 at the Nottingham Conference on Faith and Order they were designated "Areas of Ecumenical Experiment." The resolution passed at Nottingham called upon the BCC's member churches

> to designate areas of ecumenical experiment, at the request of local congregations or in new towns and housing areas. In such areas there should be experiment in ecumenical group ministries, in sharing buildings and equipment and in the development of mission.[3]

The Conference's section on ministry explains this in more detail:

> Some experiments are already in being in the field of group ministry (an ecumenical group of ordained men) and of team ministry (a group of full-time workers, ordained and non-ordained men and women, which might be denominational or ecumenical). Many more are required to provide a new common strategy in downtown areas and on new estates, with the cooperation of several churches.

In the early days, the Areas of Ecumenical Experiment (AEEs) were truly experimental. There were few guidelines, and there was no legal structure, certainly from the Church of England's point of view. Many of these experiments involved a number of churches sharing the same buildings for worship. In 1969 the churches promoted a bill in Parliament in order to provide a legal basis for the sharing of church buildings in AEEs. By 1973 it was agreed that the experimental phase was passing to something more permanent and that such schemes should be renamed "Local Ecumenical Projects." In 1973 the Department of Mission and Unity of the British Council of Churches (itself a significant title in its assumption that the two went together) sponsored the Consultative Committee for Local Ecumenical Projects in England (CCLEPE). Later in 1994 a Consultation on Local Ecumenical Projects sponsored by Churches Together in England decided that the term "ecumenical project" was itself too provisional a word and adopted the term "Local Ecumenical Partnerships."[4]

---

3. Davies and Edwards, *Unity Begins at Home*, 79.

4. In *Pilgrim Post* 22, July–August 1994, 19.

In 1978 in response to the Ten Propositions of the Churches' Council for Covenanting the Roman Catholic Church found itself able to agree only to three of the propositions. These were:

> Proposition 3: We believe that this search (for visible unity) requires action both locally and nationally.

> Proposition 8: We agree to continue to give every possible encouragement to local ecumenical projects and to develop methods of decision making in common.

> Proposition 9: We agree to explore such further steps as will be necessary to make more clearly visible the unity of all Christ's people.[5]

This, therefore, did open the way for Roman Catholic involvement in local unions and by 1992 6 percent of Catholic churches were part of LEPS (compared with 2 percent of Anglican churches and 23 percent of URC churches).

In practice, there were to be two main forms of local initiative. In some cases a number of denominations worshipped together in one building. In others, churches of different denominations covenanted together and integrated parts of their worship and mission. By the end of 1966 there were 170 such projects.[6] That number increased more slowly than ecumenical enthusiasts hoped. Ten years later it was still only 289.[7] Not everyone was unambiguous in their enthusiasm. Donald Coggan feared that they would simply lead to "an epoch of lawlessness." Even Oliver Tomkins, the Bishop of Bristol and the leading ecumenical figure for the Church of England, was ambiguous. His biographer, Adrian Hastings, comments,

> In theory Oliver was entirely in favor of LEPs, as they came to be called. In practice, however, he was not a man happy to let go of control here or anywhere within his diocese. There was a continual tension within him between the desire to encourage, and identify with youthful and prophetic enthusiasm and the anxiety to follow regulations and remain personally in control. In practice the latter usually won.[8]

---

5. Huxtable, *New Hope*, 30.

6. Hastings, *Oliver Tomkins*, 127.

7. Ibid., 154.

8. Ibid., 129

Throughout the history of LEPs Anglican bishops were to prove uncertain in the degree of enthusiasm with which they supported them. When in Sutton, Anglican, Methodist, United Reformed, and Baptist churches voted on a proposal to unite in the Anglican building, the Free Church leaders were outspoken in their support. All that Mervin Stockwood, the Bishop of Southwark, could manage was, "I commend you to study this booklet."[9] There were also practical problems with the LEPs. There was often little mentoring and a number collapsed.

Nonetheless, for their supporters high hopes were invested in the LEPS. There was a strong belief that they would contribute to mission. The CCLEPE Constitutional Guidelines of 1990 gave the rationale of LEPs as:

> The sharing of resources at the level of the local church in a partial but natural expression of the unity of all Christians. It provides an opportunity to explore more deeply the essential relation between mission and unity . . . (they) add a new dimension to the discussions between the Churches . . . such projects represent a response to the considerable, continuing movement and growth of population; a recognition of the inadequacy of provision by the Churches separately; a recognition that even where local churches are strong their resources of manpower, money and plant can often be deployed to greater effect; and an opportunity for the churches to discover new ways of undertaking their mission.[10]

Such views were shared in the LEPs themselves. In Old Town Swindon effective mission was the key to the hope of Anglican Margaret Williams. The LEP would meet "the criticism often made that we are fragmented, that the church up the road is different from that one here," they would be "more effective because we did things together, not vying with each other."[11] In the ecumenical flagship of Milton Keynes, James M. Cassidy, who was a Catholic priest for sixteen years, argued that the ability of Christians in LEPs to maintain diversity in unity was a sign of what was possible for the whole church.

> The LEPs strive to manifest the ultimate unity of those who are baptised into the one body of Christ which is made present in the body of the Church. They are a stage in the process of the growth of the Church, for if the church is considered as a living organism

9. Gooch, interview..

10. CCLEPE, *Guidelines*, 6–7.

11. Brain and Williams, interview.

there seems to be no reason to expect the denominational boundaries to be fixed in stone until the end of time. (In the LEPs) the differences have been marginalised and the reality of the common inheritance has become more obvious as the partners have grown together. . . . The same remedies can also be applied to the grief of the divisions of Christendom. With the power of the Spirit of the Risen Jesus they can be overcome.[12]

It was hoped that the reconciliation and inclusiveness of the Local Ecumenical Partnerships could offer the church a model of how diversity could be celebrated and affirmed. So Elizabeth Welch and Flora Winfield, in *Travelling Together: A Handbook on Local Ecumenical Partnerships*, argue that,

at their best LEPs are a foretaste of the unity of all God's people. . . . At their best LEPs provide models of reconciliation for the wider community of the church and of the world. In LEPs it is possible to look again at the way in which disputes are handled and resolved.[13]

Sometimes the language used was virtually eschatological in the change it expected LEPs to deliver. So the consultation on the future of LEPs organized by Churches Together in England in 1994 declared:

LEPs are grit in the system, irritants capable of producing pearls of reconciliation and renewal. Reconciliation will express the mutual acceptance of all members, ministries and sacraments in forms we cannot yet see in detail, but we are conscious that, as they are reconciled, the traditions of the Churches will be reshaped by the Kingdom to come, and unite the Churches in mission.[14]

It might be wondered how, after the failure of Anglican-Methodist unity and the Covenant, and the growing sense that people were turning away from organic unity, such unqualified enthusiasm could still be generated for LEPs. But as we have seen ecumenism was a faith commitment. Deeply held beliefs as to what God is doing are no more easily given up, or necessarily evidence based, by ecumenicists than by Jehovah's Witnesses. Beliefs like that are not easily set aside and hopes frustrated in one form easily take another.

12. Cassidy, "Membership of the Church," 514–15.
13. Welch and Winfield, *Travelling Together*, 66–67.
14. In *Pilgrim Post*, May–June 1994, 15.

So in this case the failure of the Covenant and the evident fact that organic unity nationally was not going to happen in the foreseeable future did not initially deter the growth of LEPs. In fact the numbers grew quite dramatically, reaching a peak of fifty-five new LEPs in 1989.[15]

New LEPs Established

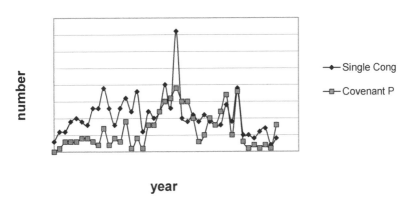

At this point a caveat needs to be entered. It was not simply belief that was promoting the growth of LEPs—practicality was doing so as well. One critical question that needs to be answered is, how much of this growth was really theologically motivated and how much was down to the increasing weakness of the church?

John Bradley, Field Officer (South) for Churches Together in England, stresses the positive:

> I think there has to be an element of both. But those that were formed out of weakness remain weak. There has to be more than just putting together two jaded congregations and assuming that life will emerge.[16]

This is to oversimplify. Certainly there were some LEPs that were simply founded out of a principled commitment to ecumenism. One of the most significant covenanted partnership LEPs was Old Town Swindon, involving Anglican, Methodist, and Congregationalist (later United Reformed) churches. Adrian Hastings says this became "something of a

---

15. Bradley, "LEP Establishment Statistics."

16. Bradley, interview.

model."[17] In his history of Immanuel United Reformed Church, Stephen Brain, who first came onto the ecumenical council in 1969, writes:

> What was so special about the coming together of the three churches was that they were established, large churches who were developing a common life not out of weakness, but out of a firm commitment to ecumenism. Elsewhere, perhaps, churches were being obliged to come together and join in a joint life together out of weakness and falling numbers but such was not the case in Old Town Swindon. All three churches were sizeable, influential and perfectly viable in terms of an independent existence.[18]

In fact, at the time the congregations of the three churches were of a size that could not have fit into any one of the buildings. Indeed, when in covenanted partnerships such as Old Town Swindon the LEP neither increased the provision of ministry, diminished the number of buildings, nor reduced the expenditure it is hard to see how expediency could have been the primary factor.

Expediency however was often a factor in single-congregation LEPs. These fall into two main categories: either a union between two or more existing congregations in a new building or one of the existing premises, or in a new site development. In the former case it is almost invariably the case that weakness was a primary initial motivation. So, for example, the motivation behind Palm Grove Methodist Church's union with Trinity United Reformed Church in Birkenhead is clearly recognized by the author of the history of the combined church:

> In the end geography, biology and arithmetic proved too much for the congregation. Palm Grove was only ten minutes' walk from the new Methodist Church at Charing Cross, itself formed by the union of three hard pressed congregations. The old building had been on clay soil on the site of an old pond and this cannot have helped the struggle against dry rot. The congregation's numbers had fallen below the point at which it could still hope to maintain and heat its buildings.[19]

In Sutton, the union of Sutton Congregational Church with Trinity Methodist Church was occasioned by the compulsory purchase of the

17. Hastings, *Oliver Tomkins*, 127.
18. Brain, *Ever-Flowing Stream*, 59.
19. Jones, *Portrait of Trinity*, 18.

Congregational building for the building of a new police station. The local historian, Colin Howard, records:

> It was largely practical considerations that provided the impetus for the two churches in question to come together, at a time when both of them were under financial pressure imposed by the ever-rising costs of the maintenance of their buildings.[20]

George Gibson's account of the origin of the Emmaus Church Centre in Chatham follows a similar pattern:

> We had a situation involving Chatham URC and the Parish Church. Both were in elderly buildings which were beginning to fail and neither had enough money to do much about it. . . . It was a matter of expediency but with goodwill behind it.[21]

While it is impossible to be statistically precise, the probability must be that such motives very frequently played a major part.

The planting of churches in new estates or towns introduces a different set of factors. Since, apart from the United Reformed Church, all the mainstream churches chose to develop more churches denominationally than ecumenically, it cannot be said that for national churches ecumenical development was a theological commitment. Often it certainly was a matter of practicality. The CCLEPE statement explicitly recognizes the problems caused by the growth and movement of population as a significant motivation behind LEPs. The large developments of the 1960s and after posed real financial challenges even for the larger churches. R. M. C. Jeffery, who was Secretary of the Department of Mission and Unity of the British Council of Churches from 1968 to 1971, notes that the expense involved in church building was increasingly problematic. The Anglicans, for example, built three churches in Corby at the cost of £1,000,000. By 1970 these were running at a deficit of over £20,000 a year with a church-going population of 250.[22]

Linked with finance was the preference of developers for ecumenical rather than denominational churches. In the vast housing estates of West Swindon, for example, four ecumenical churches were planted involving the United Reformed, Methodist, and Baptist Churches and the Church of England. George Gibson, one of the URC ministers involved, is clear that

20. Howard, *History of Trinity Church*, 90.
21. Gibson, interview.
22. Jeffery, *Case Studies in Unity*, 80.

the preference of the developer for ecumenical working was fundamental. "When the new ecumenical partnership was set up in West Swindon the developers did a deal. They said that the churches could have 0.2 of an acre but must work together."[23] Similarly, in Milton Keynes, the largest new site ecumenical development in the country, the land for the ecumenical Church of Christ the Cornerstone was provided by the Milton Keynes Development Corporation. Today some developers are even pressing for interfaith sites. The Field Officer for Southern England of Churches Together in England, John Bradley, comments:

> I think the pressure today is more than ecumenical—it's multifaith. It's the faith space—for those who like that sort of thing. That's been a struggle in some places. There is a new plant near Bedford where the developer wanted a multi-faith space, to which my response is to say, "OK how about having something similar for the political social clubs and have one place for the Labour club, the Liberal club and the Conservative club."[24]

Rather than being a theologically motivated option, the increasing number of Local Ecumenical Partnerships was often a practical strategy for a declining church, or a recognition that there was simply no option but to work ecumenically if a development was to take place at all. So George Gibson, after a lifetime's ministry in ecumenical churches, realistically reflects, "In all the occasions I have been involved it came out of weakness, either out of buildings which were falling down or when repairs couldn't be afforded."[25]

At the same time it would be wrong to dismiss theological belief as irrelevant. Some of the covenanted partnerships, as we have seen in Old Town Swindon, had no expedient reason for their creation. Similarly, in Central Sutton the longstanding secretary of the ecumenical council, David Gooch, argues, "There was also the idealism that together we could do things for the wider community which separately we couldn't.[26]

Even where weakness was a primary motivation the ecumenical option would rarely have happened had there not also been a theological commitment to ecumenism. A good number of declining churches chose an ecumenical survival strategy, but others in equally desperate situations

23. Gibson, interview.
24. Bradley, interview, 7.
25. Gibson, interview.
26. Gooch, interview.

did not. George Gibson, at the beginning of his ministry in the Medway towns, found a situation in which:

> The churches were all in various stages of death and one was in a condition I can only describe as *rigor mortis*. We closed a village church which had only three members because we couldn't find an ecumenical way through. What happened was I spoke with the congregation and said we can't go on, what I would like to do is talk to the parish church and with the Methodist Church and see if we can't get something going here. We have excellent premises. I already had an excellent relationship with the local vicar. The Bishop wouldn't wear it so that didn't happen and we approached the Methodist Circuit which was virtually bankrupt and they couldn't bear the idea of taking any kind of risk at all. So it didn't happen and we had to close the church.[27]

In Birkenhead problems with the premises may have led Palm Grove Methodist Church to unite with the URC, but in the same locality Oxton Congregational Church, with a tiny handful of people worshipping in the vestry of a 400-seat church,[28] did not seek to unite with the nearby ex-Presbyterian church and stayed out of the United Reformed Church altogether. Only when the congregation had completely imploded was the building bought by another, not markedly ecumenical, church. Many declining churches where ecumenical commitment was lacking chose to continue an independent life. In Wallington the United Reformed and Methodist churches might be only a few hundred yards apart but they chose extensive renovation of their own buildings rather than a joint project. In Epsom the declining United Reformed church chose a shared ministry with United Reformed churches in Ewell and Tolworth rather than uniting with the Epsom Methodists. Unity did involve belief, what David Gooch in Sutton described as "the idealism of the age that you could not in all conscience talk to people outside the Church and defend the differences."[29]

George Gibson recognizes the interplay of expediency and commitment that created ecumenical churches when he says of his united church in Chatham:

> Yes it came together out of weakness—both buildings were in difficulty, neither congregation was very large—but there were fifty

27. Gibson, interview.

28. *Congregational Year Book 1969–70*, 136.

29. Gooch, interview.

years of good will lying behind the merger, twenty years of active consideration, and about five years of deep discussion and involvement between the two churches and one another. Ultimately, it did come out of weakness, and you could call it expediency, none the less the deep strength in the desire to work together became obvious as the new church came together.[30]

Without that commitment very few ecumenical churches would have happened.

Unmistakably, the role of theological belief is most clearly demonstrated by the United Reformed Church. Having come into being in the belief that God might use it to break the ecumenical logjam, the reality of this belief is shown clearly by the commitment the church gave to Local Ecumenical Partnerships in a way that no other denomination did.

If we take the LEP total in August 201[31] we find that:

> Local Ecumenical Partnerships in England with the United Reformed Church August 2011
>
> The URC is a partner Church in 492 out of 895 LEPs in England.
>
> Of those 307 are Single Congregation Partnerships
>
> Of those 171 are with the Methodist Church only
>
> 29 are with the Baptist Church only (including 4 Union Churches pre-1972)
>
> 15 are with the Church of England only
>
> 1 with the Moravian Church and
>
> 1 with the Presbyterian Church of Wales
>
> 25 are with the Church of England and the Methodist Church
>
> 13 are with Baptists and Methodists
>
> 139 are Covenanted Partnerships, of which 39 are also Single Congregation Partnerships
>
> 22 are Shared Building Partnerships only
>
> 42 are Chaplaincy Partnerships

Since in 2010 the United Reformed Church had 1,545 churches this means that approaching a third of its churches are in an LEP—a figure way beyond that of any other denomination. This is partly down to local initiative, and partly to national policy in that the United Reformed Church, alone of all denominations, adopted a policy that all new church plants

---

30. Ibid.

31. Churches Together in England, 2011, cte.org.uk.

would be exclusively ecumenical. By comparison the Methodist Church planted about 100 new churches in the 1990s. Of these only 40 percent were ecumenical.[32] In the Church of England LEPs account for only around 9 percent of plants since 1967.[33] This is an impressive commitment to ecumenical church renewal by the United Reformed Church and can only be accounted for by theological principle.

HOW EFFECTIVE WERE LOCAL ECUMENICAL PARTNERSHIPS?

Evaluating the effectiveness of Local Ecumenical Partnerships is difficult and little serious attempt has been made to do so. It is certainly clear that they did not play the role in encouraging organic unity that some hoped for. The number of LEPs never reached the number its supporters hoped. In 1977 R. M. C. Jeffery called for the number to be brought up to 1,000 because only then would they be a sufficient force to seriously promote national organic unity.[34] Even in 2011, when the critical moment had long since passed, there were still only 895 LEPs. By then any thought of serious organic unity was no longer on the agenda. Despite the Anglican-Methodist Covenant it is significant that when a group of younger theologians in 2009 set out their hopes for the future none of them looked to organic union.[35]

An analysis of the rate at which LEPs were opened suggests the initial wave of optimism they engendered did not last. After the 1989 peak the number of new LEPs fell back. If we look at this in terms of five-year periods the trend is clear:

New LEPs	
1985–1989	161
1990–1994	88
1995–1999	100
2000–2005	64
2005–2009	39

32. Lings and Murray, *Church Planting*, 8.

33. Church of England, *Mission-Shaped Church*, 25.

34. Hastings, *Oliver Tomkins*, 154.

35. Curran and Shier-Jones, *Methodist Present Potential*.

Nor did all the LEPS survive. A number reverted to single denominational status or closed. In *Case Studies in Unity* one of the case studies was of Roundshaw, a new housing development in the borough of Sutton. Jeffery suggested that in such developments as this "The traditional denominational divisions seem to disappear altogether. . . . The gospel and not allegiance to any particular Christian community, becomes the point of unity."[36] The reality was quite different. In 2001 a Churches in South London review found that:

> The "Constitution" and "Introductory Statement and Declaration of Intent" (Oct 1981) clearly states that St. Paul's is an LEP and implies that it is a thorough-going ecumenical church, whereas all the evidence suggests that in reality it functions more or less entirely as an Anglican church. This is particularly so at present but appears to have always been the case, in large part. . . . It was evident to the Group, from all the feedback it received, especially its own experience of attendance at the mid-week Communion, that worship is offered only in an Anglican form. The Minister in Charge, Rev'd John Gould, makes no pretence about being anything other than an Anglican priest.[37]

The Baptist representative complained:

> I honestly don't think anyone dropping in would guess that it is, in fact, an ecumenical project. John Gould (the vicar) is aware of this himself and somewhat plaintively says "I really don't know how to do it any other way." The URC contingent is also concerned about this as they had contributed a non-stipendiary minister (Jean West) who left amid some accusations that she felt she was treated like a junior curate.[38]

Much the same point was made by Janet Sowerbutts, who was Ecumenical Officer for the Southern Synod: "Jean West the URC minister has recently resigned as the Free Church person. She has had an unhappy time as there was no real opportunity for Free Church worship to be expressed. Roundshaw has become an Anglican Church."[39] In 2002 therefore the LEP was dissolved, showing that in some cases the smaller denominations simply dissolved into the larger.

36. Jeffery, *Case Studies in Unity*, 115.
37. Churches Together in South London, *Review of St .Paul's Roundshaw*, 2–3.
38. Email, 14 June 2001, Churches Together in South London Archive.
39. Letter, 25 November 1999, Churches Together in South London Archive.

There were several factors contributing to the declining enthusiasm for LEPs. As Roundshaw illustrates, if the resources committed to an LEP come predominantly from one denomination there is a real danger that the ecumenical nature of the church becomes difficult to maintain. The Churches in South London review commented:

> Contributions from other denominations have been intermittent. Throughout the LEP's history, only the URC church has made a contribution in the form of an ordained minister. . . . The relevant denominations have recently been approached regarding the possibility of future financial resources but none has indicated any intention of providing this.[40]

As church resources dwindle, maintaining real contact with LEPs can be challenging.

Crucially the hope that LEPs would by virtue of their unity be more effective turned out to be illusory. Though it is difficult to be precise as to the relative performance of ecumenical churches to non-ecumenical churches, there was certainly no positive advantage. Over the period 1995–2000, for example, the united URC-Methodist churches in the URC's Southern Province declined by 14.2 percent compared with a decline of 13.97 percent for Southern Province churches in general.[41] The difference here is statistically insignificant but suggests that once two denominational churches unite (as will have been the case with most joint URC/Methodist LEPS) they decline or grow exactly as any other church. "We always thought once we became an ecumenical church that would attract people. Why isn't it happening?" That question from a long-time member of Trinity United Reformed/ Methodist Church in Sutton reflects a common experience in LEPs.

When it comes to new ecumenical church plants there is no evidence that these are more successful than denominational plants and some suggestion that the reverse is the case. One salient fact that helps explain the fall in the number of new LEPS is that progressively the percentage of church plants that were ecumenical declined.

> Whereas over half the earliest plants used an ecclesial venue, by the 1990s it was only one third. Many of the latter were either already redundant or under threat of closure. Over the same period the proportion of plants that were LEPs steadily declined from 1 in 7 to 1 in 20. They made sense on green field sites but their

40. Churches Together in South London, *Review of St .Paul's Roundshaw.*

41. URC, *Year Book 1995* and *2000.*

cumbersome procedures and internal preoccupations earned them a bad name among the planting fraternity.[42]

As the commitment to organic unity declined so the theological motivation for LEPs also declined (although the United Reformed Church is an exception in that it maintained an exclusively ecumenical development policy). Linked with this was the fact that most church growth was found not in the ecumenical churches but in Charismatic or conservative churches that were frequently little interested in ecumenism. Lings' suggestion that there were internal problems with the new ecumenical churches needs to be taken seriously. The growth in numbers in the new Local Ecumenical Partnership church plants has been unspectacular at best.

In Swindon, which was one of the most nationally important ecumenical areas, there were four new church plants in the ecumenical parish of West Swindon and the Lydiards, the first of which opened in 1978. By 2007 the four churches together had a total membership of 129 and an average total attendance of 145. There were 31 children in worship. Two of the churches have no children at all despite being in new housing areas, where young families might be expected.[43] This can hardly be regarded as impressive when four denominations, including the Church of England, are involved in an area housing a total of 28,000 people. By contrast the largest churches in West Swindon are outside the ecumenical parish—the Roman Catholics and Freshbrook Evangelical Church.[44]

The other major ecumenical development in Swindon was the building of a new Central Church uniting five denominational churches on a new site (Methodist, Baptist, and three United Reformed churches, formerly Congregational, Presbyterian, and Churches of Christ). Its membership collapsed from 297 in 1990 to 135 in 2009, a decline of 54 percent. To keep this in context, whenever churches unite there is a tendency for the church to decline even if no ecumenical factor is involved. So in Southampton when Avenue United Reformed Church united with St. Andrews in 1986 the new church had 345 members but by 2009 this was 139, a decline of 59.7 percent, which compares with a decline of 47.5 percent nationally over the same period.[45] This suggests that while there may be no necessity

---

42. Lings, unpublished manuscript.

43. URC, *Year Book 2008*.

44. Gibson, interview.

45. URC, *Year Book 1986* and *2009*.

to suggest that ecumenism was a hindrance to church growth, the hope it would have a positive effect was not sustained.

Milton Keynes was the most important ecumenical center in the country. Christopher Baker, who was cofounder of the Wells Community in Milton Keynes, records:

> New congregations struggled to resource new buildings which in the early days were far too numerous to be sustained. They were often poorly sited, tight budgets meant that building materials were cheap, and designs were often inadequate thus producing buildings with a lack of spiritual luminosity inside and external presence and visibility outside. Absence of clear management structures hampered a proper integration of community and use in the later multi-or dual- purpose buildings. Ecumenical ventures often foundered on different levels of expectation, resourcing and management by the parent denominations.[46]

In 2007 there were 21 Local Ecumenical Projects in Milton Keynes with a total membership of 1,292, an average membership of 61.5 per church and a total of 1,057 worshipers, an average of 50.3 per church. The significantly higher attendance than West Swindon may partly be explained by the fact that in four of the ecumenical churches in Milton Keynes, unlike in Swindon, there was Roman Catholic involvement and that the Milton Keynes ecumenical churches included pre-existing Anglican churches. Even so it is less than impressive in comparison with a Milton Keynes population that in 2009 was estimated at 243,000,[47] suggesting that only 0.53 percent of the population are members of united churches—though these statistics should be treated with some suspicion since concepts of church membership are widely different across the denominations. This conclusion is supported by Baker in his PhD thesis, "Towards a Theology of New Towns,"[48] who found that LEPs had only a limited success.

The central ecumenical church in Milton Keynes is Christ the Cornerstone, which in 2007 was served by three clergy and had a membership of 205. This compares with a membership of 218 in 2000, suggesting a fundamentally static congregation.[49] Attendance figures, however, do suggest

46. Vincent, *Faithfulness in the City*, 90.

47. Milton Keynes Intelligence Observatory, "Population Projections," online: http://www.mkiobservatory.org.uk/page.aspx?id=1914&siteID=1026.

48. Baker, "Toward a Theology," 2002.

49. URC, *Year Book 2000*.

some decline, down to a morning congregation of around 100 at the main service and around 80 at the Catholic Mass.

Church Attendance: Christ the Cornerstone[50]

	Sat Mass	Sun 9am	Sun 1030am	Sun 6pm	Mon Mass	Tues Euch	Wed Mass	Fri Peace
2003	124	41	137	41	32	9	13	5
2004	145	42	142	49	37	11	15	5
2005	134	44	127	47	35	12	26	7
2006	106	43	110	42	29	14	28	7
2007	84	48	91	35	31	21	34	7
2008	85	48	105	32	30	16	33	7

This is hardly impressive for the flagship city center ecumenical church in the country. There is some suggestion that its influence in other ways was less than had been hoped for. The 2009 LEP review commented:

> Christ the Cornerstone is the first ecumenical city centre church in the United Kingdom. In spite of the fact that a number of volunteers are drawn from the other churches across Milton Keynes, we have found it commands no particular affection or respect from other churches.

By contrast the fastest growing church in Milton Keynes is a Pioneer Charismatic church.[51]

We need as ever to be careful here, because the relative failure of the hopes invested in a church like Christ the Cornerstone must be set in a context in which most mainstream churches were in serious decline. Christ the Cornerstone has at least broadly maintained its membership, which is better than the national average. But the reality here as elsewhere is that the ecumenical church plantings disappointed the hopes they gave rise to in the bright morning of the ecumenical movement.

The Church of England's report *Mission-Shaped Church* supports its generally negative attitude to LEPs by arguing that the need to work with a variety of denominational structures and the tendency to become focused on ecumenism rather than mission were problematic.[52] It is possible the

---

50. Ecumenical Church, *LEP Review Report*.

51. Steele, interview.

52. Church of England, *Mission-Shaped Church*, 129.

theological bias of this report needs to be considered. So John Hull in his *Mission-Shaped Church: A Theological Response* characterizes the report as very Anglican orientated with a highly "church-centric" view of cultural and social change. He argues the report casually ignores other denominations in England and that there is no attempt to furnish an ecumenical overview of what might be the calling of the church in a paradigm and culture that has changed dramatically.[53] Even if this is true the fact that a Church of England report shows such little enthusiasm for Local Ecumenical Partnerships is itself a sign of the waning of the ecumenical hope. A significant number of Anglican churches, such as Holy Trinity Brompton, pursue their own particular policy of church planting.

Nor is it necessary to have any insular Anglican bias to recognize the frustrations of having to relate to a variety of denominational bureaucracies necessary within an LEP. In the covenanted partnership decision making is also often cumbersome. Some initiatives will first have to be agreed ecumenically, then referred to each participating church for ratification, then referred back to the ecumenical level for final approval. This inevitably slows action. Frequently clergy in ecumenical appointments will find themselves having to attend the committee meetings of more than one denomination and so have less, not more, time for mission or outreach. Many who work in LEPs will identify with the frustration that Methodist Karen Jobson expresses when she argues, "over the years they have become institutionalized and often find themselves boxed in excessive legalism and bureaucracy, unable to be responsive to their localities in the ways they would like to be."[54] The United Reformed Church Moderator's Report to the Assembly in 1994 recognized the same problem:

> There is a pain and a cost to ecumenism of which we are all too well aware. . . In some places ecumenical ventures have failed and some LEPs have come apart. . . . The frustrations of Local Ecumenical Projects as they live with joint membership rolls and the covenanted congregations which still have to give time, energy and finance to supporting the separate denominations. . . . To those involved in these ecumenical ventures, the structures and necessary legalities to enable ecumenical action are ponderously heavy and slow and difficult to operate. It is no wonder that some ecumenical ventures have lost their first vision.[55]

53. Hull, *Mission-Shaped Church*.
54. Curran and Shier-Jones, *Methodist Present Potential*, 128.
55. URC, *Annual Reports, Resolutions & Papers* (1994), 90.

Looking from a wider ecumenical perspective, the Churches Together in England Field Officer John Bradley sees the problems caused by ecclesiastical boundaries not being coterminus. "It's what Bishop Michael Doe called discoterminosity. This is the frustration that we work with different maps. Our boundaries don't coincide so we look in different directions."[56]

Hull's suggestion of some hesitancy from the Church of England towards LEPs is also significant—Church of England support for LEPs has not been without some ambiguity, sometimes with differing levels of support from different parts of the church. A major disappointment for local ecumenism was the Church of England's failure to deliver on hopes for an ecumenical bishop proposed for Swindon, a highly significant proposal in the area of joint leadership, oversight, and decision making. The negative outcome reduced the energy for a similar venture in Milton Keynes, which instead established the model of "Ecumenical Moderator." Similarly, a proposal for a Welsh ecumenical bishop was accepted by the United Reformed and Methodist Churches but failed to get a majority with the Anglicans in Wales despite the support of the bishops.

Some diocesan bishops have been more open to ecumenism than others. In Chichester, for example, George Gibson found the High Church Anglican diocese negative towards LEPs. There the URC and Methodist congregations united.

> At one point the town center parish church was going to be part of it but the Bishop stood very firmly against. This was the diocese which once had Bell as its Bishop, one of the heroes of the ecumenical movement. But it's quite the opposite now. . . . Basically the Anglican hierarchy don't want to have anything to do with ecumenism. There is only one Anglican LEP in the whole of the diocese."[57]

And even where Anglicans are committed their background as the national church can cause complications. So Karen Jobson writes:

> At the time of writing I minister to two Methodist/Anglican Local Ecumenical Partnerships (LEPs). What is very apparent even when the congregations and clergy are deeply committed to shared working is that there are still disparities. My Anglican colleague sits on the Circuit Meeting with full voting rights; I attend Deanery Synod as an observer. He is authorized to serve within

56. Bradley, interview.

57. Gibson, interview.

the whole of the Methodist Circuit; no equivalent is extended to me. The buildings too are regarded in different ways; while the Anglican building is on consecrated ground and therefore subject to infinitely more bureaucracy, the Methodist building is not. There is still a sense that the Methodist Church is the inferior partner at every level and this causes frustration and resentment throughout. This local example is replicated throughout the country and can be observed in most of the practical efforts to engage with the Anglican Church.[58]

Ironically, some in the United Reformed Church felt somewhat similar concerns at working with the Methodists. From her perspective as Secretary for Ministries from 1996 to 2008 Christine Craven felt that:

Although we had loads of LEPs with the Methodists I'm not sure that the working relationship is as close as people think. And I think we are often seen by the Methodists as little brother, and small fry. There are all kinds of undercurrents.[59]

At local level it is clear that even in the most ecumenically committed denominations the appeal of Local Ecumenical Partnerships to many church members was limited, and that those with a pre-existing church commitment would frequently seek out churches that reflected their denominational worship preferences rather than joining LEPs. In Swindon this is recognized both by the LEPs and by the denominational churches. George Gibson notes that URC, Methodist, and Baptist residents of West Swindon mostly went to established churches elsewhere in the town, with the result that ecumenical churches largely served those with no real denominational link. "I went there 12 years after it started and by then already more and more who were part of the Church had no particular denominational affiliation."[60] In Old Town Swindon Stephen Brain noticed the same phenomenon from the receiving end: "Quite a number chose to drive past ecumenical churches. I think they wanted to keep their denominational roots."[61] In Chatham, where 30 percent of the uniting church was Anglo-Catholic, a significant number did not join the new ecumenical church.

Of that 30 percent we lost half before the merger even happened. They took the opportunity to join a local church that was more in

58. Curran and Shier-Jones, *Methodist Present Potential*, 127.

59. Craven, interview.

60. Gibson, interview.

61. Brain, interview.

tune with where they were liturgically. And then we lost the other half of that third in the first four or five months. And this came down to theology—they had previously been high church. The rector who came across was an evangelical as was his successor and I think that people were realizing they were never going to get back what they had had.[62]

In Milton Keynes too people sometimes sought out churches with which they were more familiar. John Reardon was the first General Secretary of the Council of Churches for Britain and Ireland and chose to retire to Newport Pagnell. One might have expected him to join the Church of Christ the Cornerstone at Milton Keynes, which was in easy reach, but in fact he chose to stick with his denominational roots. "Locally I go to Newport Pagnell and I am glad I am still in a United Reformed Church."[63] Apparently just because CCBI supports LEPs that does not mean you have to attend one. URC theologian Alan Sell does attend Christ the Cornerstone, but not without some tension.

> We belong to the Church of Christ the Cornerstone where we have five traditions and we try to honor all of them. But you do occasionally get dreadful things happening as when our curate got up and said, "The Bishop has a free Sunday and can come and give confirmation, so we shall begin confirmation classes." I accosted her afterwards and said, "What about Methodist, Baptist, or United Reformed people who want to be received as members?" :Oh," she said, "I didn't think of that." Well don't you think in a Church of this sort you ought? And don't you think in a church of this sort, all five churches and their heritage should be studied in such courses?[64]

In a society where physically mobile people can choose where they want to worship over a significant geographical area the often monochrome choice of an ecumenical church will not universally satisfy. The diversity sought may sometimes be theological as well as denominational. In West Swindon, for example, the ecumenical churches are exclusively evangelical.

---

62. Gibson, interview.

63. Reardon, interview.

64. Sell, interview.

> I think there was a strong theological homogeneity around the five churches. There was a distinctly evangelical flavor to the whole of the partnership and all of the ministers were in that tradition.[65]

Indeed today the website of the West Swindon and the Lydiards Church Partnership is explicit: "We are evangelical—in doctrine and its application to contemporary life. . . . We depend upon the dynamic power of the Holy Spirit—to renew us and impart charismatic gifts for healing, deliverance and other ministries."[66] In Gibson's time all the clergy were deliberately chosen only out of one theological tradition: "I think there was a bit of string pulling going on behind the scenes by a particular man who had a lot of experience of church life at a national level."[67] The same partisan choice of clergy appointments took place in Chatham. "Norman Warren . . . manipulated to get evangelicals into as many of the parish churches as he could possibly could."[68]

This tendency to theological homogeneity did not simply operate where evangelicals were manipulating appointments. At the more liberal end of the theological spectrum there was a tendency in LEPs for like-minded people to work together more effectively. In Sutton the Baptist minister, Michael Dales, observes,

> It works within our own LEP because we are all more or less the same theologically. We are all theologically slightly to the left of center. We are all thoughtful, open-minded, and inclusive. There is a natural tendency among people with an ecumenical involvement to be happier with people who think more or less as they do.[69]

The LEP in Sutton might include Anglican, Methodist, Baptist, and United Reformed churches but it certainly did not include the evangelical gospel hall or the Charismatic church worshipping in the local cinema. If you wanted to sing choruses you needed to go elsewhere.

This raises a significant question as to what real ecumenism is. A simple definition of ecumenism might be activities that involve more than one denomination. But in a deeper sense the ecumenical hope was that

---

65. Gibson, interview.

66. wswinlyd.org.uk.

67. Gibson, interview.

68. Ibid.

69. Dales, interview.

diversity in unity would enrich the life of all. Pope John Paul II set out this hope when, while Archbishop of Cracow, he told the 1969 Roman Synod,

> Communion in fact designates unity in its dynamic aspect. It is this kind of unity that is obtained between diverse members by a communication that tends always to be profound and abundant. Consequently, plurality, even diversity itself, is to be understood in relation to communion, with the tendency towards unity.[70]

This same conception of diversity as fundamental to communion is affirmed by Welsh and Winfield, who believe that within the LEP "the diversity of shared lifestyle demonstrates once more that Christianity is not a monochrome religion but embraces the wide variety of life in God's gift of creation."[71]

It is clear that in most LEPs the reality is rather different. There may be denominational diversity, but there is often theological homogeneity rather than a real experience of diversity in unity. George Gibson is explicit that for him it was easier to work with a fellow evangelical who was an Anglican than with a liberal member of the United Reformed Church: "It's just easier to have an understanding."[72] This is certainly a limited form of ecumenism—an ecumenism that operates across denominations but not between differing theologies. Michael Dales sees evidence of this in the success of Spring Harvest:

> It appealed to a particular type of churchmanship, more conservative, more charismatic. . . . What it showed is that within the confines of a particular kind of churchmanship nobody cared what denomination you belonged to. . . . Spring Harvest were all happy with each other because they shared a generally evangelical theology.[73]

Former Methodist General Secretary Brian Beck is perceptive here when he writes of LEPs,

> Created to resolve denominational differences and witness to the one Church in each place, they often accommodate the differences without reconciling them. Not only is their relationship to denominational parent bodies an uneasy one, but they tend to an

70. Cited in de Lubac, *Motherhood of the Church*, 223.
71. Welch and Winfield, *Travelling Together*, 66–67.
72. Gibson, interview.
73. Dales, interview.

independent outlook which is in effect an option for one particular ecclesiology.[74]

This may be ecumenism but it is a less significant form of ecumenism
than was originally imagined.

The sometimes limited degree of genuine ecumenism going on in
Local Ecumenical Partnerships can also be observed in a different way in
the covenanted partnerships. Here it cannot be assumed that the existence
of the LEP is significant for all those involved in the individual churches.
At the most basic level this is apparent in the unwillingness of significant
numbers of the congregations to support united services in another church.
Old Town Swindon has been in existence since 1969 but Stephen Brain's
estimate is that only "Thirty percent of Immanuel members would make a
united service elsewhere." Margaret Williams is slightly more positive about
the Church of England. "I think it would be more at Christ Church—perhaps 40 or 50 percent."[75] If these estimates are at all accurate they suggest
that at least half of those in one of the oldest LEPs in the country would
simply stay at home rather than attend worship in another church.

Churches Uniting in Central Sutton reflects something of a similar
pattern. Consider the following attendances (C=child, A=adult):

	Trinity	St Nicholas	Sutton Baptist
October 12	C46 A168	C20 A85	C12 A86
October 19	United Service at Sutton Baptist C26 A204		
October 26	C35 A120	C20 A97	C9 A62

The weekly fluctuations mean these statistics must be treated with
caution but the average attendance at the three denominational services
was 71 children and 314 adults, which means that the united service at-
tracted only 36 percent of average child attendance and 65 percent of average adult attendance. The number of children at the united service was
actually lower than the number that attended at Trinity on either of the
other two Sundays. It is difficult to see that much more than 50 percent of
the Trinity and St. Nicholas people attended the united service at the Baptist church. Although no single service is necessarily representative, in fact
on this occasion there was comment on the better-than-average attendance
at the united service for both adults and children. An indication of the

74. Podmore, *Community, Unity, Communion*, 229.

75. Brain, interview; Williams, interview.

problems of such services is that Trinity posts a deacon at the church door to direct those who are unaware of the venue to the correct church only a few yards away. At least some of these always go home when informed that the service is at another church.

The post-1989 decline in enthusiasm for LEPs is multi-causal. Nationally the more ecumenically committed churches were in numerical decline, and the growing churches were mostly more conservative theologically and less committed to the ecumenical movement. The lack of success of some of the LEPs is almost certainly no more than a local reflection of the decline of the national denominations. But the LEPs rarely lived up to the hopes that the enthusiasts had for them. Most of the churches were ambiguous in their support of them. The non-churched were not impressed by the sight of Christians working together. In practice LEPs could be cumbersome and time consuming. They lacked appeal to some who valued traditional denominational options and frequently exhibited a theological homogeneity rather than a rich diversity. While they had practical uses it got increasingly hard to get excited about them. As Michael Dales observed in Sutton, "now nobody talks about it anymore."[76] The people who had been enthusiastic for organic unity got older, and as this generation passed they were replaced by those who no longer shared the kind of commitment that had been there in the headier days of ecumenical growth.

The clear pattern in the LEPs is that the commitment to organic unity predominates in the more senior-age cohorts. In Sutton David Gooch notes, "the thing which is very noticeable is that those who are committed to the joint activities, certainly within our own church, tend to be those who were committed 30/40 years ago."[77] At Sutton Baptist Michael Dales records the ecumenical generation has nearly all gone:

> You had a traditional group who had been around for many years who were committed to it. A lot of them have now died or gone to old people's homes and the newer people who have come in are largely ignorant of the history and don't feel the commitment.[78]

In Swindon Stephen Brain notes the same phenomenon of ageing ecumenicists: "Mostly it is the people who have been ecumenically committed

76. Dales, interview
77. Gooch, interview.
78. Dales, interview.

from the beginning."[79] At Chichester George Gibson reports that those committed to organic unity "are all very elderly."[80]

More than one factor is involved in the greying of the ecumenical generation. Most congregations in mainstream churches now consist mainly, or sometimes exclusively, of elderly people. At Chichester, for example, George Gibson estimates that two thirds of his congregation is over seventy years of age.[81] It is hardly surprising therefore if a good many of his ecumenicists are old. But this can only be a partial explanation. More important is that the generation to whom organic union was a great faith commitment is dying out.

In the 1960s and 1970s organic unity was a bright new hope. Keith Clements, an ecumenically committed Baptist theologian, describes his theological background:

> I was in a circle who believed we were entering into the era of an unstoppable ecumenical advance. Undefined, maybe naive, but it was a feeling that we were all somehow "on the way to unity." We were being welcomed at each other's communion tables and altars. Extraordinary reports were reaching us from Rome as the Second Vatican Council got under way. The Abbot of Downside made history by coming to preach in Great St. Mary's, Cambridge. Bliss was it in that dawn to be alive, as over our bread and cheese lunches we argued and speculated. In such an atmosphere it did not really seem to matter which denomination you presently belonged to. It made little sense to transfer from one to another because one's real loyalty lay to the coming Great Church.[82]

The mood reflects the optimistic mood of the 60s ("It's getting better, it's getting better every day") and the great explosion of liberal theology to which it gave rise.

Something came out of that. Churches grew much close together. Fewer people believed in an exclusive heaven. But organic unity failed. The churches did not unite. The non-churchgoers did not respond. The optimism of the 60s and the liberal theology faded, and no succeeding generation felt the same excitement or the same commitment. At Milton Keynes

79. Brain, interview.
80. Gibson, interview
81. Ibid.
82. Clements, "Free Church, National Church," 423.

the Anglican Ernesto Lozada-Uzuriaga Steele argues the commitment to organic unity is now increasingly redundant:

> For many people twenty years or so ago they used to hold the dream that one day denominations would disappear. And I think with a lot of pain they are coming to terms with the fact this is not going to happen.[83]

In Methodism, the most ecumenically committed church after the URC, Martyn Atkins argues that younger ministers now see ecumenism as "nice but irrelevant"[84] and Karen Jobson uses exactly the same term: "I am under no illusions that for the majority of Methodists, the formal ecumenical movement is an irrelevance."[85]

The creation of Local Ecumenical Partnerships was always a mixture of belief and practicality. It would often not have happened without some practical reason that made it expedient. But it was this that often gave the believers their chance to break down institutional inertia and self-preservation. Today the practical reasons for uniting are greater than ever. There are many more small churches in deep decline. The developers still prefer to work ecumenically. But the belief is no longer there in the old ways. Today there is less excitement, less ecumenical faith, fewer new LEPs, and everything is in a much lower key. So at Sutton Michael Dales observes that the LEP is accepted as the way the churches work but the ecumenical council "isn't any longer a place where ideas are discussed and debated. It's more a place where we just share dates, and that's not what we were. It's sterile."[86]

So where does this leave John Huxtable's belief that without organic unity "local initiatives would end in confused impotence"? For a generation it looked wholly mistaken. Organic unity did not take place but the LEPs expanded and seemed to be able to insulate themselves from the denominational failure to achieve unity. But looking at LEPs now, fewer than was expected and no longer generating great hope, it seems possible to argue that Huxtable was partly right—once people no longer believed organic unity was possible or desirable, the LEPs no longer had the same degree of motivation, commitment, or purpose. Their practical usefulness might continue in the right circumstances, but Adrian Hastings' judgment

---

83. Bradley and Steele, interview.

84. Atkins, *Resourcing Renewal*, 41.

85. Curran and Shier-Jones, *Methodist Present Potential*, 132.

86. Dales, interview.

that "by and large the LEPs have achieved less and been fewer than Oliver (Tomkins) and his ecumenical colleagues hoped"[87] is difficult to dispute.

LEPS AND THE UNITED REFORMED CHURCH

For the United Reformed Church the relative failure of the LEPs was to prove highly significant. As we have seen, no denomination committed itself to LEPs in the way the United Reformed Church did. It alone exclusively chose the ecumenical option for the planting of new congregations. A higher percentage of its congregations entered LEPs than was the case with any other church. The fact that this did not actually prove to be the effective missionary strategy that was hoped for does not take away the integrity of the commitment that the church showed. But this exclusively ecumenical strategy for church planting had implications for the life of the United Reformed Church itself and its prospects for growth.

In retrospect many of those involved in the exclusive policy commitment to LEPs see its results as more negative than they had imagined. From his experience as General Secretary from 1992 to 2001 Tony Burnham reflects, "I have often thought we put in more than our share of money and sometimes more than our share of ministers. And this was weakening us."[88] The United Reformed Church's first Ecumenical Secretary, Sheila Maxey, argues that the church rushed into an exclusive commitment to LEPs without seriously thinking what it was doing.

> I've changed my mind about them since I retired. I've become very critical of them since then. I think we made a bad mistake . . . quite apart from the survival of the URC. If we think of the Christian Church we imposed on new areas where it was difficult to plant a church anyway, we put on these weak little struggling congregations, the task of having to relate to three different bodies. So we burdened what would already be difficult.[89]

The negative effect on the United Reformed Church is difficult to quantify but clearly significant. For a start it discouraged local initiatives in church growth. Historically many Congregational and Presbyterian churches had been the offshoots of strong congregations. So Immanuel

87. Hastings, *Oliver Tomkins*,169.

88. Burnham, interview.

89. Maxey, interview.

Swindon planted a church in Penhill or Trinity Claughton a mission in Brassey Street, Birkenhead. This was a way of responding to new needs and population shifts. It is today a significant source of church growth in the Church of England. The United Reformed Church's exclusive ecumenical commitment, however, effectively discouraged such initiatives. Tony Burnham says he discovered this on becoming North-West Moderator. It took "the ground from under my feet for new developments and mission initiatives. People said, 'Oh we've got to do it ecumenically.'"[90] He instances the case of Wilmslow United Reformed Church, the largest in the synod. "It was the biggest church then and I said, 'This is nonsense, you can't keep growing like this, you must form another church further out in Cheshire.' But the argument was it must be ecumenical."[91] Another former Moderator of the General Assembly, Graham Cook, argues:

> The fact we've placed so many of our eggs in that one basket means that we have not been able to take any initiative at all. Any time anyone has asked about building a new church there it's taken away all our energy and initiative.[92]

It is certainly true that the URC's exclusive ecumenical commitment led to fewer church plants than any of the main Free Churches. So in the years 1993–1999 the United Reformed Church was part of twenty-nine church plants.[93] In the same period the Baptist Union established eighty-eight church plants.[94]

Where development did take place ecumenically, the fact that the United Reformed Church was both numerically weaker and organizationally looser than its partner churches meant that it was often hard to establish any real URC presence. In actuality those with real URC connections were probably fewer than the number given to the national denomination. In West Swindon, for example, Toothill was designated as the Free Church and new members were allocated one quarter URC, one quarter Baptist, one quarter Methodist, and one quarter Anglican. But that didn't mean those assumed to be URC members necessarily had a real link with the denomination. They might be URC members, but did they know this? George

90. Burnham, interview.
91. Ibid.
92. Cook, interview.
93. Lings and Murray, *Church Planting*, 9.
94. Ibid.

Gibson is honest: "I don't think they were desperately aware."[95] Christine Craven comments, "The URC membership is often nominal and gets more so."[96] The sheer number of LEPs also inevitably meant that many churches would be served by ministers who might well have little understanding of the URC theological ethos. Noting that in 1994 one fifth of the ministers serving in URC churches were non-URC, Philip Morgan expressed concern that without their being instructed on what the URC was, "we shall cease to be anything in particular."[97]

In joint URC-Methodist LEPS the United Reformed Church frequently also lost out because, as the church with a much looser organization and normally fewer members, in practice this meant Methodist influence normally tended to predominate. URC ministers found themselves on the Methodist plan and their continuance in post depending on approval from the Methodist circuit meeting. David Lawrence, who was editor of the United Reformed Church's monthly magazine, *Reform*, from 1995 to 2006, comments:

> Joint Methodist-URC churches are one of the few ways in which Methodists can maintain their numbers—because we have no ethos they take us over and we disappear.[98]

That puts it too dramatically. But the tendency for the United Reformed Church to be assimilated into Methodism is unmistakable. Christine Craven says, "I've seen Methodist/URC LEPs where the URC started off as having most members but has become the one whose identity has disappeared." Asked the reason, she says "We're too easy."[99]

The reality of United Reformed-Methodist churches was that the pressure of the circuit, the superintendent minister, and the detailed Methodist rulebook had little counterbalance from the much looser URC structures. Graham Cook, Mersey Synod Moderator from 1994 to 2004 and Moderator of the General Assembly in 1990–1991, comments,

95. Gibson, interview.

96. Craven, interview.

97. Argent, *Transformation of Congregationalism*, 498.

98. Lawrence, interview.

99. Craven, interview.

> They expect the minister to be a minister in the Circuit. And if we say our church is part of a cluster as well, they say no, he is in the Circuit but he's not in the cluster.[100]

One of the unintended, and largely unrecognized, consequences of the URC abolition of the district council was to accentuate this imbalance. Tony Burnham's experience is that of many. "Locally all our experience has been we get sucked into their machine."[101]

Since the United Reformed Church's primary theological emphasis is on ecumenism, one might argue that this is irrelevant since what matters is the Christian gospel, not the future of an individual denomination. This case is, however, more difficult to make if there is little evidence that LEPs are more effective than denominational churches. Sheila Maxey poses a more disturbing possibility: "I think we damaged our mission but I think we also damaged the whole church because we had something to bring and didn't."[102] Tony Burnham comes to much the same conclusion. "It wasn't that there appeared to be any benefit to the Church as a whole. I had very little experience of any [LEP] that really flourished."[103] Against this, it needs to be remembered that in some cases unless development had been ecumenical it would not have taken place at all and that sometimes the United Reformed congregations would have disappeared just as surely if they had attempted to survive on their own as they did by being absorbed into Methodism. Nonetheless by choosing an exclusively ecumenical route, by investing so much money and energy in ecumenism, and by allowing many of its congregations to be effectively lost from the church, the church hindered its own growth. One reason for the United Reformed Church's precipitous decline can be found in the way that it alone so committed itself to local unity.

---

100. Cook, interview.
101. Burnham, interview.
102. Maxey, interview.
103. Burnham, interview.

6

Other Ecumenical Initiatives

THE FAILURE OF THE Covenant for Unity did not mean that the United Reformed Church gave up the search for ways to promote organic unity. At a national level there were to be new developments in the ecumenical instruments and union was achieved with the Scottish Congregationalists. Indeed initially there seemed to be new possibilities opening at the national level as a result of an apparent greater openness to ecumenism by the Roman Catholic Church. Historically the Catholic Church had been outside both the World and the British Council of Churches. In 1959, however, Pope John XXIII's calling of a new general council of the Catholic Church opened new, and at that point unpredictable, ecumenical possibilities.

SWANWICK AND THE NEW ECUMENICAL INSTRUMENTS

One of these possibilities involved the British Council of Churches. This had been formed in 1942 with William Temple as its first president and included all the main Protestant denominations. By the 1980s it had real achievements to its credit, both in terms of encouraging closer relations between the churches and a prophetic social witness, including the work of Christian aid and a not uncontroversial opposition to apartheid in South Africa. Nonetheless there was a concern that it was no longer matching the developing ecumenical agenda. Celebrating its fortieth anniversary, its president, Archbishop Robert Runcie, could not resist the temptation to quote the old song.

> Forty years on growing older and older
> Shorter in wind and in memory long
> Feeble of foot and rheumatic of shoulder
> What would it help that once you were strong.[1]

Hastings comments that "Runcie well knew that such an image was just a little too close to the bone in regard to the BCC to be entirely happily received by everyone, especially just four months after the rejection of the Covenant."[2]

Despite the strength of much of the British Council of Churches' record the absence of the Roman Catholic Church made it look increasingly anachronistic after Vatican II. When the National Pastoral Congress was held in Liverpool in 1980 it requested the bishops to reconsider membership of the British Council of Churches, but this was resisted by Cardinal Hume, who used his casting vote to block it at the Conference of Catholic Bishops.[3] The main problem was the unwillingness of the Catholic Church to be associated with policy decisions it had not endorsed. John Reardon, later General Secretary of the Council of Churches in Britain and Ireland, says,

> Philip Morgan (the General Secretary of the British Council of Churches) tried very hard during the 1980s to get the Roman Catholics to join the BCC and they wouldn't join. It was mainly the question of authority—where does the question of authority lie? I heard a Catholic once say he did not understand how Bernard Thorogood and I (I was his deputy and we were both members of the BCC) sometimes didn't vote on the same side. And he said he did not understand how it is possible for Church representatives not to agree with one another before a vote is taken.[4]

However in 1982 a papal visit increased the pressure for greater unity. At first Cardinal Hume continued to resist any move towards any commitment to the British Council of Churches. "However, in private a dialogue had opened, reflected in a protracted correspondence between Basil and

---

1. Hastings, *Robert Runcie*, 134.
2. Ibid., 134.
3. Howard, *Basil Hume*, 205.
4. Reardon, interview.

the long-suffering General Secretary of the BCC, Dr. Philip Morgan."[5] This led to the establishment of the interchurch process "Not Strangers but Pilgrims," and culminated in a major British and Irish conference at Swanwick in Derbyshire. To facilitate agreement the British Council of Churches, under Philip Morgan's guidance, agreed entirely to reconstitute itself under a new (then unchosen) name in order to accommodate Catholic reservations—and it still did not know whether or not the reward for that would be Catholic membership. In the event Cardinal Hume gave his agreement, saying that "The moment had come for the Catholic Church to move quite deliberately from a situation of co-operation to one of commitment."[6] The Swanwick Declaration was adopted by acclaim and personally signed by those present on 4 September 1987. It said:

> We now declare together our readiness to commit ourselves to each other under God. Our earnest desire is to become more fully, in his own time, the one Church of Christ, united in faith, communion, pastoral care and mission. Such unity is the gift of God. With gratitude we have truly experienced this gift, growing amongst us in these days. We affirm our openness to this growing unity in obedience to the Word of God, so that we may fully share, hold in common and offer to the world those gifts which we have received and still hold in separation. In the unity we seek we recognise that there will not be uniformity but legitimate diversity. It is our conviction that, as a matter of policy at all levels and in all places, our churches must now move from co-operation to clear commitment to each other, in search of the unity for which Christ prayed and in common evangelism and service of the world. We urge church leaders and representatives to take all necessary steps to present, as soon as possible, to our church authorities, assemblies and congregations, the Report of this Conference together with developed proposals for ecumenical instruments to help the churches of these islands to move ahead together.[7]

This seemed a moment of great hope. David Sheppard and Derek Worlock, whose ecumenical partnership in Liverpool was breaking much new ground, catch the optimistic mood:

> The atmosphere at that moment was variously described: "momentous," "historic," "electric," and "as though everyone present

---

5. Howard, *Basil Hume*, 205.

6. Ibid., 208.

7. Churches Together in England, *Called to Be One*, 1.3.

had won the pools!" The Kingdom of God had not come then and there, but a consensus was that this was the breakthrough for which the churches had been waiting.[8]

At the autumn board meeting of the Division of Ecumenical Affairs of the BCC its Moderator put it even more significantly: "the Holy Spirit has had his way."[9] The Swanwick resolutions led the following year to detailed proposals in what was called the "Marigold Booklet," *The Next Steps for Churches Together in Pilgrimage.* Then in September 1990 a new body, Churches Together, replaced the British Council of Churches. The new body was organized on two levels, the Council of Churches for Britain and Ireland (CCBI), with each of the nations of the British Isles also having their own "ecumenical instruments"—ACTS (Action of Churches Together in Scotland), CTE (Churches Together in England), CYTUN (Churches Together in Wales), and the existing Irish Council of Churches. The report also envisaged what it called an "intermediate level" of ecumenical activity which would foster local ecumenism on the understanding that, in Cardinal Hume's words, "there can be no authentic evolution which does not take place at a local level."[10]

The theological justification for the new structure, according to the Marigold Booklet, was that it represented a move from ecumenism as "an extra, which absorbs energy, to ecumenism as a dimension of all that we do, which releases energy through the sharing of resources." The problem with such a definition is that, since it depends upon the commitment of the ecclesiastical bureaucrats of the participating denominations, it might in reality mean very little. Further, if the ecumenical instruments could only voice what was agreed by all the churches, this might severely limit what could be said—indeed this was part of the intention of some who supported the new structures. On this ground there was considerable opposition among the BCC staff to what was proposed. John Reardon, who was at the time Church and Society Secretary of the United Reformed Church and was part of the Division of International Affairs at the BCC, says:

> I was opposed to the new instruments. In the late eighties all of the divisions were consulted about the new arrangements and the staff given notice. . . . I took part in a number of consultations to

8. Sheppard and Worlock, *Better Together*, 93.

9. British Council of Churches, Executive Committee Minutes, Spring 1990, 5.

10. Howard, *Basil Hume*, 209.

prepare our response to the proposals and the staff were negative every time.[11]

The creation of the new ecumenical instruments was not a direct initiative of the United Reformed Church in the way that the talks about talks that led to the proposed Covenant for Unity were. Instead the Anglican and Catholic Churches were now center stage. But the seriousness with which the United Reformed Church took its ecumenical commitment was once again demonstrated. Both John Reardon and Tony Burnham believe that the role played by the then United Reformed Church General Secretary, Bernard Thorogood, in support of the proposal was an important one. But even more important was the role of Philip Morgan, as General Secretary of the British Council of Churches. Morgan was a minister of the Churches of Christ at the time of his appointment, but already his strong commitment to the Churches of Christ joining with the United Reformed Church, and his commitment to the URC's ecumenical purpose, was well known. Without his support the scheme might well have failed. There is justice in Adrian Hastings's judgment that "Only a General Secretary of the BCC as undogmatic and flexible as Philip Morgan would have been prepared to consider sinking the BCC in its existing form to let something develop in which Catholics would feel more at home."[12]

What this illustrates is that even though, as a small church, the URC could never be more than a secondary player in the ecumenical scheme, the way that some of its best people took on ecumenical posts was to contribute greatly to the ecumenical movement. Of the six general secretaries of the British Council of Churches, two, Philip Morgan and Kenneth Slack, were United Reformed Church ministers. The United Reformed Church gave the Council of Churches for Britain and Ireland its first General Secretary, John Reardon, and the current General Secretary of Churches Together in England, David Cornick. In the same way the church also gave a number of people to work in the World Council of Churches. Michael Davies, for example, was Assistant General Secretary from 1990 to 1997. This is an impressive degree of commitment. In part this may reflect the fact that in a small church like the URC significant jobs are few, but it would be overly cynical not to see it also as evidence of what mattered to the church.

Whether the URC's contribution to the creation of the new ecumenical instruments was to make a significant contribution to the fulfilment of

11. Reardon, interview.
12. Hastings, *Robert Runcie*, 135.

its ecumenical hopes is more open to question. It is important to recognize that the hesitations about the activist role of the British Council of Churches were by no means confined to the Roman Catholic Church. Others, particularly among some of the larger churches, felt that it had become too independent of the churches. As John Reardon argues, a primary concern with the BCC had been the degree of autonomy it enjoyed. The BCC "had created the impression that it was not fully answerable to the Churches and it was this impression that the creation of the new ecumenical instruments was largely designed to end."[13]

The BCC had been willing to call for talks on sovereignty with Argentina over the Falklands, had called for sanctions against South Africa, supported the World Council of Churches Fund to Combat Racism, had met with representatives of the IRA, and called on the UK to phase out nuclear weapons. Such actions might be prophetic but they certainly offended those who distrusted a political expression of the gospel they did not share. When in 1990 the Executive Committee was asked to endorse the statement "Hearing the Cry of the Poor" from Church Action on Poverty, John Habgood, the Archbishop of York, was unwilling to sign, "as he did not think that the Church could commit itself to political statements of a kind where it is possible to take different views."[14] Impressive as the BCC's record may have seemed to some, the tensions were real and led to others looking for an opportunity to curb its activities. Even those more sympathetic had their concerns. A report by Charles Handy, "The British Council of Churches and the Way It Works," in December 1986 found "a sense of over-reaching, a confusion of accountabilities and random focusing."[15]

Bob Fyffe, who in 2006 became General Secretary of Churches Together in Britain and Ireland, puts the situation bluntly:

> The Churches wanted to regain control. The BCC had become a para-church at the very least. Many people who were disenchanted with their own churches found sanctuary in the ecumenical movement and the churches felt, rightly or wrongly, that they were getting beaten over the head with blunt instruments and paying for it at the same time.[16]

13. Reardon, *Council of Churches*, 5.

14. British Council of Churches, Executive Committee Minutes, 10 January 1990.

15. Handy, "British Council of Churches."

16. Fyffe, interview.

This is implicitly confirmed by the Church of England Ecumenical Officer, Roger Paul, who argues that the "BCC became an organization which was able to make its own policy decisions, some of which were controversial." By contrast, it was for him a virtue of the Churches Together format that "what we are identifying is a far higher level of accountability to the member churches."[17] The question was whether in practice this would leave a significant role for the new ecumenical instruments. Writing in 1991, Adrian Hastings put the hesitations of some forcefully:

> Has it genuinely opened the way to a new era? Or has it, on the contrary, simply dismantled a workable body which did much good to replace it by a nonentity in the forlorn hope of drawing the Roman Catholic leadership out of a self-imposed ghetto?[18]

The new CCBI faced immediate financial difficulties and moved into a cycle of decline both in its programs and effectiveness. At the beginning it became clear that not all planned posts could be afforded and that the burden of asking the English churches to fund both CCBI and CTE would cause problems. The problems were exacerbated by budgetary errors, the fact that not all BCC member churches joined CCBI, and fact that the Roman Catholic Church did not make the kind of financial contribution that its numbers might have suggested.[19] It all made for a difficult start.

> the most part the Churches honoured their commitment to CCBI throughout the period but not all Churches met the obligations of membership in full. One or two Churches failed to meet their financial obligations at all and largely remained on the edge or even outside the Council's life, even though they had joined the instrument at the outset or soon afterwards. A number of Churches fell short of their subscription levels, unilaterally deciding how much they would give, usually explaining their shortfall by reference to their own financial difficulties.[20]

The financial constraints the new body faced significantly affected its life. "The preoccupation with the structural and staffing questions . . . meant that too much of the first two years of CCBI was taken up with them and contributed to an impression for some that ecumenism is a burden

17. Paul, interview.
18. Hastings, *Robert Runcie*, 137.
19. Reardon, *Council of Churches*, 1.
20. Ibid., 5.

rather than a boon."[21] There were to be other problems. The presence of the Roman Catholic Church caused acute problems to those used to the style of the British Council of Churches.

> When I was General Secretary of the Council of Churches in Britain and Ireland I had to be very careful not to make statements—because statements from an ecumenical body had to have the approval of the member churches and the only authority that counts as far as Catholics are concerned is bishops. I can remember we had one instance when we did issue a statement. We had an all-day meeting with representatives from all the churches present and made a statement at the end of it. The following morning I was phoned up by the General Secretary of the Catholic Bishops Conference, saying, "Who gave you the authority to do that?" I said, "All the churches were represented around the table at which we thrashed out the position we wanted to make." And he said, "Who was there from the Catholic Church? I said, "The Social Responsibility Secretary of the Catholic Church," and he said, "He's not a bishop." So even an official was not regarded as being authoritative enough to give his consent to a statement.[22]

Reardon's fears that new body would prove ineffectual were largely realized as programs were cut back, staff reduced, and public visibility lost:

> I think the BCC had influence with governments. We were able to do some of that with CCBI but not as much because we didn't have the infrastructure to start with. This was mainly financial. The BCC had more resources than we had. You had two large churches like the Roman Catholic Church and the Church of England coming into membership. The Roman Catholics had never paid any money to ecumenical instruments before and therefore suddenly to be faced with a huge bill, which they would have been if they paid a commensurate amount to the Church of England— they just couldn't countenance it. So the budget was gradually cut back. I started with a staff of over 30—when you look at it now I wouldn't apply for a job there.[23]

The arrival of the Roman Catholic Church had proved momentous, but not in the way ecumenical enthusiasts had hoped. The church historian Clyde Binfield comments:

21. Ibid., 14.
22. Reardon, interview.
23. Ibid.

I have no doubt at all it did neuter it. The only question mark is whether that would have happened anyway because it may well be that the old BCC's ability to hit the headlines in the *Daily Telegraph* for saying the wrong things about grants to freedom fighters would have gone off the radar anyway.[24]

It had always been intended that the new body should come under review and the task was given to one person, Raymond Clarke, a member of the United Reformed Church. Again this was a sign of the role URC members played in the ecumenical organizations, but when he reported in 1997 there were no easy answers. He "detected considerable problems about visibility and communication" and commented that "ecumenism was often the first victim of financial stringency."[25] There was also the question of the relation of the national to the British ecumenical instruments. A review group was set up which led to the decision that in the future most work should be done in the national bodies, leaving the British Council with a residual coordinating function, though it was agreed it should continue to have a president and a public affairs post. The name was to be changed to Churches Together in Britain and Ireland starting on 1 April 1999.

The essential structural and financial problems remained. Financial and staff cutbacks continued, as did the unwillingness of the main denominations to give responsibility to the ecumenical instruments. In the context of devolution the Church of England's refusal to fund work outside England had a particularly severe effect. At the CTBI Bob Fyffe records:

When I took over in 2006 I came into an organization which had 26 members of staff. There were a few redundancies going through at that point. Prior to that there had been 30 odd. Today we have a full-time equivalent of about seven. So over the last seven years I have made well over 20 people redundant.[26]

The Church of England National Ecumenical Officer, Roger Paul, argues that this was a reflection of the financial stringency facing the churches.

The Churches are all feeling the pinch at the moment. . . . It is inevitable that when you have a reduction in the finances available

24. Binfield, interview.

25. Reardon, *Council of Churches*, 41.

26. Fyffe, interview.

the managers will be looking for those areas they can cut and some of them consider ecumenism to be the first thing to cut.[27]

The sheer scale of the cutbacks, however, suggests that a downgrading of the priority of ecumenical work was also an underlying motive. As far as CTBI is concerned, Keith Clements, former General Secretary of the Conference of European Churches, may well be justified in calling it "a virtually complete demolition job."[28] While the CTE may have survived better, its relationship to the main work of the churches is now peripheral.

Perhaps the greatly diminished role of the ecumenical instruments was inevitable. The activist phase of the British Council of Churches had come out of a time of radical theology and ecumenical optimism when organic unity seemed imminent. But just as the Local Ecumenical Partnerships floundered out of the context of organic union so the general ecumenical retreat inevitably affected the ecumenical instruments. As the hope of organic unity dissipated the major churches reasserted their own identities and pursued their own strategies in a way that left only a minor role for the ecumenical instruments. Bob Fyffe is explicit about this: "One of the things which was said to me very early on was that it was quite clear that many of the churches wanted the ecumenical instruments to work, but not work too well."[29]

In particular, any hope that the entry of the Catholic Church might lead to a major ecumenical breakthrough was frustrated by a conservative retreat from the hopes of the Second Vatican Council. "As soon as the bishops left Rome, the Roman Curia, although made more representative of the world than before, carried on along strikingly similar lines; such that the legacy of the Council may now be regarded as in peril."[30] Few in the main churches wanted an influential Council of Churches. If the Christian case needed putting before the public, the person to do this was a denominational leader, not the General Secretary of an ecumenical body. "In the old days the BCC had its own stance and the General Secretary would promulgate that view. What happens now is that you have church leaders in the public square, engaging with public issues."[31]

27. Paul, interview.

28. Clements, *Ecumenical Dynamic*, 19.

29. Fyffe, interview.

30. Thompson, *The Church*, 1.

31. Paul, interview.

THE CHANGING DYNAMICS OF ENGLISH CHURCH LIFE

It was not simply that the denominations increasingly lacked strong ecumenical commitment. Equally important was that the whole context of church life in England had changed in a way that marginalized the ecumenical enterprise. The ecumenical movement in England had been based on the historic Protestant denominations and often pioneered by middle-class Englishmen with a shared liberal theological agenda. Today those denominations are in decline, the Roman Catholic Church has moved center stage, and there has been a rapid growth in African initiated ethnic and Charismatic congregations. In London in 2005, for example, of over four thousand churches a quarter were Anglican and a quarter Pentecostal.[32]

Just as with the involvement of the Roman Catholics, this brought a new breadth to the ecumenical movement. An increasing number of the new churches are now part of ecumenical organizations. Member churches of CTBI now include African initiated churches like the Cherubim and Seraphim Council of Churches and the Joint Council for Anglo-Caribbean Churches, while Churches Together in England includes the Assemblies of God, the Elim Pentecostal Church, and the Redeemed Christian Church of God. In total there are now something like two and a half times as many churches in the ecumenical instruments as there were in the old British Council of Churches.

These links have value both in allowing these disparate churches to interact with each other and in allowing the traditional churches to judge which of the new churches have an ordered life and a Trinitarian theology. To some the twice-yearly enabling group is a valuable contact. Roger Paul is enthusiastic: "It is going to get really interesting when we recognise there are differences and they begin to be things we can talk about, even our understanding of some of the basic building blocks of faith."[33]

Certainly this offers new possibilities. David Cornick, General Secretary of Churches Together in England, points to the way:

> Some mission focused initiatives, like *Hope* and *More Than Gold* (the churches' response to the 2012 Olympics), have a brand quality which has enabled them to gather to themselves a mixed constituency of partners who in previous decades would have shunned each other. . . . In a sense what is happening is reminiscent of the

32. Brierley, *Religious Trends No 6.*, 12.46.

33. Paul, interview.

early days of modern ecumenism, in the discovery of friendship and common purpose which (for example) marked SCM in the 1920s and 30s. If ecumenism is turning into an iterative cycle, that is an essential component of spiritual growth.[34]

But ecumenism that covers such diversity makes impossible the old goals of the ecumenical movement. For many of the new churches membership in the ecumenical instruments is more motivated by a desire to achieve ecclesiastical legitimacy than any commitment to organizational unity. Factors such as the increased facility for appointments to hospital chaplaincies could be a factor in joining. Speaking for the Church of England, Roger Paul says, "we have significant relationships with churches of many different traditions, Reformed, Methodist, Baptist, Orthodox, Oriental Orthodox, Roman Catholic, Pentecostal. To think in terms of full visible unity in terms of that is eschatological."[35]

The very diversity of the churches leaves ecumenical instruments with little more than a small enabling role.

> In the early post-war years there were small staffs who worked among the churches. Then it went into program staff who began to work on behalf of churches. Now we have come full circle to the point where the churches are saying, "We don't want you to do programs, we'll do them ourselves, we just want you to be a small little organization."[36]

Cooperating in *More than Gold* is very far removed from the radicalism of the Race Relations Unit of the British Council of Churches or the Council's part in the Northern Ireland Peace Process. As David Cornick comments, it is a sign of "a unity which is essentially relational rather than structural or institutional."[37]

This was very far removed from the kind of unity the United Reformed Church had hoped and expected to see. Writing in 1997, Arthur Macarthur, looking at what seemed to him ecumenical retreat, commented that ecumenists "had to face the truth that the straightforward assumption that these ecumenical councils could speak and act for all the member churches was a myth."[38] But this retreat from the hopes of the ecumenical

34. Cornick, "Story of British Ecumenical Endeavour," 14.

35. Paul, interview.

36. Fyffe, interview.

37. Cornick, "Story of British Ecumenical Endeavour," 14.

38. Macarthur, *Setting Up Signs*, 85.

pioneers of the British Council of Churches reflected both the priorities of the main denominations and the reality of church life. When it came to the ecumenical instruments the English churches got what they wanted—and all they were prepared to pay for. In a paper presented to the Executive Committee of the BCC in March 1987, Bernard Thorogood said,

> Perhaps in our hearts we despair of ecumenism. . . . Why are the Catholics so aloof and the black churches so hard to serve and the Church of England so hard to move in any direction?[39]

That may have been more a cry of despair than a balanced judgment but it reflected the real frustrations of ecumenical church life.

UNION WITH THE SCOTTISH CONGREGATIONAL CHURCH

There was, however, to be one further organic union involving the United Reformed Church—union with the Scottish Congregationalists. In 1798 Robert and James Haldane with others founded the Society for Propagating the Gospel at Home, out of which a number of Congregational churches developed and formed a Congregational Union in 1812. At this stage it was a grouping of fifty-five local churches that had come together "out of the will to survive."[40] Then in 1843 the Evangelical Union was founded by those expelled from the United Secession Church (founded 1820), which in turn grew out of splinters from the Church of Scotland dating back to the eighteenth century. Finally the Congregational and Evangelical Unions united in 1896.

In the twentieth century a belief that the visible disunity of the church was hampering mission and squandering resources led to a growing commitment to ecumenism. Between 1965 and 1988 the Congregational Union of Scotland explored unity with the Church of Scotland, the Churches of Christ, the United Free Church of Scotland, and the United Reformed Church. Proposals for union with the URC were approved by the URC in 1988 but only supported by a 65-percent vote in Scotland, which fell short of the legal requirement. As with the Churches of Christ in their negotiations with the URC, those committed to ecumenical union did not accept the negative result. A period of internal conflict followed and in 1993 a third

39. British Council of Churches, Executive Committee Minutes, March 1987.

40. McNaughton "Principles of Scottish Congregationalism," 44.

of the member churches (twenty-seven churches and sixteen ministers) withdrew, following a fracturing of relationships marked by suspicion and mistrust. Alan Paterson, who was Chairman of the Congregational Union of Scotland in 1993–1996 and President of the Congregational Union of Scotland/Scottish Congregational Church in 1998–1999, comments,

> Distrust, hostility, conspiracy theories and threats of litigation had clouded the debate, and at the end of the day the denomination, churches and even families had been divided. The Scottish Congregational Church emerged from the trauma of schism, scarred, brittle and weary.[41]

The Scottish Congregational Church now returned to the possibility of union. From the perspective of those who voted for the union with the United Reformed Church (and were prepared to pay a great cost in terms of fracturing of relationships within their own church) this seemed to them the only way ahead.

> Adopting the working practices of a Church, reasserting our commitment to the ecumenical journey, and achieving the unanimous vote in Assembly that brings us to this point of Union have all been costly, but it has been the price of faithfulness—faithfulness to a vision and an imperative to which there was no honorable alternative.[42]

Acting on the initiative of local churches, the CUS Assembly in September 1996 resolved by 109 votes to five to instruct the General Committee "to initiate discussions with the URC with a view to effecting the union of our two denominations as soon as possible." This request was considered by the URC's Ecumenical Committee, which encouraged the Mission Council at a meeting in October 1996 to agree to begin negotiations and to ask the General Assembly in 1997 to confirm the decision. Union was achieved on 1 April 2000. One feature of the new church was that both Scotland and Wales became national synods with greater autonomy. To the General Secretary of the Congregational Union in Scotland, John Arthur, this was part of its rationale.

> I believe that, in these heady devolution days, this aspect of the Proposals promises the opportunity to witness to how different national identities, styles and traditions may be recognized,

41. Paterson, interview.
42. Ibid.

respected and preserved, and yet belong together for the enrichment of all in the oneness of God's people. In other words it promises the possibility of *celebrating diversity in unity*.[43]

Nonetheless, the union was not unproblematic. It was of a different kind to that with the Churches of Christ and other projected ecumenical unions in that, apart from six former Churches of Christ congregations, the United Reformed Church had no presence in Scotland. Scottish Congregationalists uniting with an English (largely ex-Congregational) church was neither a union across confessional boundaries nor a meaningful step towards local church unity. It also posed difficulties for former Presbyterians, including the former General Secretary, Arthur Macarthur, who found themselves in the anomalous position on visits to Scotland of having to choose between their loyalty to the United Reformed Church and their historic loyalty to the Church of Scotland.

In 1929 the Scottish Congregationalists had on a previous occasion approached the English about the possibility of union. This had been rejected by the English Congregationalists on the grounds that Scottish Congregationalism was "born of Presbyterianism and native to the soil." If they no longer felt they had an independent mission surely they should rejoin the Church of Scotland.[44] It might well be asked if, especially at a time when national sentiment was deepening in Scotland, that was not still the more ecumenical and logical choice. On the other hand, it was also a fact that Scotland had seen twenty-five years of Multilateral Church Conversation, eventually followed by the Scottish Church Initiative for Union. None of this had led anywhere. Ecumenical progress was proving as hard in Scotland as it was in England.

Unlike in 1929, this time the approach from Congregationalists in Scotland was positively received, but questions remained. Tony Burnham, who was the General Secretary of the United Reformed Church from 1992, was skeptical:

> The ecumenical case from our point of view was that we had this handful of former Churches of Christ in Scotland. But the cost was significant. All sorts of things—supporting the synods, assemblies and how far is any of that going to deliver any kind of unity?[45]

43. Arthur, *Reflections on the Way*, 2.

44. Paterson, "Origins of the Scottish Congregational Church," 5.

45. Burnham, interview.

Stephen Orchard, who was involved in the negotiations for union, recognizes some of the same difficulties.

> Cost was certainly under consideration with the second negotiations. It was thought then that the investments of the Congregationalists in Scotland would support the Synod and it is the failure of investment policy in recent years which has undermined this. It was argued that the union would strengthen Scottish ecumenism. The Scottish and Welsh Synods make much of their national roles but each is now wholly dependent on English subsidies to function.[46]

The ecumenical commitment of those who worked for the union was real and faith driven.

> I have described to others that on the afternoon of the Uniting Assembly I felt a need to weep for joy and if I had been told it was my last day on earth I still would have wanted to finish it singing. Union was not just an end in itself however and we were sure that both partners had gifts to share and work to do together for the Kingdom.[47]

But this was very much the opposite of a union from strength. The membership of the Congregational Union in Scotland in 1945 was 37,283, and by 1970 still 25,284.[48] Decline and opposition to the union, however, meant that only 50 churches came into the URC, adding an increase of 4,154 members.[49] In fact the number of active people involved may have been less than this figure suggests since the ratio of "main service average congregation" to membership is lower in the URC Scottish Synod than the URC average (51.53 percent compared to 96.42 percent).[50] Carluke, in the Mid-Scotland area for example, might appear with a membership of 264 in 2002 to be the seventh strongest congregation in the United Reformed Church, however, its average congregation was only 53.[51]

Alan Paterson may argue:

---

46. Email to M. Camroux, 22 June 2011.

47. Paterson, interview.

48. Currie et al., *Churches and Church Goers*, 150–51.

49. URC, *Year Book 2000* and *2001*.

50. URC, *Year Book 2001*, 17.

51. URC, *Year Book 2002*.

It was far from inevitable that the CUS was collapsing either in 1988 or in 1998, but there was a track record of ecumenical pursuit dating much further back. From the 1970s ecumenists were suggesting to denominations that the Holy Spirit was talking to them about church union through their balance sheets.[52]

But it is clear that for the Scottish Congregationalists, with a declining membership and financial problems (including questions about the pension fund), the options were narrowing. Tony Burnham suggests that this was the context of union: "we had to do a lot of sorting out."[53] Even Alan Patterson acknowledges that the pressure for union came partly through financial pressure.

There is no doubt that a genuine desire for church unity was a factor. But the fact that the Scottish Congregationalists had raised the question of union with English Congregationalism as far back as the 1920s (and indeed the fact that the dissenting Congregational churches who opposed union chose to join the English-based Congregational Federation) suggests that a long-standing interest in union with the larger sister church south of the border was also involved. Though now advocated in terms of ecumenism the union might well have been pursued in the interests of shared Congregational polity even if the ecumenical agenda ha not existed. Further, unlike the Churches of Christ, for whom union had meant effective dissolution into the United Reformed Church, and unlike what would have been the effect of a union with the Church of Scotland, the creation of the overwhelmingly ex-Congregational national Synod of Scotland meant in practice that a declining church was able to buttress and perpetuate its own organizational identity.

There was, however, a real price for the union not only in the financial support required from the United Reformed Church for the Scottish Synod but also in the divisiveness that the proposal for unity brought in Scotland.

> Everybody felt wounded. . . . We hemorrhaged about a third of our member churches in a time of divergent visions, differing agendas, and fear, suspicion and mistrust.[54]

As John Arthur commented in a speech to the executive of the Council for World Mission in June 1998, "that was a very bitter and traumatic

52. Paterson, "Origins of the Scottish Congregational Church," 5.

53. Burnham, interview.

54. Paterson, "Origins of the Scottish Congregational Church," 2–3.

time in the life of the denomination." It left a divided church and bitterness that was to last for years. To John Arthur the attraction of joining the United Reformed Church was that it showed "the possibility of *celebrating diversity in unity*." In terms of a new working relationship between churches in England and Scotland that may be true, but in Scotland it showed the reverse—Christians unable to celebrate diversity in unity but rather going their own separate ways and becoming more theologically monochromatic. One consequence of the schism was that those who had consistently opposed unions with other churches seceded from the denomination, and so what became the Synod of Scotland is possibly the most liberal synod in the URC.[55] This was not how ecumenism had originally been envisaged to work.

FREE CHURCH RELATIONSHIPS

Apart from the Congregationalists in Scotland, and with the Anglican option closed, historically one possibility for organic union might have been the Baptists, with whom Congregationalists shared a common ecclesiology and history. Writing over fifty years ago, Ernest Payne, once General Secretary of the Baptist Union, said:

> The history of Baptists and Congregationalists is . . . one and indivisible. They are both parts of the same movement in Christian history. The inspiration and roots of their church life are the same. Their basic interpretation of the gospel and of Church order is the same. The type of Christian character which they have nurtured is essentially the same. By and large in doctrine, worship and polity they are so closely similar that to a stranger they are at first indistinguishable unless he happens to be present when the rite of baptism is being administered or discoursed upon.[56]

In both 1886 and 1901 the two churches met together in a joint assembly. Opening the latter, the Congregationalist Joseph Parker, minister of the City Temple, advocated a union of the two churches: "I cannot but hope that Independents and Baptists will soon be earnestly thinking under what conditions they can come together as the United Congregational Church."[57] From the Baptist side the General Secretary, J. H. Shakespeare, advocated

55. Ibid.

56. Payne, *Free Churchmen*, 93.

57. *Congregational Year Book 1902*, 31.

a federation of Congregational and Baptist churches as a first step to a united Free Church.[58] A number of union churches jointly sponsored by the Baptist Union and the Congregationalists were opened in new towns or housing estates and as late as 1955 thirty churches were affiliated with both denominations.[59]

From the second half of the nineteenth century onwards, however, the two churches began to diverge theologically. The Baptists became increasingly conservative and were in the twentieth century strongly influenced by the Charismatic movement and ambiguous in their commitment to ecumenism. Clyde Binfield sees the decisive moment here in the influence of Spurgeonism, which he calls "a comforting, understandable, proven, but inturned thing . . . it is not clear that it was the obvious development for Baptists to follow, and an observer can only regret it."[60] John Briggs, by contrast, believes the theological influence of the liberal Congregationalist Baldwin Brown was more decisive in opening up the breach.[61] Under either hypothesis the fact remains the Baptist ethos became increasingly conservative and resistant towards ecumenism, rejecting the Covenant for Unity and never opening serious unity negotiations.

Congregationalists, on the other hand, from the time of the Leicester Conference onwards, took a strongly liberal and ecumenical theological direction. As David Thompson argues, "There was an openness to modernism (or Liberal Protestantism), that was greater than in any of the Free Churches apart from Unitarianism."[62] At the same time, under the influence of the New Genevans in particular, the Congregationalists moved away from the independence of the local congregation and gave increasing influence to moderators, synods, and national church bodies. A decisive step was taken when Congregationalists moved from a Congregational Union to a Congregational Church in 1967 so that Congregationalists and Baptists were now distinct organizationally and theologically. The creation of the United Reformed Church only accentuated this differentiation. While there was some Baptist involvement in LEPs, especially in new housing developments, and while there were still some liberal Baptist churches, the Baptist church was never a credible candidate for a wider union with

58. Briggs, *Two Congregational Denominations*, 24.

59. Argent, *Transformation of Congregationalism*, 20.

60. Binfield, "Congregationalism's Two Sides," 130.

61. Briggs, *Two Congregational Denominations*, 27.

62. Thompson, "Motivation of the Ecumenical Movement," 25.

the United Reformed Church. The disparity in theological ethos between the two churches was starkly illustrated when a significant minority of Baptists opposed participation in the new ecumenical instruments because of the prospect of Roman Catholic membership and the measure only passed by a 73-percent majority.[63] David Thompson puts it bluntly: "The Baptists have not actually been interested in talking to anybody really but certainly not to the URC."[64]

The Methodist church was a much stronger possibility. Historically the two traditions were distinct. Both Congregationalists and Presbyterians were rooted in Calvinism, including for many the doctrine of predestination. Methodism by contrast began as an Arminian Holiness movement. For John Wesley its most distinctive doctrine was a belief in the possibility of perfection, in entire sanctification, in what he called "deliverance from the plague of our sinning." Calvinists totally rejected this, just as Wesley denied the doctrine of predestination. In his sermon "Free Grace" Wesley asserted that predestination contradicts Scripture, is blasphemous, making Christ's "come unto me all ye that are weary and heavy laden" a mockery, and destroys God's attributes of justice, mercy, and truth.

> This is the blasphemy clearly contained in the horrible decree of predestination! And here I fix my foot. On this I join issue with every assertor of it. You represent God as worse than the devil; more false, more cruel, more unjust.[65]

Even today, William Willimon, one of America's most influential Methodist theologians, can write, "Wesley differed not because of his rosy view of human nature but because of his huge faith in the power of the Holy Spirit."[66]

Time sometimes changes perspectives, however. Arminianism was an intra-Reformed debate and most Reformed churches modified their attitude to the Westminster Confession from the 1860s onwards. By the mid-twentieth century most Congregationalists had forgotten that their tradition had ever included predestination, even if they knew what it was. Similarly, few British Methodists any longer had any real understanding of the Holiness tradition, and even those who did frequently only did so in a

---

63. Briggs, *Two Congregational Denominations*, 42.

64. Thompson, interview.

65. Wesley, "Free Grace," quoted in Rack, *Reasonable Enthusiast*, 200.

66. Willimon, *This We Believe*, 21.

form so demythologized as to be almost unrecognizable from the original doctrine. As one President of the Methodist Conference, John Vincent, put it, "Perfection is a specific religious experience of 'second blessing' which Methodists today (with exceptions so rare as to be ignored) do not have."[67] More positively, both churches were ecumenically committed and had supported the Covenant. While the Methodists were perhaps less liberal than the United Reformed Church the spectrum of theology in both churches was not greatly different and their worship often indistinguishable. At the local level 300 of the URC's 1,500 churches were part of LEPs with the Methodists. Surely therefore a union between the two churches would be logical and welcome? The remarkable fact, however, was that neither church showed any enthusiasm for such a union. Inevitably the prospect was raised. Tony Burnham, then General Secretary, records:

> There was a stage soon after I became General Secretary when we were instructed by the Assembly that the senior staff of both churches were to have meetings. And we had meetings and they were incredibly and totally boring . . . after I think about a couple of years of regular meetings we all agreed we were wasting our time and getting nowhere and we each asked the Assembly and Conference to let us off the hook.[68]

In a sermon in 1992 Burnham recalled earlier discussions and said, "Let us recall most of us were reluctant to act with all speed in the face of discussions with the Methodists."[69] Sheila Maxey, who was the United Reformed Church Secretary for Ecumenical Affairs in 1993–1994 and then Moderator of the General Assembly in 2004–2005, remembers:

> I came to office in the middle of that, and I can't remember if the approach came from them or us, but there was a questionnaire sent out to all the joint churches. We tried to look at this questionnaire; the result was there wasn't enough enthusiasm in either church.[70]

Brian Beck, the Secretary of the Methodist Conference at the time, confirms the lack of enthusiasm:

67. Vincent, *Christ and Methodism*, 44.

68. Burnham, interview.

69. Ibid.

70. Maxey, interview.

> There was a proposal. It fizzled out for more than one reason. . . . The Methodists were much divided. A lot of voices were raised who feared a union with the URC would actually take us further away from possibilities with the Church of England.[71]

Various factors were involved. Both denominations knew that uniting two such disparate structures as the United Reformed Church and the Methodists would be an arduous and difficult process that in the end would have only a marginal effect on English church life. On the United Reformed Church side there was also the sense that any such merger would inevitably mean the loss of much of what they valued in their own church. Michael Dunford, Secretary of the Church Life Department from 1980 to 1984 and of Ministries from 1984 to 1992, is quite frank as to his hesitations:

> I am a Congregationalist and I am not keen on a structure of Methodism. . . . Deep down the answer to your question why haven't we joined with the Methodists is this feeling that we are going to be taken over and they will tell us what to do and we are going to lose the vestiges of what we have.[72]

That may not have been an obvious expression of the theology of an ecumenical breakthrough church but it was how many people actually felt.

The fact is that the connectional principle in Methodism is very different in both practice and theology from the much looser structure of the United Reformed Church with its greater emphasis on the local congregation. David Thompson argues,

> Methodism is the most conservative church structurally in the UK. It has the most rigid central organization, and really is so attached to it, it can't imagine breaking with it.[73]

Perhaps the truth is that intellectually and intuitively both traditions found it quite hard to understand the other. Sheila Maxey says,

> Methodist and URC people are very like each other, our place in society is very similar and so on, and that fools you into thinking we have more in common than we do. There are significant differences.[74]

71. Beck, interview.

72. Dunford, interview.

73. Thompson, David, interview.

74. Maxey, interview.

Though at a personal level Methodist and URC might relate well, even in LEPs there were misgivings among that minority strongly committed to the URC that the stronger Methodist organizational model would mean a loss of Reformed identity. Close as the URC and Methodists often are in worship and belief, important as the many joint congregations are, real as the URC commitment to ecumenism was, its desire to preserve its own organizational life and ethos made the United Reformed Church unenthusiastic about a Methodist union. Breaking the ecumenical logjam was one thing, union with the Methodists quite another.

On the Methodist side there was an equal lack of enthusiasm, but for largely different reasons. There was a shared sense that in practice the time spent on amalgamating the two organizations would not produce a commensurate ecumenical benefit. But in any case, as Brian Beck makes clear, Methodism tended to look far more towards the possibility of Anglican-Methodist unity rather than a joint Free Church. The first Methodist target had been reuniting with the Anglicans, not with Congregationalists or Presbyterians, and that priority remained. Another former Secretary of the Methodist Conference, Kenneth Greet, confirms this preference:

> There's never been any enthusiasm at all for that union at the national level. I suppose it's due to the fact that some of us, those of us who were most enthusiastic for the Anglican-Methodist scheme, felt a sense of shame there had ever been the break between the early Methodists and the Anglicans. We believe it ought not to have happened. So the idea of bringing these two parts of what was one family together has seemed the right and logical way.[75]

The Methodist preference for close relations with the Church of England later found expression in the search for an Anglican-Methodist Covenant. In 1995–1996 a series of informal conversations was held between the Anglican and Methodist churches. This led to proposals for "An Anglican-Methodist Covenant," which, after consultation within the respective churches, was agreed by the Methodist Conference and the General Synod, both meeting in July 2003. The Covenant states:

> We affirm one another's churches as true churches where the word of God is authentically preached, and . . . Baptism and the Eucharist are duly administered and celebrated. We affirm that one another's ordained and lay ministries are given by God as instruments of God's grace; to build up the people of God. . . . We

75. Greet, interview.

commit ourselves, as a priority, to work to overcome the remaining obstacles to the organic unity of our two churches, on the way to the full visible unity of Christ's Church. In particular, we look forward to the time when the fuller visible unity of our churches makes possible a united, interchangeable ministry. . . . We commit ourselves to encourage forms of eucharistic sharing, including eucharistic hospitality, in accordance with the rules of our respective churches.[76]

Whether in practice there was much reality to the Covenant may be a matter of dispute, since it has led neither to organic unity negotiations nor even mutual recognition of ministries. But clearly it raises the question, why was the United Reformed Church not included? After all, was not promoting such unity its primary mission as a church?

It is clear that to some in the United Reformed Church that being left out was a shock. Sheila Maxey says:

We were hurt. We complained. . . . I don't think either of them wanted us because we complicated the matter. We raised issues they hoped they wouldn't have to deal with. The Anglicans always hoped that the Methodists would take episcopacy on Anglican terms. And the Methodists who were strongly in favor of the Covenant were quite keen on that. . . . We were very upset about the Covenant talks.[77]

The actual sequence of events is quite complicated. Brian Beck says, "I remember talking to Tony Burnham at Swanwick and telling him what we had in mind, and getting from him a go-ahead to see what we could do."[78] This was confirmed by Tony Burnham. "Brian was correct in saying that I encouraged him at that stage to take it up with the Anglicans, remembering—*to take all steps etc*."[79] "When Brian told me this, it was in confidence, because it was before the Methodists had discussed it in their appropriate committee. He was telling me what at this stage was going to be on their agenda, not what had been formally decided."[80]

76. *Anglican-Methodist Covenant*, 60–61.

77. Maxey, interview.

78. Beck, interview.

79. Email to M. Camroux, 3 August 2011.

80. Email to M. Camroux, 17 July 2012.

That Tony Burnham knew of this approach did not mean there was not deep disappointment in the United Reformed Church. Burnham remembers:

> I said something like, are you going to invite us too? Well no, he said, they feel that this is about Methodists and Anglicans. I argued the Anglicans are much stronger relative to the Methodists and it would be a far more significant meeting if it was URC and Methodist. After the meeting I went back to the office and put some of my politer thoughts in a letter. I said here we are, a united church, eager to engage in talks about further unity with the Methodists and others, and it is very important that you let us in on this. I also reminded Brian that Churches Together in England was presently working on visible unity. So I asked if it would not be worth seeing what convergence there might be between the responses before going ahead bi-laterally? I also reminded him that, when in 1992 the URC decided not to open talks with the Methodists, one of the reasons was that we were moving 'from cooperation to commitment' with all the other churches on the pilgrimage and so bi-lateral talks were not appropriate.[81]

Matters got worse when the initial discussions between the Methodists and the Anglicans led to an announcement of formal talks for a Covenant without the URC being informed in advance. Brian Beck remembers:

> It went very badly wrong at the end for which I carry some responsibility. It was inadvertent. David Thompson was Moderator at the time I think. We had let the URC know when we expected to make an announcement about these exploratory talks. But on the day the talks ended we found the press at the door, and could do nothing but make a statement. And in that pressure we forgot to let David know that we'd been overtaken by events. And David was put to the embarrassment of saying we won't know until such and such a day, and then finding it all over the newspapers. And I deeply regretted that. It wasn't deliberate and I got in touch with David afterwards and tried to explain how it came about.[82]

The Methodist exclusion of the United Reformed Church needs to be understood historically. Methodism is a product of more than one tradition. To many in the URC it may appear a Nonconformist church like themselves. But to anyone from a Wesleyan heritage it is quite different.

81. Burnham, interview.
82. Beck, interview.

Many of these would have remembered that John Wesley saw himself as an Anglican to his dying day and that Charles Wesley had never left the Anglican Church. For such Methodists the natural partner for ecumenical dialogue was always the Church of England.

> When we united in 1932 that brought together one strand of Methodism which still had very strong sentimental attachments to the C of E and quite strong streaks of Anglican tradition in it, with two other branches of Methodism which lacked that. And ever since Methodism has exhibited a love-hate relationship with the Church of England depending which voice was being raised. And we are not a typical Free Church. We are not dissenting. We have not got that history.[83]

To the majority of Methodists the union that mattered was with the Anglicans and in opening up the Covenant talks they felt they were simply continuing what they had begun. And contrary to Tony Burnham's suggestion that involving the URC would make matters easier, it seemed to them it would actually make a successful outcome more difficult. As Brian Beck puts it,

> There was a strong case for including the URC but the other side was we believed we would make more progress if we narrowed the field. . . . As I recall we thought there were enough contentious issues to resolve without bringing in more like lay elders.[84]

His predecessor Kenneth Greet echoed the same outlook: "I think if I am absolutely honest, and I speak with affection and respect, the URC as such has tended to take rather rigid positions while we have been a little more open."[85] That argument still is felt by the Anglican Ecumenical Officer, Roger Paul, to have force:

> Now the question, is how much work needs to be done before the relationship with the Church of England and the URC has got to the point where a three way relationship becomes appropriate, and how much work needs to be done between the Methodist Church and the URC for that other leg of the three cornered stool to be ready for a relationship . . . The complexity of three is not just adding on one other church, it's adding to other relationships, so you

83. Ibid.
84. Ibid.
85. Greet, interview.

are trebling the complexity, whether we can handle that is another question.[86]

Some in the URC see the same situation from a different angle. So Alan Sell suggests that sometimes it "is dangerous to leave Methodists and Anglicans alone together in a room lest the Methodists be too easily persuaded."[87]

There is no doubt that these reasons for excluding the URC did have a logic to them. Anglican-Methodist unity was a long-pursued goal. It is always more difficult finding agreement with three parties than it is with two. And on difficult questions like the eldership, lay presidency, or episcopacy, involving the United Reformed Church did increase the theological divergence. But the conviction of the Covenant for Unity proposals that the United Reformed Church had agreed to had been that unity should be pursued at the widest possible level. Why had this principle been discarded? There is some point in Graham Cook's protest that "to begin talks between two churches only is a backward step. My problem is not that these talks are taking place today—my question is why haven't the rest of us been invited to join in?"[88]

The proposals in the Anglican-Methodist Covenant were not particularly radical, less so indeed than the Covenant to which the URC had agreed. There was no move in the foreseeable future to organic unity, no initial adoption of episcopacy, or even a full recognition of each other's ministries. Would the presence of the United Reformed Church really have made agreement impossible? Or did unity with the United Reformed Church simply not come high in the priorities of either of the other churches? Perhaps the reality was that in whatever area of church life you looked—national unity schemes, national ecumenical bodies, bilateral relations between churches, or local ecumenical partnerships—the tide of ecumenical commitment had turned. Following the failure of the organic unity schemes there was, as Kenneth Greet puts it, "a steady drip of enthusiasm away."[89] Organizational bureaucrats could assert themselves and denominations pursue their own agendas. Ecumenical believers were discouraged and more hesitant. David Lawrence remembers talking with Philip Morgan:

86. Paul, interview.
87. Sell, *Nonconformist Theology*, 121.
88. Cook, interview.
89. Greet, interview.

> I remember saying to Philip Morgan that the ecumenical thing
> had been basically a bit of a cul-de-sac. . . . The point of the story
> is the hurt that the comment produced in him. "If that were true
> then I have wasted my life."[90]

Such a conviction was beginning to have a dated air to it.

The exclusion of the United Reformed Church from the Anglican-Methodist Covenant indicates the church's growing insignificance. Its leaders had always exaggerated the importance the URC's formation gave it in the ecumenical scene. But at least at Westminster Abbey and with the Churches' Unity Commission there had been a moment when it could give a lead to the churches. However, as interest in ecumenism waned, and its own numbers diminished, the United Reformed Church mattered less and less. Individuals might still play important roles in the residual ecumenical organizations, and General Assemblies still passed resolutions, but the church's moment had passed.

90. Lawrence, interview.

7

A Church in Decline

THE FAILURE OF ITS ecumenical hopes was a serious blow to the United Reformed Church, frustrating its central purpose and leaving it facing Arthur Macarthur's challenge of finding an identity and reversing the decline of its predecessor churches. There were those in the church who were not without hope this could be done. Kenneth Slack had felt able to say, "It is not, however, merely a foolish optimism to conceive that our kind of Church is singularly well-placed by tradition and so much else for ministering to the post-Robbins Society. Union between the two churches, conceived as a radical re-ordering of our resources for deployment in mission . . . could create for this task a wonderful instrument for God's hand."[1] Could it still not be the case that uniting the resources of two churches might produce a church better organized for mission? Might not its unmistakable ecumenical commitment find a response from those alienated from the churches by their disunity? The United Reformed Church was heir to a serious tradition of Reformed theology—might this not offer a fruitful possibility of renewal?

Further, as we have seen, although the leaders of the new church had imagined their church would only be an interim one before a wider union, they had not in practice designed it with that in mind. The theological agenda might be for a church that was seeking unity, but the organization meanwhile was planning its own future on the unspoken assumption it would always be there. The boundaries of district councils and synods were carefully established, with Ron Bocking working out where people shopped

1. Speech delivered 12 March 1964, Westminster College Archives.

as a reliable help to where the boundaries should be drawn, "which is why North Suffolk is in Norwich."[2] A pension fund with a long-term brief was being established. As John Sutcliffe argues, "the structure of the URC was Harold Banwell's devising and it was the structure of a Church that came into existence to be in existence. It wasn't the structure of a church we were soon to say goodbye to."[3] Before long the first Ecumenical Secretary of the United Reformed Church would be worrying whether it was losing out to other denominations in the way membership was recruited in Local Ecumenical Projects.[4] In essence what had been created was the Reformed church for which Congregationalists and Presbyterians had been working since the end of the Second World War. Just because its stated *raison d'être* had failed, might the church still not thrive?

Any such hopes were soon dashed and the church was to face accelerating decline and severe identity problems. The church was unfortunate to come into being at a time of general church decline. The *UK Christian Handbook* companion volume *Religious Trends 1999/2000* records that regular church attendance in Britain fell from 4.74 million in 1989 to 3.71 million in 1998, an annual decline of more than 2.5 percent.[5] As a percentage of the population church membership fell from 19 percent in 1960 to 13 percent in 1980 and 10 percent in 2000.[6] The statistics of decline affected churches in all areas of their lives, with reductions not only in membership but in congregations, clergy, and baptisms. Writing in 2002, Brierley reports that in the previous five years a church closed every three days and the number of ministers dropped by one every two days.[7] Between 1895 and 1950 the Church of England baptized about 63 percent of English babies. In 1962 it was 53 percent. In 1993 it was 27 percent. In 1971 60 percent of weddings were religious. By 2000 it was only 31 percent.[8]

Both the Congregationalists and the Presbyterians were declining churches at the time of union. They continued to decline thereafter. In January 1973 the United Reformed Church had 192,136 members. By January 2003 (despite further unions with the Churches of Christ and the

2. Bocking, interview.

3. Sutcliffe, interview.

4. Maxey, interview.

5. Brierley, *Religious Trends No. 1*.

6. Ibid., tables 2.12.

7. Brierley, *Religious Trends No. 2*, 22.1.

8. Bruce, *God Is Dead*, 70.

Congregational Union of Scotland) membership had fallen to 84,963, a decline of 107,200 or 59.79 percent.[9] Over the whole period that is an annual decline of around 2.9 percent, even if one takes into account the two new ecumenical unions.

If one breaks this down into five-year periods the statistics are:

Year	No. Members	Numerical Decline Over 5 Years	Percentage Decline Over 5 Years
1973	192,136		
1977	166,378	25,758	13.4
1982	143,648	22,730	13.66
1987	129,141	14,407	10.09
1992	114,692	15,449	11.96
1997	96,917	17,725	15.45
2002	87,732	8,185	8.44

The regional variations in this decline are well illustrated by statistics given by David Thompson:[10]

URC Synod Statistics, January 1973 and October 2011					
Province	Number of Churches		Number of Members		Membership Decline
	1973	2011	1973	2011	
Northern	147	77	18882	3323	82%
North-Western	194	138	20151	6430	68%
Mersey	119	89	13446	3974	70%
Yorkshire	173	105	15060	3831	75%
East Midlands	144	138	10926	4198	62%
West Midlands	193	129	14933	5524	63%
Eastern	179	139	12080	5276	56%
South Western	181	120	11875	4009	66%
Wessex	184	138	15957	6737	58%
Thames North	181	140	20082	5708	72%
Southern	213	161	26234	8317	68%
Wales	172	104	12675	2545	80%
Sub-Total	2080	1478	192136	59872	69%

9. URC, *Year Book*.

10. URC, *Year Book 1973–74* and *2012*; see Thompson, "Church" 5.

Thompson does not include the Scottish figures since the Congregational Union of Scotland was not part of the United Reformed Church in January 1973.

COMPARATIVE PATTERNS OF DECLINE

To assess URC decline rigorously we need to compare this decline both with the constituent churches prior to the union and with other churches in the same period.

The first is simply done. Between 1947 and 1972 the Presbyterian Church of England lost 29 percent of its membership, the Congregationalists 32 percent, and the Churches of Christ 56 percent, an annual loss of 1.36 percent, 1.53 percent, and 3.23 percent respectively. This compares with an annual average decline of around 2.9 percent for the United Reformed Church.[11] Steve Bruce's claim that "The URC has shown a faster rate of decline than did any of its components before the merger"[12] is not true of the Churches of Christ but is applicable to both Congregationalists and Presbyterians. Rather than ecumenical commitment generating growth it has coincided with accelerating decline.

The second comparison is more difficult to make. Although the format of membership in the United Reformed Church is similar to that of the other Nonconformist denominations, there can be no direct comparison with either the Anglican or Catholic Churches, where membership is not measured in the same way. It is certain however that church attendance was in general decline and it does not appear that the United Reformed Church did exceptionally worse than the others.

A simple comparison is with the Methodist Church.[13]

Membership	1987	2007	Decline
Methodist	436,810	267,257	38.12%
URC	129,149	73,503	43.08%

---

11. URC, *Year Book*.

12. Bruce, *Religion in the Modern World*, 86.

13. URC, *Year Book*; Methodist Church, *Minutes 1990*, 57; *Minutes 2008*, 30.

Looking at more recent figures:

Membership	2008	2010	Decline
Methodist	252,000	238,000	5.55%
URC	70,508	66,746	5.33%

Depending on what years one considers, the relative position of the two churches will differ. Although over the longer period URC decline appears slightly greater, the certainty is that for both churches the decline is dramatic. Indeed the latest Methodist figures indicate a rapidly worsening position for the church. During the last ten years both membership and attendance have fallen by a third; membership from 304,971 in 2003 to only 208,738 in 2013, while attendance has fallen from 326,400 in October 2003 to only 224,500 in October 2013. Numbers on community rolls, which include the church "fringe," have fallen even further, by 48 percent; the number of children has fallen by 58 percent. The age structure is equally alarming—eighteen percent are over 81 and 51 percent are between 66 and 80.[14]

With the Church of England comparisons are more complicated since there is no equivalent category to membership. Since 1968, however, Sunday attendances have been collected centrally. As a percentage of the population these have almost halved in three decades, declining from 3.5 percent in 1968 to 1.9 percent in 1999.[15] MARC Europe Research suggests an even faster decline, from 3.6 percent of the population in 1979 to 2.0 percent in 1998. Other statistics reveal much the same picture. Baptisms per thousand live births fell from 446 in 1970 to 275 in 1990. Between 1960 and 1982 Anglican confirmations fell from 191,000 to 84,500—a fall of more than 50 percent. As Adrian Hastings observes, between 1860 and 1960 Anglican decline was "steady but seldom appeared calamitous."[16] From then on things changed. "It is not exaggerated to conclude that between 1960 and 1982 the Church of England as a going concern was effectively reduced to not much more than half its previous size."[17]

The Roman Catholic Church has a very distinct history of secularization. For most of the twentieth century it was the great exception to church decline. In 1851 total Catholic attendance in Britain represented

14. *Methodist Recorder*, 27 June 27 2014.

15. Gill, *Empty Church Revisited*, 247.

16. Hastings, *History of English Christianity*, 551.

17. Ibid., 603.

just 3.8 percent of all church attendance; in 1989 it represented 35.2 percent. Catholic attendance peaked in the 1960s. From then all the relevant statistics declined rapidly. Mass attendances declined from 1,934,853 in 1970 to 1,461,074 in 1985,[18] an annual decline of 1.85 percent. From 1990 to 2002 attendance fell from 1,351,342 to 947,845, a fall of 29.85 percent or an annual decline of 2.91 percent.[19] Between 1965 and 1985 adult converts halved and "the number of child baptisms, confirmations and marriages declined by over two-fifths."[20] From 1990 to 2002 the number of priests in England declined from 5,712 to 5,120, a decline of 10.3 percent.[21] Despite recent Catholic immigration this decline still continues. The Catholic Directory in England shows that between the 2009 and 2010 counts there was a drop of 1.5 percent in Catholic attendance.[22] Again, therefore, this is a rate of decline not totally out of line with the URC.

It is true there are some churches that did not share in this calamitous decline. In the Baptist Union of Great Britain, for example, in the period 2002 to 2008 membership fell by 7 percent from 149,685 to 139,244, an annual decline of just under 1 percent.[23] It is, however, at this point worth noting the caution introduced by John Briggs that "Baptist statistics may not be as favourable as they seem, being bolstered by some very large essentially ethnic churches."[24]

The Congregational Federation, the largest grouping of the Congregational Churches that remained outside the United Reformed Church, also shows slower decline.

Year	Churches	Members
1974	269	10,532
2013	272	7,737
Loss/Gain	+1.2%	−26.5%

This is significantly better than the URC decline over the same period, from 192,136 to 61,627 members, a decline of 68.4 percent. At the same

18. Gill, *Empty Church Revisited*, 156.

19. Brierley, *Religious Trends No. 4*, 8.5.

20. Hornsby-Smith, *Changing Parish*, 207.

21. Brierley, *Religious Trends No. 4*, 8.5.

22. *Official Catholic Directory* (2012).

23. *Baptist Times*, 19 February 2010.

24. Briggs, *Two Congregational Denominations*, 40.

time the figures are not entirely comparing like with like and almost certainly overestimate the differential since in the 1970s a number of churches joined the Congregational Federation having deliberated after the union and in the nineties the number of churches and members joining from the Scottish Congregationalists made a significantly greater addition of strength than was the case with the URC. If one takes the more recent figures for the Congregational Federation:[25]

Year	Churches	Members
2009	294	8932
2013	272	7737
Loss	−7.4%	−13.3%

This compares with URC figures of:

Year	Churches	Members
2009	1587	70508
2013	1512	61627
Loss/Gain	−4.7%	−12.5%

While over the longer period Congregational decline may be slower, the difference is not enough to be significant.

In some sections of the church there was even numerical growth. From 1990 to 2002 attendance at independent church congregations (for example Vineyard and Cornerstone) in England grew from 74,838 to 154,900, a rise of 93.6 percent.[26] The total membership of Pentecostal churches in England rose from 142,806 in 1990 to 233,065 in 2002, an increase of 63.20 percent.[27] A major, though not the only factor in this was a strong increase due to immigration in the membership of African-initiated churches. By 2005 one person in six going to church in England was non-White, half as much again as the estimated proportion of non-Whites in the population in that year.[28] If we concentrate on the Black population the increase is even more striking, with an attendance three times their proportion in the population, and an increase in attendance of 23 percent between 1998 and

25. *Congregational Year Book.*

26. Brierley, *Religious Trends No. 4*, 9.9.

27. Ibid., 9.13

28. Brierley, *Pulling Out of the Nose Dive*, 90–91.

2005, compared with a decline of 19 percent among White worshipers.[29] These have disproportionately strengthened Pentecostal churches. Thus the number of Black churchgoers in Pentecostal churches rose from 69,500 in 1998 to 114,300 in 2005, an increase of 64 percent. In the same period the number of black attenders in United Reformed churches fell from 5,200 to 3,200, a decline of 38 percent.[30] One result of the changing ethnicity of English Christianity has been to increase conservative evangelical influence. So between 1998 and 2005 non-evangelical church attendance declined twice as fast as evangelical church attendance (19 percent to 9 percent). This was almost entirely due to changes in ethnicity. White evangelical attendance declined almost as much as non-evangelical (−17 percent and −21 percent), while non-White evangelical attendance rose 35 percent and non-White non-evangelical by only 3 percent.[31]

The other major change in the pattern of English religion in this period, again significantly linked to immigration, was the rise of non-Christian religions, especially Islam. The United Kingdom had 23,000 Muslims in 1951, rising to 369,000 in 1971, topping a million by 1991 and reaching 1.6 million by 2007.[32] The Pew report on *The Future of the Global Muslim Population: Projections for 2010–2030* estimates the net inflow of Muslim immigrants in 2010 at 64,000, representing 28 percent of all immigrants to the UK in the year.[33]

Looked at overall, while the United Reformed Church may be declining slightly faster than most other comparable churches, the comparative rate of decline is not *sui generis* and is less than the Congregational Church was experiencing in the earlier part of the twentieth century. The accelerated decline of the majority of churches in the second half of the twentieth century is evidence of how difficult the culture was for any church. If the URC is in difficulty it is in good company. Two related conclusions might be drawn. Firstly, there is no statistical evidence that the United Reformed Church's ecumenical commitment produced any positive impact on membership. Secondly, while we cannot be certain what the precise rate of decline for the Congregational and Presbyterian Churches would have been

29. Ibid., 91.

30. Ibid., 95.

31. Ibid., 98

32. Jenkins, *God's Continent*, 118.

33. Pew Research Center, *Future Global Muslim Population*, 20.

without the union, there seems no reason to suppose it would have been substantially different from that of the United Reformed Church.

THE STATE OF THE UNITED REFORMED CHURCH

The fact that the United Reformed Church is not alone in facing decline does not diminish the seriousness of the situation it finds itself facing. Dramatic as its statistics of membership decline are, it is doubtful if they really convey how weak most URC congregations now are.

The perilous nature of the URC's situation is emphasized when we consider the age structure of the church. According to the "Church Life Profile" of 2001 the most numerous age group in the URC was the 65–74 cohort, which comprised nearly 25 percent of those attending. Another 20 percent was in the 75–84 age range. By contrast only 3 percent of the church was in the 25–34 age range.[34] Part of the reason for this age imbalance has been the collapse of children's work in the URC. In 1973 there were 102,027 children in URC churches (or approximately one child to every two members). In 2005 there were 21,852 children in worship (or one child to every four members). This figure is the total number of children on the register—the actual number attending on any given Sunday will almost always be less. In 1998 Brierley found the average age of attenders as 49, the same as the Methodists, and the equal highest of any denomination (the overall average is 43).[35] If we take the city of Norwich, formerly an area of some Reformed strength, in 1973 there were six United Reformed churches with a total membership of 1,105.[36] By 2012 there were four churches left with a membership of 254—a catastrophic decline of 77 percent. Of these 254 members,[37]

> 53 were below the age of 65
> 108 between 65 and 80
> 77 between 80 and 90
> 16 were over 90

The unbalanced age structure of the church not only means that membership decline will inevitably continue but that it can be expected to

34. "Church Life Profile," published in Gelder and Escott, *Faith in Life.*
35. Brierley, *Religious Trends No. 3,* 2.13.
36. URC, *Year Book 1973–74,* 95.
37. URC in Norwich, "Way Forward," 3.

accelerate. The National Church Life Survey concluded that URC membership might expect to halve again in the following twenty years. There is already evidence of this. The URC's 2012 *Yearbook* reported that the rate of decline of an "average congregation" had increased from 11.3 percent in the period 2001–2006 to 18.3 percent in the period 2006–2011. The average decline in the number of worshippers had increased from 12.9 percent in 2006 to 18.3 percent in the period 2006–2011. In the last five-year period the number of children associated with the church declined by 28.5 percent and the number of children in worship by 13.3 percent.[38] It may be that at some point the United Reformed Church membership will stabilize but it will certainly not be at anything like the current level.

The severe nature of the difficulties facing the church can be seen by comparing the United Reformed Church with the Presbyterian Church at the time of union. Their memberships are not now very different, but the Presbyterian Church was organized in a relatively small number of numerically strong congregations, most with their own minister. The United Reformed Church by contrast is spread over a much larger number of weaker, smaller congregations, to whom it is increasingly difficult to minister satisfactorily.

Arthur Macarthur recalls that when he first met with Howard Stanley, then the Congregational General Secretary, the Congregationalists had 2,990 churches and 212,017 members, the Presbyterians 346 churches and 71,329 members.

> I recall some anxiety on our side as Howard Stanley described some of those village churches and indeed the number of churches of all sorts with less than 50 members, closing at the rate of fifty a year. Presbyterians, used to a central finance system, trembled for the economic future.[39]

Another senior Presbyterian minister, Kenneth Slack, warned:

> I must bluntly say that reflection . . . has convinced me that such a union will be virtually irrelevant unless it is followed by a large-scale closure of redundant churches and a drastic attempt to drag many others, in membership and fabric, into the latter half of the 20th century. . . . I recognise that any such process will fall far more hardly on the Congregational Churches.[40]

38. URC, *Yearbook 2012*, 16–17.
39. Cornick, *Under God's Good Hand*, 173–74.
40. Slack, "Our Potential Union," 2.

In fact the number of churches fell at a significantly slower pace than did the membership. In the first 30 years membership roughly halved, as did the number of ministers, but the number of churches fell by 20.8 percent.[41]

	Members	Buildings	Ministers
1972	200,000	2,080	1,841
2002	90,314	1,745	884

By 2012 the average United Reformed congregation had only 41 members, compared with around 200 in the Presbyterian Church of England. As for large churches, it was increasingly hard to find any. Not including ecumenical congregations, by 2012 only ten United Reformed churches had at least 200 members, which had been the average in the more than 300 Presbyterian congregations.[42] Writing in 1962, in what was generally a rather pessimistic book, Christopher Driver could write:

> Looking at the Zephyrs, Minxes and Gazelles parked outside the more prosperous chapels of Mill Hill and Bournemouth and Ealing and Purley, it might seem premature to contemplate the obituary of the species . . . And indeed, there are some localities, mostly conspicuously among the middle-class suburbs of large cities, where Free Churches are imitating the best features of their booming American neighbours.[43]

By the beginning of the twenty-first century the obituary would not have seemed so premature. The churches in the suburbs might still be stronger than those in the inner cities, but their members were older and the numbers slipping. Purley, for example, which in 1972 was the fourth largest United Reformed Church with 594 members and 121 children, by 2011 had 145 members, an average congregation of only 75, and only seven children in worship.

Of course there are churches that have held their own or in a very few cases grown. But the scale of the catastrophic implosion that the URC has experienced needs to be grasped. In most churches there are now congregations of elderly people carrying on with diminishing numbers and declining hope. The question "How much longer can we go on?" is a real one in many

41. Cornick, "Vocation of the United Reformed Church," 4.

42. URC, *Yearbook 2012*.

43. Driver, *Future for the Free Churches?*, 17.

congregations. David Thompson comments, "We are now smaller in size in England and Wales than the Presbyterian Church of England was in 1972. This means that we have changed from being a small 'large Church' to being a large 'small Church.' That may require further changes in structure."[44] That puts it as positively as anyone can. The United Reformed Church is not facing imminent dissolution—indeed the evidence of bodies such as the Free Church of England or the Wesleyan Reform Union is that declining religious organizations can continue forms of residual life long after they have lost social significance. Nonetheless any projection of the future must assume (unless the church enters an ecumenical union) accelerating membership decline, an increasing inability to maintain national and synod structures, the closure of the majority of the remaining churches, and a relegation of whatever remains to increasing ecclesiastical insignificance. Whether we consider the dream it embodied, its numerical strength, or its identity and vitality, the failure of the United Reformed Church is stark and unmistakable. Born in illusion, without real purpose or coherence, it has declined to the point where its future is, at best, problematic. It is hard to dispute Michael Davies' judgment that the state of the United Reformed Church today is "pretty awful."[45]

A poignant moment for the church came in 2009 when ordination training ended at Mansfield College in Oxford. Mansfield had opened in Oxford in 1886 after the ancient universities were opened to dissenters. Its Champneys neo-Gothic building was an assertion of Congregationalism's intellectual and social status. Of the 154 students admitted by the first principal, Fairbairn, to courses of at least two years, all were already graduates and 54 were graduates of Oxford or Cambridge.[46] Scholars such as Fairbairn, Selbie, and Cadoux personified Congregationalism's liberal theology, Micklem led the New Genevans, Routley was Congregationalism's most eminent musicologist, C. H. Dodd and George Caird were distinguished New Testament scholars, and John Huxtable was a Mansfield man. The decline of Congregationalism in the twentieth century, however, meant that even by the 1920s the college was in financial difficulty and short of intellectually adequate students. Facing possible bankruptcy under John Marsh, the college moved to admit non-theological students. Inexorably the college secularized, with George Caird, who left in 1977, as the last

44. Thompson, "Church," 3.
45. Davies, interview.
46. Kaye, *Mansfield College Oxford*.

URC minister to be its principal. The Sunday congregation, which under Selbie had been one of the largest in Oxford, dropped away. Elaine Kaye remembers as a post-war student at Oxford the college chapel was three quarters full on a Sunday. "Then when I came back to Oxford in 1972 and went to Mansfield on a Sunday I was appalled because there was George Caird, an out-standing preacher, and there were fifteen people."[47]

After Caird's departure to be Dean Ireland Professor in the university there was no longer a major URC theologian in the college, reflecting in part the declining academic resources of the church. The intellectual standards of the ministerial students declined too with ordinands no longer having to be graduates and at one point taking only a certificate. Tony Tucker, Assistant Director of Education and Training at Mansfield from 1989 to 1996, discovered "there were many people in the college who felt that the theological link was a hindrance. They felt students were coming in as ordinands who might not have won a place there otherwise."[48] Finally the declining number of ordinands in the United Reformed Church led, after a period of equivocation, to the end of ministerial training at Mansfield. By 2014 the now secular college had turned the chapel into the dining hall, moving the tables to the side when there was a service. Many of the students and perhaps even some of their tutors no longer knowing who these saints and scholars were who looked down on them from statue or stained glass. If Mansfield's opening epitomized Congregationalism's moment of Victorian pomp, the end was a sign of the extent of its decline. Clyde Binfield says:

> What I think was tragic beyond measure is that we did not find new uses for Mansfield. I think the pass had been sold considerably earlier—but here was plant in the University of Oxford, one of the great universities of the world, that could be used for Reformed scholarship. It didn't have to be for ordination training, there were all sorts of other possibilities. And the moment it is lost we will never return to it. The College will become, one hopes, a most distinguished college of the university, but if ever it remembers its religious origins it will assume it was some sort of milk and water Anglicanism. I regard that as an unmitigated tragedy.[49]

47. Kaye, interview.
48. Tucker, interview.
49. Binfield, interview.

This possibly overstates the matter. Westminster College, which also had a distinguished intellectual history, remained open at Cambridge, although now increasingly as a resource center for the United Reformed Church and a conference center, rather than simply a theological college. But nothing spoke more eloquently of the URC's decline than the failed hopes of Mansfield.

UNITED REFORMED CHURCH: CHARACTER AND IDENTITY

The other challenge the United Reformed Church faced as a uniting ecumenical church was to discover a shared identity. Initially there seemed little need to do so if the church was simply a staging post on a journey to a united church—that alone would surely give it identity. Of course the church had named itself "Reformed," but what exactly did that mean? As Arthur Macarthur put it, "The word Reformed in our title represented only a very general nod to the past and was certainly not a defining banner under which we were prepared to fight."[50]

Congregationalism in particular was already facing a severe loss of identity. Traditional Congregational ecclesiology seemed increasingly inappropriate to many and the church was developing new structures of government. Micklem felt able to claim that changes he had seen in Congregationalism "amount almost to a revolution"[51]—though there was a tradition of Congregationalism, as represented by Selbie, Cadoux, and Geoffrey Nuttall, who felt deeply alienated by them. In the Commons debate on the United Reformed Church bill, Tony Benn, whose mother was an ardent Congregationalist, had argued, "Congregationalism is synonymous with the right of people to decide for themselves how they will worship God, organise their affairs, and run their affairs."[52] Something like that might well have been said by many Congregationalists, but it was becoming less and less adequate as a description of the church.

In the most recent history of English Congregationalism, *The Transformation of Congregationalism 1900–2000*, Alan Argent (who it is relevant to note is a minister of the Congregational Federation) sees the twentieth century as having been a period in which the great historic traditions of Congregationalism were largely discarded. As a result the Congregationalists,

50. In *Reform*, January 1994, 16.

51. Micklem, *Box and the Puppets*, 136.

52. *Hansard*, 21 June 1972.

and then even more the URC, suffered a crisis of identity. For him the evidence for this is not simply the move away from Independency but can be seen in the adoption of "formal clerical dress, following the Anglican pattern."[53] He offers an analysis of the obituary photographs in the Congregational *Year Books* from 1900 to 1957, which shows that whereas none were wearing dog collars in 1900 the practice became common after 1920. Then too more ministers were wearing gowns. "Probably they did this because they wanted to be seen as equivalent to Anglican clerics."[54] Similarly, in worship there were changes such as the introduction of crosses, the use of the lectionary, and the practice of the pulpit no longer being central but at the side. The word "chapel" was increasingly being replaced by the word "church." The increasing use of service books, he believes, represented "a loss of confidence and inspiration."[55]

As it stands this argument is in danger of suggesting that only an ossified tradition can maintain an identity, which would be a strange inversion of a theological tradition based upon the concept of *Ecclesia reformata, semper reformanda*. The New Genevan preference for cassock, gown, and bands expressed a distinctive form of reformed identity that it would be grossly misleading to describe as "following the Anglican pattern." Its rationale should be found instead in a belief in the significance and dignity of the ministry. Nor should a greater stress on the importance and dignity of the Communion service be seen as uncongregational; indeed the increasing use of a common cup for Communion was in fact a return to the practice of the eighteenth century. As for the negative effect of written prayers and liturgies, it is difficult to believe these were less inspirational than what, all too frequently, were the repetitive rambles of the Congregationalists' "long prayer." None of this amounted to an adoption of Anglicanism. Argent singles out Leslie Weatherhead's placing of the pulpit at the side in the rebuilt City Temple, and formal clerical dress, as examples of the changes. No one worshipping at the City Temple, however, would have imagined this was anything but Free Church worship.

Nonetheless, Argent is right that there was a crisis of identity in Congregationalism. As the independence of the local congregation eroded, Congregationalism did become less distinct. The change from a Congregational Union to a Congregational Church represented a major theological reversal. Some of the old justification for a separate existence went with

53. Argent, *Transformation of Congregationalism*, 239.

54. Ibid., 243.

55. Ibid., 249.

it. What is more, as Argent, from his somewhat uncritical position, fails adequately to recognize, the whole *raison d'être* of the Free Churches was becoming more problematic. Congregationalists had increasing difficulty explaining exactly why patterns of church life and identity originating in the Reformation still had any lasting significance in the very different religious and human context of the twentieth century. For Presbyterians there had been a greater sense of identity, if largely as an English version of the Scottish kirk, but they too now had to explain who they were, and why it mattered to belong.

When the early hopes of union proved illusory the question of what the United Reformed Church's distinguishing characteristics were was now fundamental, but instinctively it seemed unecumenical to explore it. For many years there was an almost total lack of serious published work on the church. It was not until 1998 and the publication of David Cornick's *Under God's Good Hand* that a history of the traditions that came together in the United Reformed Church was published. Today it is no longer in print. It was 2002 (thirty years after the church's foundation!) before the United Reformed Church published David Peel's *Reforming Theology*, which set out to explore the theological ethos of the United Reformed Church.

In reality, creating a United Reformed Church out of Congregationalists and Presbyterians was always a more difficult problem than most people realized. This was not simply a union of two very similar Reformed churches. Congregationalism was never a classical Reformed church but a blend of Reformed and radical Anabaptist. As Forsyth points out, if Calvinism was the father of Independency, Anabaptist theology was its mother.[56]

Stephen Mayor lists five main areas of divergence:

> Congregationalism has never committed itself to a theological system in the way the Reformed tradition has.
>
> Congregationalism does not have any single historical founding figure comparable to Calvin.
>
> Congregationalism has been less conscious of Church and creed than the Reformed tradition.
>
> In Congregationalism the final authority is the Church Meeting not the General Assembly.
>
> Congregationalism and the Reformed Churches have divergent understandings of the ministry.[57]

56. Forsyth, *Faith, Freedom and the Future*, 120–21.

57. Mayor, "Congregationalism and the Reformed Tradition," 207.

History deepened the divide. In the eighteenth and nineteenth centuries Congregationalism was renewed first by the Evangelical Revival and then by liberalism. Calvinism was abandoned and almost forgotten. As David Cornick has reminded us, at the beginning of the twentieth century Charles Silvester Horne could write a history of the Free Churches with only one reference to Calvin—and then only that his influence had hindered the development of church music!

The new United Reformed Church was thus largely comprised of people who had never seen themselves as Reformed. Even had they been eager to familiarize themselves with the concept they would have found it, as Philip Benedict's history shows, "a multi-vocal" tradition[58] that has given rise to incompatible theologies, and, if it makes sense to talk of it as existing at all, is more a series of theological tendencies than any defined set of beliefs. For many Presbyterians "Reformed" meant they were the English version of the Scottish kirk, an option not open to the URC. To expect the new church to find the motivation and flair to explore a shared contemporary expression of this tradition was an ambitious project, especially as its theological resources diminished. The difficulty of self-identification was complicated by the fact that the new church was led by denominational leaders who felt the need to downplay their heritage, partly for ecumenical reasons and partly because if they were ex-Congregationalists their life's work had been to edge away from the traditions of Independency in order to create a Reformed church. Put this church in the individualistic consumer culture of late modernity, where all religious identities are eroded, and it was inevitable the church would have an identity problem.

This is evidenced by the extreme difficulty most respondents felt at being asked what the United Reformed Church stood for. Asked the question, David Lawrence's "I don't know, I really don't know"[59] and Stephen Orchard's "I don't know. I find it baffling"[60] may be the extreme but it is clear that everyone found this difficult. When they did attempt to define it there was no single response. Graham Cook: "a biblical people committed to the priesthood of all believers." Colin Thompson: "a church both Catholic and Reformed." Martin Cressey: "the witness to a united church" David

---

58. Benedict, *Christ's Churches*, 55.

59. Lawrence, interview.

60. Orchard, interview.

Lawrence: "I would have hoped a willingness to be radical coupled with a fierce attachment to the rights of the individual."[61]

It is clear that many members of the church simply looked back to the tradition in which they had grown up. Church historian Elaine Kaye, for example, when asked how she would explain what the URC meant to her, replied, "I am an ex-Congregationalist."[62] Michael Dunford, for twelve years a departmental secretary for the United Reformed Church, gave a similar reply: "it may be true that I am still a Congregationalist at heart—I hardly dare whisper such a thing. By that I mean the belief in the local church meeting, to me that is paramount."[63] When David Thompson was asked what his greatest regret about the United Reformed Church was, he indicated it to be the failure to develop the pattern of weekly Communion, which he grew up with in the Churches of Christ.[64] To Ernest Marvin, on the other hand, there was a sadness that the URC seemed to him to have lost the essential marks of a Presbyterian church.[65] This is hardly surprising. Churches are organic bodies that over time develop their own life. New identities cannot simply be adopted overnight.

If the old Congregational identity had already become increasingly problematic, the creation of the United Reformed Church accentuated the dilemma for both traditions. As the new church developed, the de-emphasizing of the Congregational heritage continued. The autonomy of congregations was further reduced and power centralized towards the moderators, the synods, and the central church. To those who remembered Congregationalism this was a different church. Some of course welcomed the changes. General Secretary Roberta Rominger could mark the church's fortieth anniversary by celebrating "40 Things I love about us."[66] Many ex-Congregational ministers welcomed the coming of centrally paid stipends. But others felt displaced in the new dispensation. Tony Tucker, who was a URC minister in Oxford and Associate Director of Education and Training at Mansfield College from 1989 to 1996, argues:

> Nobody was satisfied. Congregationalists didn't like what we'd got and the Presbyterians certainly didn't like it. . . . I think with my

61. Interviews.
62. Kaye, interview.
63. Dunford, interview.
64. Thompson, interview.
65. Marvin, interview.
66. In *Reform*, October 2012, 11.

generation there is a lot of grieving going on for the loss of our Congregational identity. It's a feeling that our identity was taken from us.[67]

To Donald Hilton, Moderator of the Yorkshire Province from 1987 to 1997 and of the General Assembly from 1993 to 1994, it seemed that "organic union robs us of our real Congregationalism" and that the church he grew up in had died.[68]

This did not mean there was no continuity. Local congregations were still more autonomous than in Methodism. Old Congregational habits of mind lingered, including in some ex-Presbyterian churches that still showed a considerable ability to make independent decisions. Few URC members would address the moderator as "Sir," as Methodists would the district chair, or show the deference to a moderator that Anglicans would to a bishop. Most congregations were still tolerant of theological diversity and creeds were still not much used in worship. But the cost of entering the United Reformed Church was the end of Congregationalism. Geoffrey Nuttall, one of Congregationalism's most perceptive theologians says, "Nowadays my mind often turns to the title of Grandfather Hodgson's pamphlet, *Congregationalism Played Out—Then Cometh the End.* I fear that Congregationalism has folded up, and it's ecumenical claptrap to suppose that it has "died in order to live."[69] The majority of Congregationalists may have joined the United Reformed Church but their new church had a theological tradition they didn't really own and a structure that contradicted what had until recently been for many of them their own deeply held beliefs. In such circumstances a degree of confusion and uncertainty was inevitable.

For the Presbyterians the change seemed more straightforward. Despite being the smaller of the uniting denominations, the Presbyterians could apparently recognize much of their heritage in the new church, with its General Assembly, conciliar structure, and even an ordained eldership on which they had insisted against considerable Congregational opposition. But their identity too proved difficult to maintain within the new church.

The Presbyterian Church of England had a twofold focus of identity. Firstly its basis as a historic Reformed church on the Genevan model was reflected in its conciliar structure, its commitment to the parity of ministers, and to the understanding of biblical doctrine set out by Calvin in his

67. Tucker, interview.
68. Hilton, interview.
69. Nuttall, "Geoffrey Nuttall in Conversation," 287.

Institutes of the Christian Religion and crystallized in statements of faith such as the Heidelberg Catechism, the decrees of the Synod of Dort, and the Westminster Confession of Faith. Secondly, and just as importantly, it had a cultural identity, consisting as it did of gathered congregations that often shared a Scottish or sometimes Irish Presbyterian origin. Churches were often called St. Andrew's or St. Columba's, metrical psalms would be sung out of the Church of Scotland hymnbook, Scottish country dancing might take place in the week, and the children's address might refer to the exploits of the Scottish rugby team. The Presbyterian Church magazine, *Presbyterian Outlook*, was full of reassuring references to committee conveners with names like MacDonald or Macleod and might have pictures of Scotland in spring. Not all Presbyterians had Scottish or Ulster roots, nor were all churches culturally expatriate, but enough were for a Scot moving to England to know where to go.

Both these sources of identity were eroded in the new church. Theologically, Presbyterians were now in a minority in a church to which its Genevan traditions meant very much less. It is important here not to misread the influence of Micklem and the New Genevans on Congregationalism. For a time they held the key posts and influenced the official ecclesiology and structure of the church but their influence was more superficial than it seemed at the time. Their conviction that public worship should be ordered and dignified was, at least for a time, highly influential in the church. It became more common for churches to have a chalice on the communion table and for ministers to wear cassock and gown. The hymnbook *Congregational Praise*, published in 1951, reflected their strong commitment to hymns of a high musical standard in the tradition of the *English Hymnal's* belief that "good taste is a moral concern."

And yet how deep did their influence really go? Their belief that a rediscovery of Genevan tradition would reinvigorate the church proved to be illusory. Their influence on worship was ephemeral. The cassock and Geneva gown went out of fashion. By 2013 Michael Hopkins could reflect, rightly or otherwise, "I am probably the only minister under 50 who wears a cassock and bands."[70] Choruses projected on screens began to supplement and even replace traditional hymns. Micklem's belief that only an ordained minister should celebrate Communion gave way to an easy-going tolerance of lay presidency. This was not going to be a Genevan church.

70. Hopkins, interview.

Nor was the cultural cohesion of the old Presbyterian Church possible in the wider, more inclusive United Reformed Church. The Scottish congregations were a much lower percentage of the church. In time ex-Presbyterian churches would call ministers who were not ex-Presbyterians and had no love of metrical psalms. Scots coming to England might now find their way to other United Reformed churches or to the parish church, which as the national church might well seem more natural to them, especially now that there was not an obviously Presbyterian church they could join.

There had always been fears among some Presbyterians that the reality of the United Reformed Church would be seriously difficult for ex-Presbyterians. Such fears were largely justified. "The gathered churches in the larger centres of population in southern counties were genuinely, and as it has proved, rightly concerned about their future."[71] It is doubtful if those in the north did any better. St. Cuthbert's Whitley Bay, with 469 members in 1973, had closed by 2008. Monkseaton had fallen from 576 to 173. Fisher Street Carlisle, with 486 members in 1973, had united with St. Georges, and the united church had 93 members and an average congregation of 53 in 2011. St. Columba's North Shields had fallen over the same period from 495 to 154 members. Of all the synods, Northern had the most former Presbyterians. It was also the one with the most severe decline.[72]

United Reformed churches of all sorts declined. But in the old Presbyterian strongholds the effects of decline were dramatic. Take St. Andrews Cheam, the strongest church in the Presbyterian Church of England and at first the largest in the new United Reformed Church. This fell from 915 members in 1973 to 186 members in 2011, a decline of 79 percent. By the later date the average congregation was down to 99, mostly elderly, many of whom could remember the time the church had been, at least for Communion services, packed out.[73] Now, Sunday by Sunday, there were hundreds of empty seats. The fate of the Church of Scotland suggests that something of this sort might have happened even without union. But to ex-Presbyterian churches the reality of the United Reformed Church was the shattering of their world, making the old Presbyterian Church seem "a land of lost content" in comparison. Before long Presbyterians too would

71. Macarthur, in *Reform*, September 1997, 6.
72. Thompson, "Church," 5.
73. URC, *Year Book*.

find the conciliar structure of the new church significantly different from their traditional understanding of it.

Of course new churches develop in new directions—otherwise there would be little point in forming them. What is remarkable about the changes that took place in the United Reformed Church, however, is that they were unplanned and found their origin neither in missionary strategy nor theological principle, but in the unexpected consequences of financial decisions taken at the time of union. These changes involved ever increasing expenditure, staff, and power centered on the moderators and synods.

A Presbyterian fear before union was that by accepting moderators they would be adopting a form of "pseudo-episcopacy."

> The combination of representative democracy, exercised through the various 'courts' of the church to which Presbyterians were used, seemed to be overtaken by a pattern which left no clear way of arriving at corporate judgement. We seemed, therefore, to be vulnerable to power exercised from the office and by officials. Bureaucratic structures implied in the description of the Provinces added to this fear, as Synods were expected to meet at intervals too long to enable them to be effective in handling the duties they were given.[74]

These fears were, as David Peel records, received with "some amazement"[75] by Congregationalists, who pointed out that moderators only normally had a secretary to assist them and were a pastoral ministry. "The claim revealed as serious a misunderstanding of how Congregational Moderators worked as it did of their characters."[76] Ironically it was to be changes in the Congregational model made in response to Presbyterian fears that led to exactly what they were trying to avoid.

Any influence the Congregational moderators had was purely because of the respect in which they were held—not because they were involved in any councils of the church. The Presbyterians, however, in their concern to limit the perceived dangers of the personal ministry of moderators, insisted in creating a link between moderators and synods. As Stephen Orchard says, "And that was where these wretched synods came from, because they have become diocesan and that was never the intention."[77]

---

74. Macarthur, in *Reform*, September 1997, 6.

75. Peel, *Story of the Moderators*, 43.

76. Ibid.

77. Orchard, interview.

The key factor was financial. The bulk of trust fund money and the money from the sale of redundant churches went to the synods, and the center of gravity of the power structures of the church followed the money rather than any theological conviction. Norman Pooler was legal advisor to the Presbyterian Church of England from 1963, and a member of the Joint Committee that negotiated the union.

> What we were doing was bringing together two entities, one Congregational and the other Presbyterian, with different structures, to form one church. One of the parts I was involved with was uniting the trust funds of two denominations. With the Presbyterian Church most of the trusts were with the local churches; with the Congregationalists they were mostly with the county unions. . . . I would have preferred to have had these at the national level but was told this wasn't possible.[78]

There were a variety of reasons why this was so.

> Partly it was due to the nature and extent of the functions assigned to each council; partly to the accident of history that had left the greater part of the funds in the trusteeship of county unions for application within restricted geographical areas of benefit; partly to practical politics which required extensive "negotiation" with the legal committee of the Congregational Church and the county unions; and partly to the need to provide for the allocation by the Charity Commissioners of most Congregational funds—other than local church property—between the URC and non-uniting Congregational churches.[79]

In the end it proved simpler to place the bulk of the money neither with the national church nor the district council, but with the synod.

The other major source of funds was the proceeds of the sale of redundant churches. This too mostly went to the synods; indeed for some synods, such as the Southern, this was to be a major resource and would be used year by year to cover budget deficits.

> The Acts give two separate powers of sale for local church buildings. . . . The power which the draftsmen had in mind would be used for the sale of redundant churches did empower synods to stipulate that the proceeds of sale be added to the general synod funds. At this distance in time, I can only make the assumption

78. Pooler, interview.

79. Ibid.

that the reasoning behind it was, partly at least, that church extension is a synod function.[80]

The first moderators were used to the old Congregational model of
moderator and largely still adhered to it. Eric Allen, Moderator of Mersey
Province from 1987 to 1994, remembers:

> I was in no way executive officer of a team of paid Synod staff—
> we never aspired to such extravagant deployment of ministers
> and worked out of a port-a-cabin [sic] office based in a (church)
> car park . . . with one part-time administrator and two half-time
> secretaries.[81]

Quickly, however, synod offices and staffing levels went beyond anything that anyone had envisaged at the time of union. David Thompson
puts it powerfully:

> What is most striking is the speed with which the United Re-
> formed Church once formed departed from the intentions of the
> Joint Committee thereby creating exactly what the critics of the
> Scheme (and indeed the Committee itself) feared, namely a struc-
> ture which was more expensive to administer than that which
> either constituent Church had had before.[82]

In *The Story of the Moderators* David Peel points to the appointment
of David Jenkins in 1984 as Director of Training for the North-West Synod
by Tony Burnham as a key moment in the change from a pastoral ministry
to team leadership. "It was a significant development and it was deemed
so successful that it was taken up by other Synods. The Synod staff team
was born."[83] Moderators now became less and less pastoral resources for
the church and more the head of bureaucratic teams chairing finance and
property committees and trust bodies as well as relating to ecumenical
partners and structures. As one former Moderator, Michael Davies, put it,

> Inevitably loose associations gradually developed into stronger
> bodies with more teeth, particularly when the sharing of fi-
> nance and ministry developed . . . it was clear that the need for
> strong leadership, co-ordination and pastoral prayer produced

80. Ibid.
81. Peel, *Story of the Moderators*, 45.
82. Ibid., 45.
83. Ibid., 63.

Moderators and central staff who actually had a great deal of authority and influence in practice.[84]

Some moderators clearly enjoyed the increased power and set out to maximize their role. Eric Allen might have been happy to work from a Portakabin in a church car park, but soon synods were seeking the larger premises necessary to find room for their expanding staff numbers. By 2010 Southern Synod, for example, had seventeen synod and trust staff, including four personal assistants.[85] Other less wealthy synods had less staff. Mersey Synod for example still had only eight staff. Despite some financial sharing between synods, the availability of finance, not any theological or strategic criteria, determined the pattern of staff deployment.

As their work as team leaders and their ecumenical role increased, moderators found themselves with less and less time for pastoral care, which had been their most essential role. This development reached its apotheosis in Southern Synod in 2008 when David Skitt was appointed as synod pastor to carry out the pastoral care of ministers, which the moderator could no longer cope with. The stresses that such care created were real and there is a point to David Cornick's comment that "to expect one individual to have direct pastoral responsibility for 150 ministers and churches (as we do) is cruel."[86] There is, however, also point to David Peel's rejoinder, "At the same time, it is salutary to recognise that until quite recently moderators viewed what Cornick describes as 'cruel' as their central task, and one which they accepted as perfectly manageable."[87]

While some moderators clearly welcomed their increased role, it was the availability of finance that empowered it. As David Peel says:

> I agree that some Moderators may have been lured into empire building, but if the money had been mainly in Districts or controlled by Assembly they would not have had the money to fund their thirst . . . most past Moderators were as concerned as I was how the office of Synod Moderator had changed (largely beyond their control). Neither they nor we seem to have had the guts to say: Let's stop all this nonsense and get back to the heart of this

84. Ibid., 89.
85. URC, Southern Synod, *Handbook 2010–11*, 4.
86. Cornick, "Tensions and Modesty," 113.
87. Peel, *Story of the Moderators*, 62.

translocal ministry as it first emerged and is still needed. I do not think *they* should take all the blame.[88]

Nonetheless, the way the United Reformed Church came to operate was as remarkable as it was unexpected. As David Lawrence pertinently asked in *Reform*, "Just how did an organization of 250,000 people with offices in London plus 12 Moderators with part-time secretaries meta-morphose into one of 80,000 people with offices which keep having to be altered to fit in extra people, plus 13 Moderators supported by Synod staff of around 100?"[89] Since the formation of the URC the number of minis-ters in pastoral charge has roughly halved but the number of full-time staff employed at national and synod levels has risen to around 200. Lawrence estimates that adding up managerial and support staff at the national and synod level suggests there is one extra salary for every three to four min-isters in pastoral charge—a level that is, he claims, "beyond absurdity."[90] Some care needs to be taken here in distinguishing between the increase in national and synod staff, the latter being more marked than the former.

Further centralization was to follow with the Catch the Vision Review, which reported to the 2005 General Assembly. Its most significant conclu-sions were the abolition of the district council, leaving the church with "one level of council" between the local congregation and the General Assembly (in effect the abolition of the presbytery), and the decision that the General Assembly should only meet once every two years. The first, especially by removing the work of the pastoral committee of the district council, in-creased the power of the synod. The second had the effect of passing more decision making to the Mission Council, which, though not a designated council of the church, acted like one. David Thompson argues, "It inevita-bly moves the center of gravity towards Mission Council. The changes were ill thought through and adopted out of panic."[91]

No one had been more important in leading the Presbyterian Church into union with the United Reformed Church than Arthur Macarthur, its last General Secretary. Macarthur had a critical mind and from the first had hesitations as to how, if there were no wider unity, the church would be able to find a clear identity. The changed structures of the new church now seemed to him to challenge its Reformed identity.

88. Peel, email to M. Camroux, 21 August 2012.
89. In *Reform*, April 2005, 3.
90. Ibid.
91. Thompson, interview.

I do not know where decisions are taken. I admit that many within the church do not want to be involved in decision making and are happy that many of them are taken behind closed doors but I remain a democrat. . . . I have found Assemblies increasingly dull because the real decisions are taken elsewhere and 'presented' to the Assemblers. All the Assembly does is to pass harmless motions about sin being a bad thing. No wonder most of them are passed unanimously. . . . My Presbyterian soul revolts.[92]

In another letter he wrote, "From time to time I have a bad night repenting of past misdeeds, often with the feeling I killed the Presbyterianism that gave me my spiritual birth."[93] The personal feelings here may have been intensified because Macarthur's grandfather had been one of the founders of the PCE.

It might be argued that the Congregational or Presbyterian loss of identity was the inevitable cost of creating a new church—which would develop a new identity and purpose. Ecumenists had always said that the church must die in order to be born. Could it therefore be a mistake to look for identity in terms of tradition? Might it now come from the very ecumenical enterprise for which the United Reformed Church was created?

It is certainly true that to many in the church this above all was what the church was about. What is more here, theology did influence church life and structures. The United Reformed Church was the only church to exclusively develop its new churches ecumenically. It did take initiatives for unity, it did give some of its most gifted people to work in the ecumenical instruments and the World Council of Churches, and it was involved in a higher percentage of LEPs than any other denomination. It was the only union across confessional lines in Britain. Did this not give an identity?

Up to a point the answer is yes—this was certainly part of whatever identity the United Reformed Church possessed. But there were limits to distinctiveness and adequacy as a motivating belief. Firstly, the form it had taken, a belief in organic unity, had proved to be impossible to achieve. Although never formally abandoned even within the United Reformed Church, the reality was accepted and the enthusiasm for organic unity waned. David Peel, for example, was a young enthusiast for unity.

I actually thought there was a charisma, a spirit, about the URC, that was going to move mountains. That stayed with me for a

92. Macarthur, letter to Bernard Thorogood, Macarthur Papers.
93. Macarthur, letter to Margaret Thompson, 25 January 2001, Macarthur Papers.

number of years. It started being questioned when I went to the
United States for my fourth year ordinand's training. I saw zero
commitment to ecumenicity and I saw thriving churches of different hues in a competitive market place . . . and the real permission
that churches gave themselves to set out and be a certain kind of
church and not worry that someone around the corner were doing
something different. Here it seemed to me there was a reluctance
to want to do anything, unless we all did it together.[94]

Sheila Maxey, former Ecumenical Officer, came to doubt the way the
URC had thrown all resources into ecumenical LEPs often with very little
result. In many congregations the newer members were less likely to be
committed to organic unity and the excitement of the ecumenical vision
diminished.

Secondly, if the hopes for organic unity and the excitement of ecumenism had faded, at another level the acceptance that no church had a
monopoly of salvation and ought to work together with others was now
widespread among the churches, including to some degree among evangelicals. David Lawrence makes the point, if somewhat over simplistically.
At first the United Reformed Church was an ecumenical pioneer:

But then of course everyone else joined that game. The problem
with ecumenism is that it has succeeded only at the grass roots. The
irony about ecumenism it that it was going to be a structural thing
which would gradually bring us all into the universal church, but
what has happened is that we have all joined the universal church
and now the structures don't wish to be united because there are
too many interests. So it is an irony because, at the base, apart from
a few lunatics people don't care about the labels any more. They
are what they are, they have no problem with being a part of the
wider church.[95]

It is doubtful if faithful members of the Catholic and Orthodox
Churches, for example, should be considered "a few lunatics," but the fact is
that, in a context in which increasing numbers of people no longer limited
truth to any one denomination and often didn't care which one they belonged to, the URC's ecumenism was not a clear defining belief.

The United Reformed Church could point to its ecumenical commitment, although this increasingly was not exciting even its own members, let

94. Peel, interview.
95. Lawrence, interview.

alone the Methodists or the Church of England. But it had an inadequate sense of what a Reformed church was, little ecclesiology, and little idea how to relate to a society that no longer had many contacts with formalized religion. With a weak relationship with its own history, it is not surprising if its members were unclear what they stood for or why anyone should belong to them rather than, say, to the Church of England.

And even in terms of ecumenism, had the United Reformed Church fulfilled the hope?

The ecumenical hope had never just been that church organizations would reunite. It was that such unity would bring renewal. Ernst Lange, a former staff member of the World Council of Churches, wrote:

> The indissoluble connection between 'unity' and 'renewal' has been one of the constant formulas of ecumenical theory and practice. Unity can only come through the renewal of the "actual churches." Yet at the same time, unity is itself an ecumenical way to renewal. As the churches are radically renewed they unite. As they seek unity on the basis of the fundamentals of faith, they are renewed.[96]

Where could the United Reformed Church show it had in fact renewed its life through the bringing together of two ecclesiastical structures? In a very damning verdict David Thompson says, "In retrospect there may have been union without renewal, as far as the United Reformed Church is concerned."[97] If that is so, how successful can the URC's commitment to ecumenism be judged?

Karl Barth sees clearly the scandal of Christian disunity. "There is no justification theological, spiritual or biblical, for the existence of a plurality of churches genuinely separated—and mutually excluding each other. A plurality of churches in this sense means a plurality of lords . . . a plurality of gods."[98] Barth, however, goes on to argue that the way to unity is not by churches ceasing to take their distinctiveness seriously, "by denying and renouncing their special character for the sake of internal or external peace, by trying to exist in a kind of nondescript Christianity"—a state of ecclesiological "featurelessness."[99] In fact the continued existence of separate

96. Lange, *And Yet It Moves*, 107.

97. Thompson, interview.

98. Barth, *Church Dogmatics* 4/1, 675.

99. Ibid., 678.

churches can only be justified when they claim to represent something vital for faith and salvation.[100]

There were all sorts of things about the URC of which it need not be ashamed. Its commitment to equality of male and female within the church, or the degree of tolerance it achieved for differing points of view. Stephen Orchard points to the contribution of hymn writers like Fred Kaan or Brian Wren. Martin Cressey points to the role of United Reformed Church members in the committees of the World Council of Churches. There is no doubt that the pension and housing provision for retired ministers was improved and that stipends were increased. Through its Church and Society Department and Commitment for Life the URC has a strong record of commitment to world development and has done pioneering work with its Church Related Community Workers. The church can claim that women are well represented in its leadership. Perhaps there are, as Roberta Rominger argues, forty or more things one might love about the church. It is difficult, however, to see whether any of this can be said to be "something vital for faith and salvation." Certainly the one thing that no one could claim was that the church's ecumenical commitment justified its separate existence.

The history of the United Reformed Church demonstrates powerfully one of the problems of the organic model of church unity. Writing in 1945 in the context of possible Congregational-Presbyterian unity, C. J. Cadoux argued that "The polity of each body has its own peculiar characteristics: and before anything resembling an amalgamation of the two can profitably be effected, each of them will need to consider carefully how far its own principles can be harmonized, honestly and without serious loss, with that of the other."[101] This is not simply a matter of official theological doctrines. Churches are "communities of memory" (Bellah et al. 1985) comprised by the stories they tell, the memories they cherish, the myths they share, and the habits they own and recognize. When change is imposed from above, as is inevitable with organic unity, the memories are disrupted in a way that risks a dislocation of identity. So Clyde Binfield can say,

> I remember going to the Assembly at Cardiff and I suddenly realized there was an Assembly language and tone that wasn't mine. And I've tended to feel that every time I have been back. I'm not sure I can define it. I suddenly thought this isn't quite me.[102]

100. Ibid., 680.

101. Cadoux, *Congregational Way*, 30–31.

102. Binfield, interview.

When you unite two distinct bodies, each with its own inherent logic and tradition, you may weaken the theological vitality of both without creating anything that itself is distinctive and coherent. As Dale Turner warned in the USA, "A divided church that stands for something is better than a united church that stands for nothing."[103] The URC does not stand for nothing, but if even those within are unclear as to what its meaning is, it is unlikely to be able to communicate it to those without.

The point was to be visibly and painfully demonstrated when the United Reformed Church sought to face the dilemma. As well as ecclesiology, a significant part of Congregational identity, for some, had been its liberal heritage, summed up often at the popular level in the belief that theirs was a church that prized the freedom to think for oneself. This was still to be broadly true of the United Reformed Church. In his Moderator's Address to the 1993 Assembly Donald Hilton asserted, "I stand in the liberal Christian tradition, and rejoice to see it well-affirmed in the United Reformed Church."[104] That claim is clearly justified. The 1989 English Church census showed the broadly liberal nature of the church.[105]

	URC	Methodist	Baptist	Anglican
Evangelical	12%	32%	80%	26%
Low Church	15%	19%	4%	10%
Broad	22%	25%	6%	18%
Liberal	48%	21%	9%	20%
Anglo-Catholic/ Catholic	–	1%	–	25%

Quite what some of these terms mean may be open to question. But the URC is distinctive in having the highest percentage of liberals of any trinitarian denomination. It was not until 1991, sixteen years into the life of the URC, that an evangelical, Malcolm Hanson, became Moderator of the General Assembly.

Nonetheless, the URC was not as self-consciously liberal as the Congregationalists had been in the earlier part of the twentieth century. The influence of Barth, Forsyth, and the New Genevans had already added greater complexity to Congregationalism's theological variety and, despite Oman and Hick, the Presbyterians tended to be more conservative than

103. Quoted in Guess, "John Thomas."
104. Hilton, *To Follow Truth*, 12.
105. Brierley, *"Christian" England*, 164.

Congregationalists. The new church had an explicitly ecumenical purpose, not a liberal one, and included a significant number of Barthians in its leadership. At the grassroots level (where Barthians were few and far between) there was a new upsurge of conservative evangelicalism and even fundamentalism. When the Group for Evangelism and Renewal (GEAR) was set up in 1974, with a theology reflecting some of the "fundamentals" drawn up in Princeton in 1909, it indicated a preference for the formula, "The Bible is His written word."[106] In some congregations at least it could not be assumed that doubts and questions would be welcomed.

A broadly liberal ethos still continues. Even over sexuality, where deep divisions were revealed, most people in the church in the end were prepared to accept others who believed differently. As Colin Thompson says, "The debates on homosexuality . . . were mostly pretty ghastly, but we came through and have come to some kind of, possibly rather grudging, but at best quite deep appreciation that we can't agree with each other and want to live together."[107] What the church mostly could not do, however, was articulate a shared liberal (or for that matter evangelical) theology that could give it real self-identification and public visibility. Neither with human sexuality nor Catch the Vision was a common vision possible. As one who would welcome a radical liberal identity, David Lawrence asks, "From the point of view of someone outside the church with a vague Christian faith, what exactly would be the point of joining the URC? In the absence of a local congregation which has some particular selling point in the form of good youth work, an outstanding preacher, an extensive social life etc., I can't see that there is one."[108]

The URC's dilemma was cruelly exposed when an attempt was made to articulate a radical identity through a program that (with unintended irony) it named "Zero Intolerance." In the USA the largely ex-Congregational United Church of Christ (UCC) had at its General Synod in 2003 initiated an identity and marketing campaign called "God Is Still Speaking," which sought to present the church as a welcoming, justice-minded Christian community with a strong commitment to inclusion. Unambiguously it positioned the church as a progressive religious community and its advertising insisted that this was what made the UCC unique. To some in the URC, including its General Secretary, Roberta Rominger, and its

106. GEAR, "Faith We Hold."
107. Thompson, interview.
108. Lawrence, email to M. Camroux, 13 December 2013.

Moderator-Elect, Lawrence Moore, this seemed to offer a model of how the URC might overcome its own identity problem. Rominger did not simply want to mark time as General Secretary but use this as an opportunity to tell the British public that a church like the URC existed. "What's the point of being such a well-kept secret?," she asked. Approaches were therefore made to the UCC as to the possibility of the URC adopting the program.

It began badly and got worse. Firstly, the UCC was only willing to allow the URC, its sister church, to use its "God Is Still Speaking" program on condition that the URC signed an agreement to let them vet any changes they might make to the materials and reserving the right to revoke the license at any point. It was a clear lack of trust and put the URC in an impossible situation since it was inevitable that American material would have had to be modified for a British context. Unsurprisingly the URC declined the offered terms. Despite this serious setback the URC committed itself to develop its own version of the campaign, which it called "Zero Intolerance." A logo was developed together with six posters, adequate for eighteen months' worth of advertising. There were plans for a film to be posted on YouTube to coincide with the public launch, which was scheduled for May 2012.

As the campaign planning developed the question was raised as to whether an ecumenically minded church should really be attempting to abrogate to itself a theme of this kind. Might it not be better to share ZI outside the URC and create a coalition of churches willing to support the program? It was decided that the URC branding be removed from the ZI material allowing it to be used by churches of any denomination. This was a significant and surprising change in the concept from that practiced by the UCC and as originally conceived by the URC. What had happened to the idea of ZI acting as a focus for the URC's identity? Once more the ecumenical commitment of the URC was making it more difficult for the church to define itself. It raised other problems. The notion that some churches would opt to be ZI churches and others would not caused serious alarm. There was concern lest the effect of some ministers and churches (and not others) identifying themselves with ZI might be a major factor as to which churches a minister would be willing to serve. Roberta Rominger said, "Some of the fears about divisiveness arose from the prospect of a vocal coalition of non-conservative churches boldly (and effectively!) proclaiming a different version of the gospel."[109] There may have been a theoretical aspect to this

109. Rominger, email to M. Camroux, 22 August 2014.

debate since it was not clear whether there was in fact a significant desire in other churches for the URC to take a lead in this way—it was proving hard for the URC to recognize how little influence it now had.

The central problem had still to be faced—was there a common vision around which the church could coalesce? It was Rominger's hope that because gay people had in practice sometimes been accepted by evangelical churches, "radical welcome" might be offered by all. Indeed at first the conservative evangelicals in GEAR did make a positive attempt to engage with the program, believing that it could be a way to engage with the community. A GEAR member, Paul Stokes, joined the committee. There were hesitations about some of the literature but it seemed they might be able to live with it. There was, however, a crunch question still to face. To conservative evangelicals, "radical welcome" had to be linked with a radical call to discipleship that included the need for sexually active homosexual people to repent. To people like Lawrence Moore, however, acceptance of gay people just as they were meant exactly that—the acceptance of their God-given sexuality. Both were versions of radical discipleship—but radically different. Could the two really come together in a common program?

The decisive moment came when the steering group decided that the nature of the welcome being offered needed definition. It noted that the stated policy of the Evangelical Alliance made clear its rejection of gay sex. "We believe habitual homoerotic sexual activity without repentance to be inconsistent with faithful church membership. Where someone is publicly promoting homoerotic sexual practice within a congregation, there may be a case for more stringent disciplinary action. " This logically made nonsense of any policy of radical welcome. "We are clear that a church that would use this as a policy to guide their treatment of homosexual people would not be practicing radical welcome and could not therefore be a ZI church."[110] The committee therefore determined that no congregation that belonged to the Evangelical Alliance could be part of ZI. However, the committee concluded this did not mean that evangelical churches that regarded homosexual activity as sinful (but were not members of the Evangelical Alliance) could not be part of ZI. Such a church could qualify if it "committed itself not to preach and teach that homosexual activity is wrong."[111] It is difficult to see how any evangelical church could in conscience so limit its preaching and teaching. At this, inevitably Paul Stokes resigned from the

110. URC, Zero Intolerance Steering Group, "ZI and the Sexuality Issue," 3.
111. Ibid.

committee. He and others in GEAR felt this contradicted what had been said to them in earlier discussions and that a campaign about tolerance had itself now become intolerant.

The problem however was fundamental—if churches that regarded homosexuality as sinful were included, the campaign could not have the radical cutting edge its supporters looked for. The hope of gay Christians that at last a church was fully accepting of them would be denied and "radical welcome" would be a false promise. But if conservative evangelicals could not be part of the campaign that would exclude a significant body of those believing they were simply being true to clear biblical teaching. Rominger's belief that her advocacy of ZI could bridge the gap between the two theologies was, it was now apparent, an illusion—it had to be clear whether or not gay people were accepted in their sexual orientation.

It seemed the URC would have to decide where it stood. The debate became heated, harsh words were said, a number of people came under severe stress, and in November 2011 Denese Chikwendu, the campaign coordinator, resigned. Dismayed and confused by the turmoil, some initial supporters of the project began to doubt its wisdom. Rominger confessed, "We never anticipated the scale of the controversy which the campaign would generate"[112]—though this surprise is itself surprising since it had been so in America and she knew GEAR's views on homosexual relationships. Tracey Lewis, the convener of the Mission Committee, reported in March 2013:

> The "URC identity campaign" had, by the time the local churches were presented with it, moved on into a more edgy gospel focused venture. These elements, along with a presentation style that aimed to give leadership but was perceived as having no room for debate, meant that the advertising campaign was met with resistance, arguments became heated and personality issues became part of the debate.[113]

Should they go on? An investigation group set up to decide about the continuance or otherwise of the campaign recommended that it continue, but a resolution from Mersey Synod, strongly supported by members of GEAR and the wider evangelical constituency, proposed the opposite. The URC choose to back away. In March 2012 its Mission Council passed the following resolution: "Mission Council strongly encourages all churches to

112. URC Mission Committee Minutes, 4–5 October 2012, in URC Archive.

113. URC Mission Committee Minutes, 7–8 June 2013, in URC Archive.

continue to work on developing their radical welcome . . . but discontinues the ZI campaign with immediate effect." Roberta Rominger reported to the Council for World Mission in October 2012 (whose funding had been used)"

> As of March 2012, 500 of the URC's 1500 congregations were exploring radical welcome. However, none had completed their preparations to the point that they had affiliated as ZI churches ready to be included in the advertising. The steering group asked to postpone the public launch until September to give the churches time. However, the feeling in Mission Council was that too much momentum had been lost and it was time to admit defeat.[114]

While this was certainly part of the truth, it was not the complete picture. The request for a postponement from the steering group was partly because the materials were not yet ready and there were churches in the training process close to qualification that were hugely disappointed by the decision. The material produced for the campaign, which both individuals and churches wanted to use, was shut away, never to be seen again for fear of the divisiveness its use might cause.

The strategic decision making behind the campaign is difficult to evaluate. It might be argued that by dropping the campaign the URC was recognizing the diversity of opinion in the church and respecting the consciences of its conservative evangelical members. But in that case why was the campaign started in the first place? Was it really impossible to predict it would be divisive? Was there a failure to recognize the force and distinctiveness of the theologies involved and that sometimes prophetic choices have to be made? And in the end did the desire to protect the organization become more important than the question of what the organization was for? Lawrence Moore thought so:

> It highlighted our overriding fear of risking alienating anyone. We are in such decline that the most important principle we hold to seems to be, "Don't do anything that risks losing anyone else!" I am at a loss otherwise to explain how the abandonment of the campaign could have happened as it did.[115]

It was hugely disappointing to everyone involved. Evangelicals felt they had been met with intolerance; radicals that a visionary opportunity to

---

114. Rominger, email to M. Camroux, 22 August 2014.

115. Moore, email to M. Camroux.

articulate the gospel had been frustrated. Reflecting on the results, Rominger said, "This raises wider issues for the URC." The first on her list was, "Is it possible for a conciliar church to do something brave?"[116] That was not quite the point. The UCC is a conciliar church; that did not prevent it endorsing "God Is Still Speaking." It was not the conciliar system that was the problem—it was the lack of shared values in the church.

In her report to the Mission Council in March 2013 Tracey Lewis tried to put a positive spin on the result.

> The vision, work and aspirations of the project were engaged with by the church and many initiatives have been born out of the experience. We will gather its "fruits" as we learn from this experience for our future development of our mission.[117]

The reality was darker. Zero Intolerance was started in hope and faith and with a vision for the church and gospel but it ended in disaster. Lawrence Moore was closer to the truth: "what the campaign did was to expose the inability of the church to articulate—or live—a common identity." It may even have been worse than that. Paul Stokes puts it even more bluntly: "If Lawrence thinks we are unable to articulate a common identity, does that presuppose that one exists?"[118]

In the name of a program committed to showing what a tolerant, welcoming, and friendly church the URC was, Zero Intolerance managed to cause deep pain and factionalism. Also there were severe management failures, good people behaved badly, the Moderator-Elect resigned, and relations between some of the key participants were severely damaged. When she reached the end of her term the General Secretary was not reappointed. Above all ZI demonstrated the problem it was unable to solve. It raised hopes it could not fulfill. David Lawrence says:

> One of the tragedies of the whole "Still speaking" / ZI process is that, momentarily at least, I treasured the hope that we might have found something that would lead existing and potential members to see something unique and valuable in the URC, something that no other mainstream denomination could have offered. We failed and thus revert to the norm, that people within our churches have between zero and very little identification with the URC as a national body. . . . Our last state was worse than our first; confused,

116. Rominger, email to M. Camroux, 22 August 2014.

117. URC Mission Committee Minutes, March 2013, in URC Archive.

118. Stokes, email to M. Camroux.

indecisive and visibly unable to say anything positive to contemporary society.[119]

That is the voice of deep disappointment. The idea that the URC might stand for something unique does not have much reality in a post-denominational culture where theological ideas are rarely particular to any denomination (though the UCC did make this claim on the basis of "God Is Still Speaking"). But the angst was real and not unjustified. A church needs a reason for existence and the failure of ZI demonstrated the problem this posed for the URC. In any case, by then it was a little late. It was now a church largely dying at the roots, with many of its congregations consisting of very small groups of very elderly people not sure how long they could go on. The idea that such congregations could become centers of radical welcome to the marginalized is quite difficult to imagine.

119. Lawrence, email to M. Camroux.

8

Why Did Organic Unity Fail?

JOHN KENT'S JUDGEMENT THAT "The ecumenical movement has been the great ecclesiastical failure of our time" goes too far.[1] The relationships of the churches have changed hugely and positively in the last hundred years. Roman Catholics and Protestants now work together in a way that would have been unthinkable in the past. At the coronation of Queen Elizabeth in 1953 the papal legate sat in a specially constructed box opposite the entrance to Westminster Abbey so that it was clear that he was not participating in or condoning a Protestant act of worship.[2] Today, with the Roman Catholic Church a full part of the ecumenical instruments, we are in a different era. As Michael Davies comments,

> When I was ordained I could not take communion in an Anglican Church except with the express permission of the bishop. The only thing we could do with the Roman Catholics was to say the Lord's Prayer and it had to be their version. How different now.[3]

But there is another side to this that gives at least some credence to Kent's proposition. Insofar as organic unity was the preferred model of unity, it almost entirely failed. As Kent observes, "The churches throughout the world remain broadly as divided in the 1980s as they were in 1910 when the

1. Kent, *Unacceptable Face*, 203.
2. Sheppard and Worlock, *Better Together*, 8.
3. Davies, interview.

search for institutional unity was first systematically organized."[4] Indeed the explosion of new Black-majority and Charismatic churches since that time, both worldwide and in Britain, means that the diversity of churches is actually greater than it was in 1910. It is a sign of how far back the movement for organic unity has gone that for the Church of England even reconciled diversity with the Free Churches seems outside current possibilities. The Church of England National Ecumenical Officer, Roger Paul, puts it bluntly:

> The Church of England has found it relatively straightforward to enter into communion with the churches of Scandinavia and the Baltic because they have an episcopal structure. As there are no episcopal churches in this country (the Roman Catholic Church is of course) it would be extremely difficult to enter into that sort of agreement in this country.[5]

Even the ability to take weddings in each other's churches is in doubt.

> We don't have interchangeability of ministry so certainly a Methodist or United Reformed Church minister could not take a Church of England wedding, . . . By the same token the Church of England minister cannot take a Methodist wedding.[6]

The expansion of the ecumenical instruments has made them more inclusive but only at the cost of making them less significant; indeed this was the intention of some of the denominational bodies. They have retreated in their areas of operations and seen their staff and programs drastically cut back. Internationally too, ecumenical bodies have declined in influence. Michael Davies, Assistant General Secretary at the World Council of Churches from 1990 to 1997, observes that "There were five members of the General Secretariat when I went there. There are two now. They can't do it. There were 340 staff, now there are about 120."[7]

Forms of ecumenism continue. Local ecumenical partnerships still offer attractive prospects in some situations. There is cooperation at the local level on matters such as food banks or street pastors. Internationally there has been dialogue between the different faith communities leading to a series of agreed statements such as the International Lutheran-Roman

4. Kent, *Unacceptable Face*, 303.

5. Paul, interview.

6. Ibid.

7. Davies, interview.

Catholic Commission on Unity, the International Dialogue between the Catholic Church and the World Alliance of Reformed Churches, and the International Dialogue between the Anglican Communion and the Roman Catholic Church.

RECEPTIVE ECUMENISM

The theological justification for the current commitment to dialogue is sometimes found in the idea of "receptive ecumenism." The concept derives primarily from the ecclesiology of the Roman Catholic Church, where it refers to the assimilation and acceptance by the faithful of the teaching of the Magisterium. Following Pope John Paul II's *Ut Unum Sint* in 1995, receptive ecumenism was developed, especially by Cardinal Kasper, as a realistic approach to ecumenism so that Christian traditions might approach unity by learning from each other. "On the basis and in the context of what we have in common, we try to understand better what divides us, and engage in a dialogue regarding the issues involved."[8] In England the concept was significantly advanced by Dr. Paul Murray, a Roman Catholic lay theologian at the University of Durham, and has taken shape around two international conferences. The first was held in 2006 and was called "Receptive Ecumenism and the Call to Catholic Learning." This was followed by a conference in January 2009 on "Receptive Ecumenism and the Call to Ecclesial Learning."[9] For Murray the central meaning of receptive ecumenism is that churches make what he calls a programmatic shift from asking what our dialogue partners need to learn from us to asking what we can learn from our dialogue partners. Roger Paul, from the Church of England, is enthusiastic: "I have a hunch if we help people to take that on board then they are placing themselves in a position where they are truly able to receive each other's gifts."[10]

It is to the credit of receptive ecumenism that it recognizes the stagnation in the ecumenical movement and looks for a way to progress. Murray accepts that the movement for organic unity has "run out of steam"[11] and that there are tendencies in the churches to respond to secularization by adopting a more inward-looking preservationist mentality. But does this

8. Kasper, *Harvesting the Fruits*, 5.

9. See Kelly, "New Ecumenical Wave," 1.

10 Paul, interview.

11. Murray, *Receptive Ecumenism*, 9.

mean that "reconciled diversity without structural unity is the best that can be hoped for and worked for in this context?"[12] For Murray the answer is both yes and no. Structural unity is an eschatological hope, not about to be realized.

> But it would be a poor eschatology that led us to conclude that it is, therefore, a reality that is of no relevance to the contingencies of our present existence. On the contrary, when understood as a destiny breathed out in the original fiat of creation, Christian existence is properly viewed as a living from and towards this promised end.[13]

Living with this hope, Christians need to place at the heart of the ecumenical agenda the question, "What, in any given situation, can one's own tradition appropriately learn with integrity from other traditions?" One expression of this, for Murray, was the invitation by Pope John Paul II in *Ut Unum Sint* to theologians in other Christian traditions to help rethink the Petrine ministry so that it might become a focus for unity for the whole church—"An invitation which itself exemplifies the strategy and virtues of Receptive Ecumenism."[14]

A willingness to learn from others is integral to any real ecumenism, and it might well be argued that ecumenism is an iterative cycle, with every generation needing to start its own exploration of the riches of other traditions. No doubt Murray is correct that "The logic is that if we believe the Holy Spirit is really at work in other Christian traditions sustaining real elements of the Church of Christ there . . . why need we wait for full ecclesial unity before being enriched by them?"[15] In practice, however, all this has very clear limitations. The very diversity of Christian belief means that confessional dialogue runs up against hard differences that resist elimination. For Roman Catholics the dialogue must and can only take place in the context of the Magisterium, which is "authoritatively binding . . . on the Catholic side."[16]

When it comes to the Petrine ministry, the very idea of a single head of the one universal church of Christ contradicts what many Protestants believe about leadership in the church and what they would see as the

12. Ibid.,11.

13. Ibid.

14. Ibid., 13.

15. Murray, "Hands across the Tiber," 14–15.

16. Kasper, *Harvesting the Fruits*, 7.

God-given right of individuals to participate in decision making. If structural unity is to wait till agreement is found on doctrine such as this, it would put any such unity into the eschatological future. Progress in confessional dialogue is inevitably limited and incremental and unlikely to engender the radical Christian renewal that ecumenism promised. The fact that Murray offers the Anglican-Methodist Covenant as a hopeful sign, when even in many LEPs the practical effects of it are invisible, is an illustration of how limited the effects of such dialogues are.

What is more, because it inevitably centers on work done with very little visibility by church functionaries, it represents the clericalization of the ecumenical movement, removing it from the grass roots, what Martin Marty calls "ecumenism by committee." As Kinnamon puts it,

> Unless the movement becomes less clericalized, less dominated by "professional ecumenists," ecumenism will seem increasingly remote and irrelevant to persons in our congregations—and its protest character will be further diminished.[17]

A very large number of papers and agreed statements have been issued. Many of these are significant documents that seemed important to those who wrote them and have played some part in a reconciling process. All are, however, compatible with forms of ecumenism that leave the visible unity of the church still a distant goal. Diarmaid MacCulloch argues that the mistake of the twentieth-century ecumenical movement was "diverting its energy into committees and prepared statements."[18] Jurgen Moltmann puts it more emphatically in reference to the World Council of Churches:

> From conference to conference Faith and Order had splendid study programmes on which excellent theologians from all over the world worked. At the onset I was most enthusiastic about what emerged theologically in these studies in the ecumenical world format. The studies were always accepted and their praises sung at the next full Assembly. But then the new study arrived and the old one disappeared. As time went on I saw through the method. The way was supposed to be the goal because no goal outside it could be reached. Ecumenical cooperation was the main point irrespective of what one worked on. And for that reason these studies have been long since forgotten.[19]

17. Kinnamon, *Vision of the Ecumenical Movement*, 84.

18. MacCulloch, *Silence*, 228.

19. Moltmann, *Broad Place*, 86.

Significant as these documents may have seemed, they did not affect the Anglican unwillingness to accept reconciled diversity with non-episcopal churches or prevent the Roman Catholic Church setting up an ordinariate for Anglican clergy who wanted to change churches. Vatican II had broken much new ground in ecumenical relations but the changes were less that had sometimes been hoped for. John Buchanan records:

> I was part of a Presbyterian delegation to a Reformed–Roman Catholic dialogue at the Vatican. Our delegation decided to gently raise the issue of sacramental exclusion. We agreed with our Catholic counterparts that the church has been given responsibility for the sacrament. As we pressed this issue, it became clear that we had not resolved disagreements about the nature of the church. Lewis Mudge, a Presbyterian theologian, spoke up: "You're still saying that we are not a true church, aren't you?" We remained, for them, an "ecclesial community," not a church—so no sharing of communion.[20]

The limited nature of receptive ecumenism means that it can be endorsed by churches that in practice are not willing to make serious efforts to achieve even reconciled diversity. Such dialogue is entirely compatible with the Roman Catholic Church maintaining the authority of the 1896 encyclical *Apostolicae Curae*, which condemned Anglican orders as defective in both form and intention. It is an ecumenism that is compatible with churches that do not accept each other as churches, with a refusal to accept others at the Lord's Table, and with Roger Paul for the Church of England objecting to Anglican clergy taking weddings in Methodist churches even in an LEP. To describe this as "the new ecumenical wave," as Gerald Kelly of the Catholic Institute of Sydney does, is to forget what has been before. More realistically it reflects a reality described by Rena Karefa-Smart: "incremental gains, carefully chosen schedules, and imposing publications all add up to churches still separated in their ecumenical life."[21] When adopted in a minimalist way by churches not serious about real change, it becomes what Albert Outler called "ecumenism within the status quo."

Today it is clear that the hopes not only of Nottingham but of Swanwick have not been realized. Those committed to organic unity are of a diminishing age cohort and organic unity is no longer realistically on the agenda. As Keith Clements comments, "It is apparent . . . that today, both

20. *Christian Century*, 26 September 2013.
21. Karefa-Smart, "Future of the Ecumenical Movement," 154.

in these islands and in the wider world, the ecumenical movement is seen by many as a failing, lost or irrelevant cause. Some talk of an ecumenical winter."[22] Few would dispute the conclusion of Konrad Raiser, former General Secretary of the World Council of Churches, that "the contemporary moment is marked by uncertainty, stagnation, and a loss of direction and vision."[23] In their more honest moments even the more reflective members of the United Reformed Church knew it had all gone wrong. As the URC Moderator's Report commented in 1994, "It is unlikely that the person in the street cares two brass buttons whether the Church is united or not."[24]

The reality of failure is visibly demonstrated by the hopelessness of the task the United Reformed Church set itself when it sought to break the ecumenical logjam. Taken together with the failure of Anglican-Methodist unity and the Covenant for Unity, the emasculation of the ecumenical instruments, and the diminished commitment to the World Council of Churches, the reality of ecumenical retreat and disappointment is unmistakable. In the remainder of this chapter I want to summarize why this great reversal occurred. The answer is complex, with a variety of factors all leading to the same end.

A LACK OF A CRITICAL AND REALISTIC APPRAISAL OF THE TASK

All believers find objective intellectual analysis difficult because it relates to who they are and what they hope and believe. In particular this is true of the religious believer, who often makes a direct link between their own beliefs and the will of God. If you believe that something is the will of God, it is easy to believe that it must happen, just as Jesus seems to have imagined an imminent eschatological event that never in fact occurred. That human contingency and decision are involved is often overlooked and critical problems are ignored or minimized. When it came to ecumenism there was a lack of a critical and realistic appraisal of the task. As Paul Avis puts it, "The 'halo' of transcendence around the idea of unity tends to disarm our critical faculties and can sometimes reduce ecumenical documents to the

22. Clements, "Open Letter to the Churches," 1.

23. Raiser, *Ecumenism in Transition*, 33.

24. URC General Assembly, *Annual Reports*, 1994, 89.

mere invocation of a hazy idea—an ideal that is incapable of being implemented in practice."[25]

The first of the resolutions of the Nottingham Conference stated that the theological differences between the churches "though important, are not sufficient to stand as barriers to unity. They do not separate us at the point of our central affirmation of our faith, and they can be better explored within a united Church."[26] This proved untrue. Episcopacy, for example, was a real barrier. As Roger Paul says, "It is fundamental to our vision within the Lambeth quadrilateral."[27] What this means is that any united church will be episcopal in direct continuity with Anglican traditions (though these traditions may of course develop). Similarly, while it is possible—perhaps probable—that one day either the process of secularization or the growing multifaith nature of British society will lead to the disestablishment of the Church of England, this was never going to be given up in exchange for organic unity with the United Reformed Church. As the then Bishop of Leicester, Ronald Ralph Williams, put it bluntly but honestly in 1966, ecumenically "the purpose would quite frankly be the building of a united Church round the fabric of the existing Church of England."[28] The nature of English history, the relative numerical strengths, and the theological beliefs involved meant a united church could only be a modified version of the Church of England—unless of course the Roman Catholics were involved, at which point unity could only mean accepting the supremacy of the Pope and other core Roman Catholic beliefs—impossible to accept for almost any historic dissenter, and many Anglicans.

On the question of episcopacy there was a great deal of wishful thinking in the United Reformed Church. There were many who, like John Reardon, "were willing to embrace it as long as the episcopacy of the Anglican Church could be reformed . . . we thought that maybe if they were willing to accept Methodists presidents and chairs, and our moderators as on the same level then some of us felt it would reform itself."[29] There must be at least a suspicion that what this meant was that bishops would be acceptable provided they became more like URC moderators. This was an extraordinary failure to understand Anglicanism. John Sutcliffe is wither-

25. Avis, *Reshaping Ecumenical Theology*, 39–40.

26. Davies and Edwards, *Unity Begins at Home*, 75.

27. Paul, interview.

28. Quoted in Jennings, *What's Still Right*, 20.

29. Reardon, interview.

ingly accurate when he says that the United Reformed Church's ecumenical commitment "was all very romantic. There was a desperate lack of rational thought about it."[30] Very little of the talk about unity looked objectively at the hard questions that would have to be solved. Quite a few were initially enthusiastic for a unity that they did not want to be part of when they saw what it meant.

Fundamental to what happened was a striking failure to understand other traditions and what mattered to them. Many in the United Reformed Church did not understand the Anglican commitment to episcopacy and wholly overrated their own significance in the Anglican mind. They did not recognize the way the powerful pull of unity with Rome would, for Anglo-Catholics, act as a disincentive to union with dissenters. Similarly, not everyone recognized the logic of the tradition of Wesleyan Methodism, which meant that some Methodists were much more inclined to a reunion with the Church of England than to one with the United Reformed Church. Presbyterians did not always understand how an ordained eldership was viewed as a denial of the role of the laity by some Methodists, and not all Methodists understood the essentially lay nature of an ordained eldership. High church Anglicans misread the chances of the Roman Catholic Church being willing to accept Anglican orders. Silvester Horne's old comment about P. T. Forsyth's theology, that it was "fireworks in a fog," is even more applicable to much ecumenical debate.

ORGANIC UNITY CAN LEAD TO NEW DIVISIONS IN THE BODY OF CHRIST

The ecumenical movement sought to restore the visible unity of the church in such a way that it could be a credible witness to God's reconciling power. In a very small way the United Reformed Church demonstrated this and it was the hope of the Nottingham and Swanwick Conferences. However, what the history of the United Reformed Church also demonstrates is how divisive organic unity can frequently be. The United Reformed Church was created to unite, but both its genesis and expansion led to the creation of new churches, and to division within the uniting churches and some considerable ill feeling. Both the union with the Churches of Christ and the Scottish Congregationalists led to secessions from those two churches. Had

30. Sutcliffe, interview.

the Covenant proposals been accepted there would have been those who, like Donald Hilton, would have left the United Reformed Church.

It may be argued that on each of these occasions statistically more members came together in the uniting churches than split off into dissenting churches. So perhaps there was overall gain. It could also be argued that in any creation of a united church among those left behind there will always be the irreconcilables who will simply never be part of it. The kind of Congregationalism that could recognize no authority beyond an often ill-attended Church Meeting might be seen as a kind of negative atomistic Independency that could no longer express the challenge of the gospel. Of those lost to the URC some might well have left anyway due to an evangelical theological agenda. But this understates the loss. Had the Covenant been accepted the withdrawal of people like Donald Hilton would have meant the loss of a significant ecumenically minded tradition within the United Reformed Church. It would have been a lesser church. Churches are coalitions, and organic unity will often have a price in terms of the disunity it creates. That price often includes division, hurt, and some public disunity, which demonstrates the power of religion to divide—the exact opposite of ecumenism's stated *raison d'être*.

It is not simply that there is a painful cost to organic unity—it is that this prospect is a deterrent to those considering adopting it. Any organization is concerned to maintain its own structural integrity and unity, and churches are only going to be willing to pay the price of the potential divisiveness of unity if there is some significant advantage to be gained or a strong motivating belief. For the creators of the United Reformed Church this was essentially theological—their conviction either that unity was the will of God or that a united church could provide a stronger witness to the Reformed tradition. For those like Philip Morgan and David Thompson in the Churches of Christ, unity was the fulfilment of the theological vision that underlay their church life. There were also more practical concerns. The Scottish Congregationalists were in drastic decline, and their very weakness suggested that their life might be better preserved as a synod in a wider church than in an autonomous church. The ecumenically minded in the Churches of Christ had little to lose.

Very often, however, churches were unwilling to risk the divisiveness of organic unity. This may have been one reason why the Baptists were so unenthusiastic about possibilities of union with the Churches of Christ. So David Thompson argues that they "feared that any movement which involved significant change in the structure of the organization would provoke division."[31] That motive was to be seen above all in the rejection by the Anglican Church of both the proposals for Anglican-Methodist union and the Covenant. The theological diversity of the Church of England means that it contains both an evangelical and a Catholic party. Congregationalists, Presbyterians, and Churches of Christ might be willing to accept internal fragmentation as the price for unity; the Church of England was not. Even at Nottingham, John Moorman, the high church Bishop of Ripon, was alienated and the Anglo-Catholic wing of the Church of England was never willing to accept a union that might complicate unity with the Roman Catholic Church. On the other hand, any serious move towards Rome would be unacceptable to the evangelicals. Thus the Church of England became, as Huxtable saw it, "The bridge church over which no traffic ever flows."[32] David Thompson says that he early came to see that, for the foreseeable future, this meant the end of any hopes of organic unity.

> I felt instinctively at the Uniting Assembly at Birmingham in 1981 that it would be the last organic union I would see in my lifetime. That was because I had been deeply involved at the center of the Covenant discussions and had come to the conclusion that the Church of England would be unable to move ecumenically in relation to the Free Churches because of the question of the ordination of women, and that it was reluctant to do that because it was going to mean either a split or a loss of members.[33]

In one detail this is wrong—the Anglicans did finally decide to risk the dissension caused by the ordination of women. It is fundamentally accurate in that the Anglican state of ecumenical stasis does reflect the problems of a complex multi-theological church.

THE CHANGING NATURE OF THE CHURCHES

Our period saw major changes in the theology, diversity, and relative strength of the British churches. The churches became more conservative theologically and the center of gravity in church life shifted away from the traditional denominations to a growing range of Black-majority and

---

31. Thompson, *Let Sects and Parties Fall*, 190.
32. Huxtable, *As It Seemed to Me*, 71.
33. Thompson, interview.

Charismatic or evangelical churches. Taken together, this made organic unity significantly less likely or even possible.

The relationship of ecumenism to liberal theology is, as we have seen, complex. The Orthodox churches that joined the World Council of Churches were not liberal, nor were all the churches who welcomed ecumenism in Britain. The Churches of Christ, in particular, was mostly a conservative church and, according to David Thompson, felt some misgivings about the liberalism of Congregationalists:

> I think it would have been very difficult for us to join anything without the comfort of knowing that there were Presbyterians there as well. . . . I could never see what Congregationalists stood for.[34]

There were evangelicals working within some of the LEPs. West Swindon was an evangelical enclave. The Pentecostal churches that have now joined the ecumenical instruments cannot easily be seen as liberal. Nor were all liberals necessarily committed to ecumenism. Nonetheless, the degree of liberalism in a denomination is usually an indication of the likelihood of an ecumenical commitment, and vice versa. The churches that have withdrawn from or not joined the ecumenical movement, such as the Southern Baptists and the Missouri Synod of the Lutheran Church in the United States, are normally evangelical. Though it is now diminishing, there is an anti-ecumenical element in evangelicalism in Britain, reflected for example in those who will not join councils of churches if the Roman Catholic Church is in membership. Christians of all theological persuasions, including liberals, can be intellectually intolerant, but the central dynamic of liberalism as exemplified by Schleiermacher is to adapt belief in the light of changed circumstances and new ideas. This is inherently conducive to ecumenical openness. As David Hollinger argues, the normal liberal response to the theological other is "to treat inherited doctrines as sufficiently flexible to enable one to abide with them while coexisting "pluralistically," or even co-operating, with people who do not accept these doctrines."[35] By contrast, the more conservative the theology the greater the likelihood of exclusive truth claims. Evangelicalism's commitment to ecumenism is also moderated by its tendency to sit light to structures and

34. Ibid.

35. Hollinger, *After Cloven Tongues of Fire*, 6.

its frequent preference to promote alliances with those who share its belief system.

Because of the inherent organizational conservatism of organizations, and because any move towards organic unity is by nature divisive and carries significant dangers for the unity of the organization, organic unity requires a significant motivation. The liberal mood of the 1960s, with its atmosphere of hope and rather naïve optimism that the church could be renewed, provided exactly that stimulus. It was a time when it seemed there was nothing that could not be done—probably by next week, and if not at least by 1980.

The heady moment passed remarkably quickly. As the failure of the attempt to achieve organic unity indicated, the institutional church was deeply resistant to real change. What is more, it soon became apparent that however many people were reading *Honest to God*, it was not prompting any revival of church attendance nor indeed halting the decline. As John Kent rather cynically observes, "If radicalism had proved effective in rescuing institutions in decline it would have continued to receive ecclesiastical support, but when the decline continued, writers like Edward Norman soon discovered that radicalism was one of the major causes of the problems of the churches."[36] Within the Roman Catholic Church the limits of radicalism became clear. In 1968 the encyclical *Humanae Vitae* condemned artificial methods of birth control. Liberal Catholic theologians such as Hans Kung, Edward Schillebeeckx, Charles Curran, and Archbishop Hunthausen were disciplined. The 1960s, therefore, which had begun as an optimistic decade, grew darker as the Vietnam War poisoned political life and radicalism began to become socially less fashionable. Sandbrook titles the last chapter of *White Heat*, his history of Britain the 60s, "The Carnival Is Over."

The signs of the loss of liberal self-confidence were everywhere. John Robinson was not offered a diocesan bishopric by the Church of England and in 1969 returned to Cambridge as dean of chapel at Trinity College. By 1965 Nick Stacey was recommending that "most of the clergy now engaged in parochial work should leave their parishes and take secular jobs,"[37] advice he soon took himself. In his autobiography he admitted, "I plead guilty to underestimating massively the depth and significance of social pressures which keep the English working class away from the worshipping

36. Kent, "Shadow of a Grove," 135.
37. *Church Times*, 28 May 1965.

community of the Church."[38] *Parish and People* published its last edition in 1968, and in 1970 merged with a number of other small reform groups to form "One for Christian Renewal." "It was wholly ecumenical. It was also almost wholly insignificant."[39] *New Christian* folded in 1970. The SCM was taken over by radical Marxists and collapsed.

The sense, which was clearly felt in the discussions leading to the creation of the United Reformed Church, that people were no longer as interested in ecumenism as they had been, that as Arthur Macarthur worried, we were too late, is an indication that the liberal moment was already passing and with it the hope and theological momentum required for drastic organizational change. As Keith Robbins observes, "In 1972 prospects looked remote. A certain weariness, or perhaps disillusion began to set in."[40] The denominations could begin to settle back into their own concerns and the radicalism of the British Council of Churches could be curtailed. As Michael Kinnamon, who was General Secretary of the American Consultation on Church Union, says, "To put it bluntly, ecumenism has been, to a large extent, brought under control by the churches it was intended to reform."[41] Though he was speaking about this experience in the United States the point has wider validity. "For my generation," lamented Visser't Hooft in 1974, "the ecumenical movement had all the attraction of something unexpected and extraordinary. For the present generation it is simply part of the church's design."[42] The creation of the United Reformed Church was a cause that long predated the liberal optimism of the 1960s and was still possible. Little else was. As Andrew Chandler puts it:

> The confident liberal, ecumenical visions of the earlier century were by the close of the age looking hesitant and even bewildered. So many of the great new themes brought the Churches not opportunities, but reasons for doubt.[43]

A second major factor that substantially changed the prospects for organic unity was the changing balance of the British churches, in which the traditional ecumenically committed denominations lost some of their

38. Stacey, *Who Cares?*, 77.

39. Hastings, *History of English Christianity*, 549.

40. Robbins, *England, Ireland, Scotland, Wales*, 367.

41. Kinnamon, *Vision of the Ecumenical Movement*, 84.

42. Visser't Hooft, *Has the Ecumenical Movement a Future?*, 40–41.

43. Chandler, *Church of England*, 481.

dominance as church diversity increased with the emergence of new Black-majority or Charismatic churches. Demographically, Britain changed radically in the period under discussion. Between 1951 and 2000 the number of members of ethnic minorities resident in Britain rose from just under 100,000 to 4,039,000, by which time they made up 7.1 percent of Britain's population.[44] By the 2011 census 13 percent (7.5 million) of residents in England and Wales were not born in the UK, with just over half (3.8 million) having arrived between 2001 and 2011, the largest numbers coming from India, Poland, and Pakistan.[45] The effects were seen most dramatically in the major cities. Only 44.9 percent of London's residents are now White British, with 37 percent of the population born outside the UK. This significantly increased the multifaith context of British society, with the number of Muslims, for example, rising from 1.5 million or 2 percent in 2001 to 2.7 million or 4.8 percent in the 2011 census. There was also major Christian immigration from countries such as Ghana or Nigeria, which had neither the same experience of secularization nor of the ecumenical movement as had the long-established British churches. This was to be a major factor in the changing ecumenical landscape, with a rapid growth of new churches outside the old ecumenical consensus.

The 1985 English census showed that in the previous seven years church attendance had been in steady decline, but in that period over a thousand new churches had been opened, many of them linked to denominations or individuals from Africa.[46] So, for example, the Redeemed Christian Church of God began in Britain in 1988. In April 2004 there were 161 churches with a membership of 45,377. By 2010 there were 440 churches with approximately 85,000 members.[47] In Birmingham, to give another example, a survey by Birmingham Churches Together showed that that their churches represented only 60 percent of the places of worship in Birmingham and Solihull; the other 40 percent included Black-majority Pentecostal churches, new Charismatic churches such as Vineyard and New Frontiers, and 50 other churches with origins across the world.[48] The complexity and pace of change has been dramatic. A study by Colin March-

44. Rosen, *Transformation of British Life*, 89–90.

45. *The Guardian*, 11 December 2012.

46. British Religion in Numbers, "Findings from the English Church Census 2005," online: http://www.brin.ac.uk/figures/findingsfromtheenglishchurchcensus2005/.

47. Goodhew, *Church Growth in Britain*, 129–30.

48. Ibid., 193

ant of Churches in the London Borough of Newham found in 1999 that 72 of the 180 Christian congregations were Pentecostal and of these 39 had been unknown in 1995. On the other hand 18 of the churches existing in 1995 had disappeared five years later. Calvary Charismatic Baptist Church in Newham had grown from 40 to 700 members in the same period.[49]

These churches no doubt differ in theology and organization but most could be described as theologically conservative, often, for example, with strong gender differentiation in their leadership. The very mention of the possibility of interfaith relationships could lead to some churches breaking fellowship with others. In his study of churches on the Barking Road, Greg Smith concludes, "Most of the black majority Pentecostal Churches are fiercely independent if not sectarian, and not even well networked with similar groups, let alone with mainline Christianity."[50] Some have joined councils of churches and are open to ecumenical contact. Sometimes they work practically together in mission or social service. But organic unity is not of interest. As John Vincent comments, "This growing and chaotic pluralism is the opposite of the orderly 'growing into unity'" that the ecumenical pioneers anticipated.[51]

Among the host culture too, the emerging Charismatic churches were equally less inclined to be part of the old consensus. In a study of new churches in York, David Goodhew notes that their ecumenical involvement is on their own terms, and they have created their own ecumenical structure, One Voice York, which grew out of a prayer meeting and which, despite its title, does not speak for all the York churches. It does include those from traditional denominations among its membership but it has a clear Charismatic/evangelical emphasis. Goodhew writes, "One leader commented to the author in private that its stress on intercession was a means of sorting out what he saw as the theological 'sheep' from the 'goats,' since he believed, liberal Christians would have little use for such a practice."[52] The stress is on ecclesiastical entrepreneurism rather than structural ecumenism. In this very changed situation the kind of unity possible is fundamentally different from that of the world of the Nottingham Conference.

A third factor that tended to lessen interest in ecumenism was the increasing multifaith diversity of British society and the resultant search for

49. Vincent, *Faithfulness in the City*, 211.

50. Ibid., 108–9.

51. Ibid., 226.

52. Goodhew, *Church Growth in Britain*, 188.

interfaith dialogue. Hans Kung gave the classic expression of this when he said, "There can be no peace among the nations without peace among the religions. There can be no peace among the religions without dialogue between the religions"[53] These words took on a new and added urgency after the terrorist attack on the New York World Trade Center on September 11, 2001. One might argue that logically this did not in any way detract from the importance of Christians rediscovering the unity they had in Christ. Indeed one might well argue that interfaith dialogue is something done best ecumenically, in that Christian/Muslim dialogue, for example, makes more sense than Methodist/Muslim dialogue. But in practice a great deal of effort that might earlier have gone into ecumenism now went into interfaith dialogue. On October 27, 1986 Pope John Paul II led a multidenominational and interfaith gathering at Assisi and the phrase "interfaith—the new ecumenism" began to be heard. It was increasingly argued that *oikoumene*, understood as the whole inhabited earth, extends beyond the Christian church to the wider dialogues. The methodology of ecumenism—building relationships, trust, dialogue, shared experience, even shared witness—can be applied in the new context. As Keith Clements argues, "It has become almost axiomatic that intra-Christian ecumenism is now far surpassed in importance by interfaith-relations and inter-religious dialogue.[54] He himself argues that the two should be seen as complimentary not interchangeable. This point may intellectually be conceded, but a visit by a Methodist to the mosque is much more challenging than a visit to the Anglican parish church. In the interfaith context the unity of Presbyterians and Congregationalists finds itself profoundly marginalized in importance.

THE VALUE OF DIVERSITY

The belief in organic unity came in a particular time and context. In the 60s there was much talk about mergers, takeovers, the uniting of the small into the larger. The drive towards European union got under way. Bringing together the British car industry was going to revolutionize it. Uniting churches reflected the same mood. In the 70s, however, contemporary culture began to emphasize the local rather than the national, and a nondenominational religious culture began to develop in which the uniting of institutional structures no longer had the same priority. As Peter Steinfels

53. Kung, *Global Responsibility*, xv.
54. Clements, *Ecumenical Dynamic*, 17.

points out, "What once was the scandal of division now looks more like the virtue of diversity."[55] As one example of this changed perspective, Michael Kinnamon points out that while the United Church of Christ might still have John 17 ("that all may be one") on its logo, its website highlights its multicultural identity while "burying its historic concern for Christian unity in the last paragraph of both its Statement of Mission and Statement of Commitment for the twenty-first century."[56] As Michael Davies says:

> I think we have now concluded that if God had meant us all to be the same, he would have made us that way. I think there is a great deal that is complementary among the denominations. I think there has to be some coming together for purely practical reasons but that is a different matter. . . . I think this may be the Lord's will.[57]

A number of other factors pointed in this direction. One was biblical—a greater realization of the diversity of Scripture and the implications this had for the unity of the church. A WCC study in 1949 (at a time when the biblical theology movement was in its brief vogue) had stressed the unity of Scripture and argued, with amazing naivety, that a common reading of Scripture could help bring the church to one mind on formerly divisive issues. By the fourth World Congress on Faith and Order at Montreal in 1963, however, Ernst Käsemann was arguing:

> The tensions between Jewish Christian and Gentile Christian Churches, between Paul and the Corinthian enthusiasts, between John and early Catholicism, are as great as those of our own day. . . . To recognize this is a great comfort, and as far as ecumenical work today is concerned, a theological gain.[58]

Freed from the illusion that there was a single New Testament model for the church, people were liberated to explore a diversity that reflected the diversity of Scripture. Oscar Cullmann went so far as to argue that "the richness of the full measure of the Holy Spirit rests in plurality. Whoever does not reflect this richness, and wants uniformity, sins against the Holy Spirit."[59] In Britain this was developed especially by the work of James

---

55. Steinfels, "Praying for Christian Unity."
56. Kinnamon, *Can a Renewal Movement Be Renewed?*, 149.
57. Davies, interview.
58. Kinnamon and Cope, *Ecumenical Movement*, 97.
59. Cullman, *Unity Through Diversity*, 17.

Dunn in his *Unity and Diversity in the New Testament*. All of this may be compatible with organic unity. It does, however, invalidate any attempt to ground a simplistic theological case for denominational unity based on texts like John 17:11, "May they be one as we are one." To apply texts that were addressed to local churches experiencing factionalism to the relationships of differing denominations, as if the two issues are the same, is to misuse Scripture.

It could be that the multiplicity of belief and organization that the canon legitimizes is best preserved in a variety of churches with their own theologies and organizations. Indeed you could argue that the biblical text, insofar as it witnesses to diversity and unity within the Trinity, itself offers a model of something other than undifferentiated unity. This was reflected in the conclusions of the Nairobi Assembly of the WCC in 1975, which argued, "It is because the unity of the church is grounded in the divine trinity that we can speak of diversity in the church as something to be not only admitted but actively desired."[60] At least from this perspective the theological debate is much more open. As the Canberra Assembly of the WCC concluded in 1991, "diversities which are rooted in theological traditions, various cultural, ethnic or historical contexts are integral to the nature of communion."[61]

The fact that the expected missionary advantages of ecumenism did not materialize, and that the fastest church growth was found in those churches that were least interested in structural ecumenism, also took away a significant part of the case for organic union. Instead it now appears that a diversification of distinct religious options may be more effective as a missionary strategy than the appeal of a united church.

The experience of the United Reformed Church did little to offset this. As so often happens when two organizational structures merge, the end result in the United Reformed Church was more office jobs, a more expensive bureaucracy than either of the two uniting churches, and a financial system that arguably proved to be a disincentive from innovative fundraising. The United Reformed Church declined faster than either of its predecessor churches, though at a roughly comparable rate to similar mainstream churches. None of this can be taken as proof that the two churches would have done better separately, though it is difficult to believe they could have done significantly worse.

60. Kinnamon, *Vision of the Ecumenical Movement*, 57.
61. Ibid., 124

Diversity cannot be a value in itself but requires the commonality shared in Christ to be expressed in diversity in unity. A situation in which churches simply competed with each other or lived in isolation from each other would be an impoverishment of the Christian life and denial of the work of Christ in bringing all together as one. But as a way of maintaining unity in diversity organic union now looks fraught with difficulty. Just as single congregation LEPs often end up theologically monochromatic, so church unions can lead to a loss of diversity. This is one reason why very many members of the URC were unreceptive to a union with the Methodists, which they feared would extinguish their tradition without advancing the kingdom.

ECUMENISM IN THE POST-DENOMINATIONAL RELIGIOUS MARKET

The social and cultural conditions of late modernity are complex and ambiguous in their implications for religious institutions. On the one hand, in a globalized world the range of religious options increases. At the same time, the greater reflexivity and individualism of modern society's life means that a commitment to these institutions will more likely be personally chosen than simply received. This need not lead us to adopt rational choice theory but it does not exclude the possibility that in our contemporary culture, where increasing numbers of people lack a firm identification with an established religious tradition, religious choices may be influenced by the consumer choice criteria characteristic of a free-market capitalist economy.

More difficult to calculate, but certainly too significant to overlook, was the effect of social and economic change on religious life in general and ecumenism in particular. The extent to which religion is determined by the social and economic base of society is disputed, with Marx and Weber offering significantly different perspectives. Marx stressed the primacy of the economic infrastructure in determining the society's ideology while Weber argued for a more reciprocal two-way relationship. Irrespective of the relative value of these two perspectives it cannot be doubted that there is an influence on religious life from a society's economic culture.

In the latter part of the twentieth century, the world moved from a period of "Fordist" industrial capitalism, in which production was centered on large scale factory production, to one in which there was more globalized production, markets became increasingly segmented, and mass consumerism became a dominant economic driving force. "Mass consumption gave way to consumerism after the 1950s and has resulted in a profoundly morphed household, social and cultural reality, one in which the abundance of objects and the continuous appeal to desire is central."[62] Eric Hobsbawm argues that the marks of such a society are "an otherwise unconnected assemblage of self-centred individuals pursuing only their own gratification."[63] In such a society increasingly the basic unit is the individual as hedonistic consumer.

Once consumer satisfaction becomes dominant in a society it is likely to affect religious practice. In a study of one mainstream liberal congregation in the US, Fourth Presbyterian in Chicago, James Wellman comments:

> The religious market is wide open; there are no longer any natural monopolies. To thrive, or even survive, religious institutions must market themselves to the consumer because Americans have little or no denominational loyalty. Fourth Presbyterian knows that it is in a competitive market.[64]

In Britain Linda Woodhead argues that a commonality among growing churches is that they are "entrepreneurial, democratized, and individualised or autotomized. That is to say they take for granted the importance of the individual—and place higher value on consumer choices than on central planning by experts, elites or even representative bodies."[65] There is a need for caution here. People have always been willing to move from one congregation to another because there was a better choir or better opportunities for meeting the opposite sex. There are still churches where a sense of denomination is strong and many Roman Catholics would not consider becoming Protestant, and vice versa. But it is increasingly common to have congregations drawn from a wide variety of denominational backgrounds, with new members joining the church of their choice only after sampling a variety of other options. In such cases the particular denomination will matter less than the specific advantages of the local congregation and indeed there may be little awareness of the denominational choice that is being made.

62. Gauthier et al., "Religion in Market Society," 15–16.

63. Hobsbawm, *Age of Extremes*, 16.

64. Wellman, *Gold Coast Church*, 211.

65. Woodhead and Cato, *Religion and Change*, 19.

Christian people are not bothered by these things. They do have their preferences as to whether to have bells and smells but they don't have preferences about hierarchies and bishops and councils and things. The trouble is those who run the churches do.[66]

In such circumstances institutional unity seems increasingly unimportant, as indeed does the denomination itself.

This may be a factor in the current expansion of Neo-Pentecostal churches. Pentecostalism in its myriad manifestations is, as David Martin argues, a religion that "belongs by nature to open markets."[67] Indeed when expressed through forms of prosperity theology it offers believers the same durable goods and benefits as the capitalist economy, only linking the possession of such benefits to a religious commitment.

Robert Wuthnow draws the conclusion: "With potential congregants characterized by fewer denominational loyalties and greater tendencies to engage in denominational switching, the autonomous congregation that focuses on its own programs and local priorities is thus in the best position to succeed."[68] It is not without irony that this model has similarities with the old-style Congregationalism from which the United Reformed Church was so keen to distance itself.

This recent cultural mood does not entail the rejection of everything for which ecumenism has stood. Churches may work together on shared concerns and often people will have particular theological loyalties and concerns that transcend the church to which they happen to belong. Organic unity, however, is no longer on the cultural agenda, except possibly where declining denominations come to the conclusion that they have little viable future.

CONCLUDING THOUGHTS

Predicting the future with any degree of accuracy is always an extraordinarily difficult thing to do. "Our brains, wired to detect patterns, are always looking for a signal," writes Nate Silver, "when instead we should appreciate how noisy the data is."[69] The belief that the ecumenical movement represented the future and the hope of the church, and indeed was what God was

66. Davies, interview.
67. Martin, *Pentecostalism*, 171.
68. Wuthnow, *Boundless Faith*, 15.
69. *New Republic*, 21 December 2012.

doing to renew the church, seemed to be being realized in the search for organic unity. It was this hope that was the primary motivation in the creation of the URC. Today this hope appears increasingly archaic, and insofar as it still exists is held primarily by an aging cohort.

The United Reformed Church itself can only be regarded as part of that disappointment. The fact that to most observers the high point of the church's life was its inaugural service, before the reality of the hopeless task it had set itself became clear, is a poignant reflection of the illusions that motivated it. When, despite its hopes, the new church found itself a continuing part of the English church scene, a crisis of relevance and identity was inevitable. The church's ecumenical aspirations may even have made this more difficult to solve, just as its commitment to develop new churches ecumenically may have damaged its prospects of growth. In any case nothing stopped membership plummeting to undreamed-of depths.

Against this something more positive can be said. As Christopher Driver recognized, the rationale for the Free Churches was already in question before the creation of the United Reformed Church.[70] If the United Reformed Church never found an answer to the dilemma, it is by no means clear that its predecessor churches would have done any better. And anyone cynical enough to doubt that belief can motivate action, and even override the self-interests of organizations, might do well to look at the history of the United Reformed Church. It came into being primarily because its creators believed they were acting out God's will. That inspiration was visibly present in the life of the United Reformed Church, in the way it alone chose only to develop new churches ecumenically, in its work for unity through the Churches' Unity Commission and in its members who served both in the British ecumenical instruments and in the World Council of Churches. No other denomination had the same commitment to Local Ecumenical Projects. Wherever there were local councils of churches it was very often the United Reformed Church minister who chaired them. The United Reformed Church may have read the future inaccurately, and it grossly overestimated its own importance, but it cannot be accused of not acting on its convictions. Sadly there was some truth in the ever-sage reflection of Arthur Macarthur that the URC found itself "on a hiding to nothing, with its flag still high on the mast proclaiming its own wish for further unity and the absence of answering signals from the rest of the fleet."[71]

70. Driver, *Future for the Free Churches?*
71. Macarthur, *Setting Up Signs*, 95

Organic unity proved unachievable, and even some of those who once believed in it were finally glad it had not happened. It is important, however, to recognize that what failed was a particular model of ecumenism, not ecumenism as such, and there are many ecumenically positive aspects of contemporary religious culture. A significant part of the ecumenical case is now widely accepted. Catholic/Protestant relations have been transformed. As Paul Avis puts it,

> The ecumenical movement has not simply replaced suspicion, incomprehension and rivalry with understanding, trust and friendship—though in itself that is no mean achievement. In the form of theological dialogue, ecumenism has also significantly scaled down the extent of church-dividing issues between Christian traditions . . . and has established that there is "a certain albeit imperfect, communion" between churches that are not yet in full communion.[72]

Evangelical responses to the ecumenical movement are, in general, also more positive than they were. The willingness of someone like Billy Graham (always a bellwether of trends in evangelical theology) to move toward a style of evangelicalism in which ecumenical Protestants, Catholics, Jews, and secularists were offered respect rather than summary damnation was a sign of a changing mood. The Second Vatican Council helped to break down hostility and suspicion towards Roman Catholics. Today there are deep divergences in evangelical theology, but at least among sections of evangelical opinion some traditionally liberal theological concerns, such as ecumenism, are not viewed in as hostile a way as they were. There is some truth in the argument of David Hollinger and others that liberals are experiencing cultural victory at the same time as organizational defeat.[73] On social justice concerns such as poverty and inequality evangelicals have moved closer to positions liberals have held for generations. Today, especially among the young, what were formally controversial liberal theological ideas are now widely diffused in the religious culture. Smith and Snell even argue that "Harry Emerson Fosdick would be proud" to hear young White evangelicals "paraphrasing passages from the classical liberal Protestant theologians, of whom they have no doubt actually never heard."[74] More than a little caution is necessary here. It may be doubted if Harry Emerson

72. Avis, "Unreal Worlds Meeting."
73. Hollinger, *After Cloven Tongues of Fire.*
74. Smith and Snell, *Souls in Transition*, 288.

Fosdick would find the rise of creationism congenial and there are those who still hold the old antipathy to ecumenism or to liberals or Catholics. But a willingness to work with those of a different denominational background is now more common among evangelicals.

Nor is the wider culture destructive of all forms of ecumenism. The diversity and pluralism of late modernity may have undermined organic unity but they have also made distinctions between denominations less significant—the conviction that one can believe in the truth of one's own faith without denying the authenticity of the perspectives and beliefs of others is now widely diffused in our culture. Individualism and detachment from institutional commitment means that ecumenism is inevitably now mainly relational, but it is real. In the search for trade justice or environmental sustainability Christians of differing backgrounds happily find common cause. At the local level people move from one church to another while frequently oblivious to the distinctions that seem so significant to the institutions. Whatever the hesitations one may have about the individualism of post-denominational culture, it is open and indeed fostering of the sharing and learning and working together that is at the heart of ecumenism. Its embracing of diversity offers the opportunity for an understanding of unity that does not threaten the God-given diversity of the church.

The culture of late modernity is not unproblematic for Christian faith. A private search for meaning divorced from community worship, formation, and mission is characteristic of much contemporary culture. As singer Rosanne Cash put it recently, "I don't need to play team games in religion." This may lead to, as in her case, an interest in compassion or non-violence. It may equally lead to an interest in Buddhism, healing crystals, Mayan re-birthing rituals, or a self-selected mix of contrasting spiritualties. Absolved of the need to relate to others and without deep roots in any tradition, people can easily become inward looking and self-indulgent. By contrast, the New Testament is about the gathering of a community bound to one another by love and forgiveness, a common life together, and a shared mission to the world. The Roman Catholic Church has long maintained that there is no salvation outside the church (*Extra Ecclesiam nulls salus*) and John Calvin would have agreed. In some interpretations this can be frighteningly exclusivist but at least it recognizes that being a Christian is about discipleship in community. As John Buchanan puts it,

> No religion is about God and me. It's about God and me and you,
> all of us and our neighbours, particularly the ones who need us.

> Of course, my faith is personal and private, but it's also public and corporate. And the church, the church of Jesus Christ, has every-thing in the world to do with it.[75]

Once the communal context of Christian discipleship is accepted, it follows logically that no Christian community true to its core commitment to Jesus Christ can live its life in isolation from other such communities—that is integral to the catholicity of faith. How these communities relate to one another and work together in shared mission is vital to their own integrity and the effectiveness of what they do. As George Redford wrote in the statement of faith produced on the formation of the Congregational Union of England and Wales in 1833, "They believe it is the duty of Christian churches to hold communion with each other, to entertain an enlarged affection for each other, as members of the same body, and to co-operate for the promotion of the Christian cause."[76] The search for organic unity centered ecumenism too much on church organizations and structures, which like all organizations have only a tangential relationship to the purposes they profess. The real heart of ecumenism is in the relationships between people. But the community context in which faith is lived cannot be ignored. The shallow and self-indulgent individualism, which is a characteristic danger of the religious culture of late modernity, poses a danger to the quality of ecumenical experience but it does not invalidate it.

It is a long time since bread-and-cheese lunches at Anglican and Catholic chaplaincies at Hull University introduced me to wider vistas than the placid East Anglian Congregationalism in which I grew up. It is long time too since reading John Robinson filled me with hope that the Christian faith might be renewed. "Bliss was in that dawn to be alive, but to be young *and ecumenical* was very heaven." The optimism of those days is now difficult to recapture. Did the World Conference on Church and Society meeting at Geneva in 1966 actually say, "We know that God appears to have set no limits to what may be achieved by our generation"?[77] But then it was the decade the Beatles sang, "It's getting better, it's getting better all the time." Naivety and hubris were specialties of the time.

I have tried to face honestly in this book how such optimism met reality. I have also tried to be honest about the catastrophic implosion of my own church. It has not been easy to write. But all through this time

75. Buchanan, *New Church*, 17.

76. Walker, *Creeds and Platforms*, 552.

77. Kinnamon, *Can a Renewal Movement Be Renewed?*, 158.

ecumenism has remained for me both enriching and challenging. It has, I believe, led me to a far richer faith than I could have had in the East Anglian Congregationalism in which I grew up.

At university my small world of Congregationalism was opened out. To sit in a discussion group with Eamon Duffy (later to be one of our most important Catholic historians), get to know Anglicans, and then worship on Sunday with the Baptists was akin to the experience of changing from black and white to color television. Later at Oxford I mostly stayed away from churches of my own denomination and worshiped with Methodists, Baptists, or at college chapels where I could enjoy the wonders of Anglican choral evensong. My childhood Congregationalism had no conception of the Christian liturgical year, often treated Communion as a kind of insignificant afterthought to the main service, and was largely devoid of serious theologians. Just like the SCM had done for so many, my university ecumenical experience sent me out a quite different kind of Christian. I should have known better, however, than to ask a Quaker if he would give me a reference for entering the ministry, leaving him to explain that he didn't believe in any such thing! And how naïve of me to suggest that the local Catholic priest might lay hands on me at my ordination!

Ordained as a URC minister and having served in three ecumenical projects, I have found it natural to share ministry and worship with Anglicans, Methodists, Baptists, and (in Merseyside) Roman Catholics. In every place I was effectively sharing ministry in a team of ecumenical clergy, some of whom became good friends and to whom I very often felt closer than I did to ministers of my own denomination. Even a Methodist staff meeting was not always without any point. The idea that by being open to other traditions we diminish our own is incomprehensible to me and wholly alien to my understanding of the Reformed tradition or the Christian faith itself. On the contrary, such openness has been a huge enrichment and the willingness to respond to the new takes me to the very heart of the Reformed tradition as I understand it.

Before the Pilgrim Fathers sailed to America their pastor, John Robinson, warned them:

> For my part I cannot sufficiently bewail the condition of the Reformed Churches, who are come to a period in religion and will go at present no further than the instrument of their Reformation. The Lutheran can't be drawn to go beyond what Luther saw. . . . And the Calvinists stick fast where they were left by that great man

of God, who yet saw not all things. . . . I beseech you remember tis an article of your church covenant, that you be ready to receive whatever truth shall be made known to you from the written word of God.[78]

I would add to that: be willing to receive anything out of the worshipping life and experience of other believers that can enrich our own. Or as Calvin put it, "We are at liberty to borrow from any source anything that has come from God."[79] Reformed faith holds more loosely to denominational identity in order to hold more firmly to God and in order to better serve the world God made.

Finally, ecumenism is about the gospel. One of the functions of religion has always been to define the boundaries of the tribe—who is in and who is out, who is friend and who is enemy. The history of religion is a history of horrendous violence, intolerance of others, heresy trials and burnings, religious wars in which millions have died, torture and persecution. But in Jesus of Nazareth there is another kind of religion, a religion that transcends the boundaries and reaches out—that regards the other, whoever he or she is, as a beloved child of God—Black or White, male or female, rich or poor, Muslim or Jew, gay or straight, liberal or conservative. This is the religion of inclusion.

> Here the outcast and the stranger
> bear the image of God's face.[80]

William Sloane Coffin sees the essence of this when he says, "If faith can be exclusive, love can only be inclusive."[81] And Paul declares that the hidden purpose of God, finally and amazingly laid bare to us, is to unite all things in heaven and earth in Jesus Christ (Ephesians 1:10) This is an ecumenical agenda that goes far wider than Christian unity but can never be pursued with integrity without it, remembering that Jesus died "to gather into one the dispersed children of God" (John 11:52).

Organic unity may have been a hope that failed but we have not gone back to a pre-ecumenical world. In 1922 Harry Emerson Fosdick lamented the "shame that the Christian Church should be quarrelling over little

78. Winslow, Hypocrisie Unmasked, 97.

79. Commentary on 1 Cor 15:33, citing Paul's example; commentary on Titus 1:12, citing Basil.

80. "Let Us Build a House," words by Marty Haugen.

81. Coffin, Heart Is a Little to the Left, 7.

matters when the world is dying of great needs."[82] The shared dynamic of Christian discipleship may yet lead to new ecumenical expressions that can meet that challenge. If so the United Reformed Church may yet play some small part in achieving this.

82. Quoted in Sherry, *Riverside Preachers*, 37.

Bibliography

INTERVIEWS

Argent, Rev. Alan. President of the Congregational Federation, 2007–8. September 2012.

Beck, Rev. Dr. Brian. Former Secretary of the Methodist Conference. May 2010.

Binfield, Dr. Clyde. Church historian. June 2010.

Bocking, Rev. Ronald. URC minister. August 2010.

Bradley, John. Field Officer for Southern England of Churches Together in England. August 2011.

Stephen, Dr. Brain. Secretary of Immanuel URC Swindon. August 2011.

Burnham, Rev. Tony. General Secretary of the URC, 1992–2001. June 2011.

Cook, Rev. Graham. Moderator for Mersey Synod, 1994–2004. July 2009.

Craven, Rev. Christine. Secretary of Ministries of the URC, 1996–2008. June 2011.

Cressey, Rev. Martin. Principal of Westminster College, 1979–96. May 2009.

Dales, Rev. Michael. Baptist minister in Sutton. November 2011.

Davies, Rev. Michael. Moderator for Thames North, 1978–90; and Assistant General Secretary for the World Council of Churches, 1990–97. October 2012.

Dunford, Rev. Michael. Secretary of the Church Life Department of the URC, 1980–84; Secretary of Ministries of the URC, 1984–92. June 2011.

Fyffe, Bob. General Secretary of Churches Together in Britain and Ireland. June 2012.

Gibson, Rev. George. URC minister. August 2011.

Gooch, Dr. David. Senior Methodist Deacon of Trinity Sutton; Secretary of the Ecumenical Council of Churches Uniting in Central Sutton. July 2011.

Greet, Rev. Dr. Kenneth. Former Secretary of the Methodist Conference. August 2010.

Hilton, Rev. Donald. Moderator of the General Assembly of the URC, 1993–94. March 2009.

Hopkins, Rev. Michael. URC minister. March 2013.

Jones, Dr. Diana. Secretary to John Huxtable. February 2011.

Lawrence, Rev. David. Editor of *Reform*, 1995–2006. June 2009.

Marvin, Rev. Ernest. URC minister. August 2010.

Maxey, Rev. Sheila. Secretary of Ecumenical Affairs of the URC 1993–2003; Moderator of the General Assembly of the URC, 2004–5. October 2009.

Orchard, Rev. Dr. Stephen. Principal of Westminster College at Cambridge, 2001–7; Moderator of the General Assembly of the URC, 2007–8. November 2009.

Paterson, Rev. Alan. President of Scottish Congregational Church, 1998–99. 2012.

Paul, Rev. Dr. Roger. National Ecumenical Officer for England of the Church of England. June 2012.

Peel, Rev. Dr. David. Principal of Northern College, 1993–2003; Moderator of the General Assembly of the URC, 2005–6. September 2010.

Pooler, Norman. Legal advisor for the Presbyterian Church of England. May 2001.

Reardon, Rev. John. Moderator of the General Assembly of the URC, 1995–96; General Secretary of the Council of Churches for Britain and Ireland, 1990–99. January 2011.

Richardson, Rev. John. Ecumenical Officer for South London of Churches Together in England. January 2012.

Sell, Rev. Dr. Alan. Former Professor of Christian Doctrine and Philosophy of Religion at the United Theological College, Aberystwyth (Wales). October 2010.

Steele, Rev. Ernesto Lozada-Uzuriaga. Anglican minister in Milton Keynes. August 2011.

Sutcliffe, Rev. Dr. John. Assistant Secretary of the Congregational Church in England and Wales, 1971–72; Secretary for Christian Education of the URC, 1972–74. August 2010.

Thompson, Rev. Dr. Colin. URC minister. July 2009.

Thompson, Rev. Dr. David. President of the Annual Conference of the Churches of Christ, 1979–80; Moderator of the General Assembly of the URC, 1996–97. August 2009.

Tucker, Rev. Tony. Associate Director of Education and Training at Mansfield College, Oxford, 1989–96. March 2011.

Williams, Margaret. Lay minister at Old Town Parish Swindon. August 2011.

PRIMARY SOURCES

British Council of Churches, Executive Committee Minutes. Church of England Record Centre, Bermondsey, London.

Church of England/Presbyterian Church of England Committee Minutes. Reformed Studies Library, Westminster College, Cambridge.

Coggan, Donald. Papers. Archbishops' Papers, Archbishops' Archives, Lambeth Palace Library, London.

Congregational Year Book. Archives of Congregational Church in England and Wales, Westminster College, Cambridge.

Daily Telegraph.

Directory of the Re-formed Association of Churches of Christ. Birmingham: RACC, 1980.

Evangelical Federation of Congregational Churches. Yearbook 1996–1997. Congregational Library, Dr Williams's Library, London.

Macarthur, Arthur. Papers. Reformed Studies Library, Westminster College, Cambridge.

Methodist Church. Minutes of the Annual Conference and Directory. London: Methodist Publishing.

Official Catholic Directory. 2012 ed. New Providence, NJ: P.J. Kenedy & Sons/National Register, 2012.

Oral History. Journal of the Oral History Society.

Presbyterian Outlook. Presbyterian Church of England Archive, Westminster College, Cambridge.

Ramsey, Michael. Papers. Archbishops' Papers, Archbishops' Archives, Lambeth Palace Library, London.

Reform. Congregational Library, Dr Williams's Library, London.

Reformed Quarterly. United Reformed Church Archive. Congregational Library, Dr Williams's Library, London.

United Reformed Church. *Assembly Record*. Congregational Library, Dr Williams's Library, London.

United Reformed Church. *The Manual*. Congregational Library, Dr Williams's Library, London.

United Reformed Church. *Year Book*. Congregational Library, Dr Williams's Library, London.

United Reformed Church Archive. Congregational Library, Dr Williams's Library, London.

United Reformed Church, Ecumenical Committee Minutes. United Reformed Church Archives, Congregational Library, Dr Williams's Library, London.

United Reformed Church, General Assembly. *Annual Reports, Resolutions & Papers*. Congregational Library, Dr Williams's Library, London.

BOOKS AND ARTICLES

Abbott, W., editor. *The Documents of Vatican II*. London: Geoffrey Chapman, 1966.

Alternative Response Group. *An Alternative Response*. Norwich, 1981.

Anglican-Lutheran Joint Working Group. *Anglican-Lutheran Relations: Report [of the] Anglican-Lutheran Joint Working Group, Cold Ash, Berkshire, England 28 November – 3 December 1983*. London: Anglican Consultative Council; Geneva: Lutheran World Federation, 1983.

An Anglican-Methodist Covenant: Common Statement of the Formal Conversations between the Methodist Church of Great Britain and the Church of England. Peterborough: Methodist Publishing, 2001.

Argent, A. *Elsie Chamberlain: The Independent Life of a Woman Minister*. Sheffield: Equinox, 2013.

———. *The Transformation of Congregationalism, 1900–2000*. Nottingham: Congregational Federation, 2013.

Arthur, J. "Reflections on the Way to Unity." Unpublished paper.

Atkins, M. *Resourcing Renewal: Shaping the Churches for the Emerging Future*. Peterborough: Inspire, 2007.

Avis, P. *A Church Drawing Near: Spirituality and Mission in a Post-Christian Culture*. London: T. & T. Clark, 2003.

———. *Reshaping Ecumenical Theology: The Church Made Whole?* London: T. & T. Clark, 2010.

———. "Unreal Worlds Meeting." Unpublished paper presented at a conference in Assisi, 2012.

Baker, C. "Towards a Theology of New Towns." PhD thesis, University of Manchester, 2002.

Barth, K. *Church Dogmatics*. Vol. 4, *The Doctrine of Reconciliation*, part 1. Edinburgh: T. & T. Clark, 1975.

Bebbington, D. W. *Evangelicalism in Modern Britain: A History from the 1730s to the 1980s.* London: Unwin, 1989.

Bellah, T., R. Madsen, W. Sullivan, N. Swidler, and S. Tipton. *Habits of the Heart: Individualism and Commitment in American Life.* Berkeley: University of California, 1985.

Benedict, P. *Christ's Churches Purely Reformed: A Social History of Calvinism.* New Haven, CT: Yale University Press, 2002.

Benn, T. *Out of the Wilderness: Diaries 1963–67.* London: Hutchinson, 1987.

Bentley, M. *Modern Historiography: An Introduction.* London: Routledge, 1999.

Berger, P. "Secularism in Retreat." In *Islam and Secularism in the Middle East,* edited by J. Esposito and A. Tamimi. London: Hurst, 2000.

Bilheimer, R. S. *Breakthrough: The Emergence of the Ecumenical Tradition.* Grand Rapids: Eerdmans, 1989.

Binfield, C. "Congregationalism's Two Sides of the Baptistery: A Paedobaptist View." *Baptist Quarterly* 26 (July 1975) 119–33.

Binfield, C. "A Learned and Gifted Minister: John Seldon Whale." *Journal of the United Reformed History Society* 6/2 (1998) 97–131.

Bocking, R. "The United Reformed Church: Background, Formation and After." In *Reformed and Renewed, 1972–1997: Eight Essays,* edited by C. Binfield. Supplement no. 2 to *Journal of the United Reformed History Society* vol. 5. September 1997.

Bolden, D. "Organizational Characteristics of Ecumenically Active Denominations." *Sociological Analysis* 46:3 (1985) 261–74.

Boyd, R. *The Witness of the Student Christian Movement: Church Ahead of the Church.* London: SPCK, 2007.

Braaten, C. "The Reunited Church of the Future." *Journal of Ecumenical Studies* 4 (1967) 611–28.

Bradley, John. "LEP Establishment Statistics." Unpublished chart. Churches Together in England.

Brain, S. *An Ever-Flowing Stream: The Story of Immanuel United Reformed Church.* Swindon: Immanuel Church, 1999.

Briggs, J. *Two Congregational Denominations: Baptist and Paedobaptist.* London: Congregational Memorial Hall Trust, 2010.

Brierley, P. *"Christian" England: What the 1989 English Church Census Reveals.* London: MARC Europe, 1991.

———, editor. *Pulling Out of the Nosedive: A Contemporary Picture of Churchgoing; What the 2005 English Church Census Reveals.* Eltham: Christian Research, 2006.

———, editor. *Religious Trends No. 1, 1998/1999.* London: Christian Research, 2000.

———, editor. *Religious Trends No. 3, 2002/2003.* London: Christian Research, 2002.

———, editor. *Religious Trends No. 4.* London: Christian Research, 2003.

———, editor. *Religious Trends No. 6.* Eltham: Christian Research, 2006.

———, editor. *Religious Trends No.7.* Eltham: Christian Research, 2008.

Brown, C. *The Death of Christian Britain: Understanding Secularisation, 1800–2000.* London: Routledge, 2001.

Bruce, S, *God Is Dead: Secularization in the West.* Oxford: Blackwell, 2002.

———. *Religion in the Modern World: From Cathedrals to Cults.* Oxford: Oxford University Press, 1996.

———. "A Sociological Account of Liberal Protestantism." *Religious Studies* 20/3 (1984) 401–15.

Buchanan, J. *A New Church for a New World.* Louisville: Geneva, 2008.

Bultmann, R. "The Problem of Hermeneutics." In *Essays, Philosophical and Theological,* by R. Bultmann. London: SCM, 1955.

Cadoux, C. J. *The Case for Evangelical Modernism: A Study of the Relation between Christian Faith and Traditional Theology.* London: Hodder and Stoughton, 1938.

———. *The Congregational Way.* Oxford: Blackwell, 1945.

Camroux, M. "How Radical Was the Social Philosophy of Seebohm Rowntree?" MA diss., University of York, 2012.

Carpenter, H. *Robert Runcie: The Reluctant Archbishop.* London: Hodder and Stoughton, 1996.

Carr, E. H. *What Is History?* 2nd ed. Harmondsworth: Penguin, 1987.

Cassidy, E. "The Uphill Ecumenical Journey." *Catholic International,* 2 July 1991.

Cassidy, J. M. "Membership of the Church with Special Reference to Local Ecumenical Projects in England." PhD thesis, University of Birmingham, 1995.

Cave, S. *The Doctrine of the Person of Christ.* London: Duckworth, 1925.

Chadwick, O. *Michael Ramsey: A Life.* Oxford: Clarendon, 1990.

———. *The Victorian Church.* Part 1, *1829–1859.* Ecclesiastical history of England 5. London: A. & C. Black, 1970.

Chandler, A. *The Church of England in the Twentieth Century: The Church Commissioners and the Politics of Reform, 1948–1998.* Woodbridge: Bodywell, 2006.

Chaves, M., and P. Gorski. "Religious Pluralism and Religious Participation." *Annual Review of Sociology* 27:2 (2001) 261–81.

Church of England, Archbishop's Council on Mission and Public Affairs. *Mission-Shaped Church: Church Planting and Fresh Expressions of Church in a Changing Context.* London: Church House Publishing, 2004.

Church of England, and Methodist Church. *Conversations between the Church of England and the Methodist Church: An Interim Statement.* London: SPCK, 1958.

Churches Council for Covenanting. *Towards Visible Unity: Proposals for a Covenant: The Report of the Churches Council for Covenanting.* London, 1980.

Consultative Committee for Local Ecumenical Projects in England. *Guidelines for Local Ecumenical Projects.* London: CCLEPE, 1990.

Churches Together in England. *Called to Be One.* London: CTE, 2002.

Churches Together in South London. *Review of St. Paul's Roundshaw Local Ecumenical Partnership.* London: CTSL, 2001.

Cleaves, R. W. *The Story of the Federation: Congregationalism 1960–1976.* Swansea: John Penry, 1977.

Clements, K. *Ecumenical Dynamic: Living in More than One Place at Once.* Geneva: WCC, 2013.

———. "Free Church, National Church, Dropping Pretenses for Unity." *Theology* 113:876 (2010) 421–28.

———. *Life on the Frontier: A Life of J. H. Oldham.* Edinburgh: T. & T. Clark, 1999.

Cocks, H. F. L. *The Faith of a Protestant Christian.* London: Independent Press, 1931.

———. "Where Two or Three." *World Congregationalism* 111/8 (May 1961) 31–32.

Coffin, W. S. *The Heart Is a Little to the Left: Essays on Public Morality.* Hanover: University Press of New England, 1999.

Congar, Y. *Dialogue between Christians: Catholic Contributions to Ecumenism.* London: Chapman, 1966.

Congregational Church in England and Wales. *A Declaration of Faith*. London: Independent Press, 1967.

Cornick, D. "The Story of British Ecumenical Endeavour." In *Unity in Process: Reflections on Ecumenical Activity*, edited by C. Barrett, 60–79. London: Darton, Longman and Todd, 2012.

———. "Tensions and Modesty: A United Reformed Church Reflection." In *Translocal Ministry: Equipping the Churches for Mission*, edited by Stuart Murray. Didcot: Baptist Union of Great Britain, 2004.

———. *Under God's Good Hand: A History of the Traditions Which Have Come Together in the United Reformed Church in the United Kingdom*. London: United Reformed Church in the United Kingdom, 1998.

———. "The Vocation of the United Reformed Church: Some Reflections." Unpublished paper, 2002.

Cox, H. "The Myth of the Twentieth Century." *Japanese Journal of Religious Studies* 27:1–2 (2000).

———. *The Secular City: Secularization and Urbanization in Theological Perspective*. Harmondsworth: Penguin, 1965.

Cray, G. *Mission-Shaped Church*. London: Church House Publishing, 2004.

Crow, P. "Ecumenics as Reflections on Models of Christian Unity." *The Ecumenical Review* 39/4 (1987) 389–403.

Cullmann, O. *Unity Through Diversity: Its Foundation, and a Contribution to the Discussion Concerning the Possibilities of Its Actualization*. Philadelphia: Fortress, 1988.

Curran, L., and A. Shier-Jones. *Methodist Present Potential*. London: Epworth, 2009.

Currie, R., A. Gilbert, and L. Horsley. *Churches and Church Goers: Patterns of Church Growth in the British Isles Since 1700*. Oxford: Clarendon, 1977.

Davie, G. *Europe: The Exceptional Case: Parameters of Faith in the Modern World*. London: Darton, Longman and Todd, 2002.

Davies, H. *Worship and Theology in England: From Newman to Martineau*. Princeton, NJ: Princeton University Press, 1962.

Davies, R., and D. Edwards. *Unity Begins at Home: A Report from the First British Conference on Faith and Order, Nottingham, 1964*. London: SCM, 1964.

Davies, R., R. A. George, and G. Rupp. *A History of the Methodist Church in Great Britain*. Vol. 3. London: Epworth, 1983.

Dodd, C. H. *The Parables of the Kingdom*. London: Nisbet, 1935.

Dodd, C. H., G. R. Cragg, and J. Ellul. *Social and Cultural Factors in Church Divisions*. London: SCM, 1952.

Dorrien, G. *Kantian Reason and Hegelian Spirit: The Idealistic Logic of Modern Theology*. Chichester: Wiley-Blackwell, 2012.

———. *The Making of American Liberal Theology: Imagining Progressive Religion, 1805–1900*. Louisville: Westminster John Knox, 2001.

———. *The Making of American Liberal Theology: Idealism, Realism, and Modernity, 1900–1950*. Louisville: Westminster John Knox, 2003.

———. *The Making of American Liberal Theology: Crisis, Irony, and Post-Modernity, 1950–2005*. Louisville: Westminster John Knox, 2006.

Driver, C. *A Future for the Free Churches?* London: SCM, 1962.

Dudley-Smith, T. *John Stott: A Global Ministry*. Leicester: InterVarsity, 2001.

Ecumenical Church of Christ the Cornerstone. *LEP Review Report*. February 2009.

Elford, J., and I. Markham. *The Middle Way: Theology, Politics and Economics in the Later Thought of R. H. Preston*. London: SCM, 2000.

Evans, G. R. *Method in Ecumenical Theology: The Lessons So Far*. Cambridge: Cambridge University Press, 1996.

Evans, R. J. *In Defence of History*. London: Granta, 1997.

Figures, J. A. "Corporate Congregationalism." *The Congregational Quarterly* 35:1 (1957).

Findlay, J. F. *Dwight L. Moody: American Evangelist, 1837–1899*. Chicago: University of Chicago Press, 1969.

Forecast, K. *Pastor's Pilgrimage: The Story of a Twentieth-Century Christian Minister*. Leicester: Troubador, 2008.

Forsyth, P. T. *Faith, Freedom and the Future*. London: Independent Press, 1955.

Frost, D. *An Autobiography*. London: Harper Collins, 1993.

Garvie, A. E. *The Ritschlian Theology: Critical and Constructive: An Exposition and an Estimate*. Edinburgh: T. & T. Clark, 1899.

Gauthier, F., T. Martikainen, and L. Woodhead. "Religion in Market Society." In *Religion in the Neoliberal Age: Political Economy and Modes of Governance*, edited by T. Martikainen and F. Gauthier. Farnham: Ashgate, 2013.

Giddens, A. *The Consequences of Modernity*. Stanford: Stanford University Press, 1990.

Gill, R. *The Empty Church Revisited*. Aldershot: Ashgate, 2003.

Glock, C. Y., and R. Stark. *Religion and Society in Tension*. Chicago: Rand McNally, 1965.

Goodall, N. *The Uppsala Report: Official Report of the Fourth Assembly of the World Council of Churches*. Geneva: WCC, 1968.

Goodhew, D., editor. *Church Growth in Britain: 1980 to the Present*. Farnham: Ashgate, 2012.

Goodwin, J. *A Paraenetick, or Humble Addresse to the Parliament and Assembly for (Not Loose) but Christian Libertie*. London: Printed by Matthew Simmons for Henry Overton, 1664.

Green, S. J. D. *The Passing of Protestant England: Secularisation and Social Change, c. 1920–1960*. Cambridge: Cambridge University Press, 2012.

Group for Evangelism and Renewal within the United Reformed Church (GEAR). "The Faith We Hold." Online: http://www.gear.org.uk/about-gear/the-faith-we-hold.

Guess, J. B. "John Thomas: 'A United Church that Stands for Something.'" 11 June 2006. Online: http://www.ucc.org/john-thomasa-unite.

Hadaway, C. K., and D. A. Roozen. *Rerouting the Protestant Mainstream: Sources of Growth & Opportunities for Change*. Nashville: Abingdon, 1995.

Handy, C. "The British Council of Churches and the Way It Works." British Council of Churches archives. December 1986.

Harrison, J. F. C. *The Second Coming: Popular Millenarianism, 1780–1850*. New Brunswick: Rutgers University Press, 1979.

Hastings, A. *A History of English Christianity 1920–1990*. London: SCM, 1991.

———. *Oliver Tomkins: The Ecumenical Enterprise, 1908–1992*. London: SPCK, 2001.

———. *Robert Runcie*. London: Mowbray, 1991.

Heelas, P., and L. Woodhead. *The Spiritual Revolution: Why Religion Is Giving Way to Spirituality*. Oxford: Blackwell, 2005.

Hempton, D. *The Church in the Long Eighteenth Century*. London: I. B. Taurus, 2011.

Henderson, I. *Power without Glory: A Study in Ecumenical Politics*. London: Hutchinson, 1967.

Hilliard, D. "The Religious Crisis of the 1960s." *Journal of Religious History* 21 (1997) 209–27.

Hilton, D. *My Testimony: The Origins of a Liberal Faith.* Cheam: Free to Believe, 2008.

———. *To Follow Truth and Thus . . . an Elliptical Faith.* London: United Reformed Church, 1993.

Hinchliff, Peter. "The Future of the Church of England/Presbyterian Church of England Committee." December 1971. Westminster College Archives.

Hobsbawm, E. *Age of Extremes: The Short Twentieth Century, 1914–1991.* London: Abacus, 1994.

Hobson, T. *Milton's Vision: The Birth of Christian Liberty.* London: Continuum, 2008.

Hodgson, L., editor. *The Second World Conference on Faith and Order, Held at Edinburgh, August 3–18, 1937.* London: SCM, 1938.

Hollinger, D. *After Cloven Tongues of Fire: Protestant Liberalism in Modern American History.* Princeton, NJ: Princeton University Press, 2013.

Holmes, R. *Tommy: The British Soldier on the Western Front, 1914–1918.* London: Harper Perennial, 2005.

Hopkins, M. *Nonconformity's Romantic Generation: Evangelical and Liberal Theologies in Victorian England.* Milton Keynes: Paternoster, 2004.

Horne, C. S. *A Popular History of the Free Churches.* London: James Clarke, 1903.

Hornsby-Smith, M. *The Changing Parish: A Study of Parishes, Priests, and Parishioners after Vatican II.* London: Routledge, 1989.

Howard, A. *Basil Hume: The Monk Cardinal.* London: Headline, 2005.

Howard, C. *A History of Trinity Church, Sutton: 1907–2007.* London: Trinity Church, 2009.

Hull, J. M. *Mission-Shaped Church: A Theological Response.* London: SCM, 2006.

Huxtable, J. *As It Seemed to Me.* London: United Reformed Church, 1990.

———. *Christian Unity: Some of the Issues.* London: Independent Press, 1966.

———. "A Covenanted Fellowship of Churches." *World Congregationalism* 3/9 (1961) 14.

———. *A New Hope for Christian Unity.* Glasgow: Fount, 1977.

James, E. *A Life of Bishop John A. T. Robinson: Scholar, Pastor, Prophet.* London: Collins, 1987.

Jeffery, R. M. C. *Case Studies in Unity.* London: SCM, 1972.

Jenkins, D. *Congregationalism: A Restatement.* London: Faber, 1954.

———. "Covenant or Capitulation." Norwich: Alternative Response, 1981.

Jenkins, P. *God's Continent: Christianity, Islam, and Europe's Religious Crisis.* Oxford: Oxford University Press, 2007.

Jennings, P. *What's Still Right with the Church of England: A Future for the Church of England.* Winchester: Circle Books, 2013.

Johnson, D. A. *The Changing Shape of English Nonconformity, 1825–1925.* New York: Oxford University Press, 1999.

Joint Committee for Conversations between the Congregational Church in England and Wales and the Presbyterian Church of England. *Report to Assembly.* Presented to the Congregational and Presbyterian Assemblies, 1969. URC Archive, Congregational Library, Dr Williams's Library, London.

Jones, J. *Three Score Years and Ten.* London: Hodder and Stoughton, 1940.

Jones, R. *A Portrait of Trinity with Palm Grove, 1863–1988.* Birkenhead: Trinity with Palm Grove Church, 1988.

Jones, T. R. *Congregationalism in England 1662–1962.* London: Independent Press, 1962.

Karefa-Smart, R. "The Future of the Ecumenical Movement." In *On the Way to Fuller Koinonia: Official Report of the Fifth World Conference on Faith and Order*, edited by T. Best and G Gassmann. Geneva: WCC, 1994.

Kasper, W. *Harvesting the Fruits: Aspects of Christian Faith in Ecumenical Dialogue*. London: Continuum, 2009.

Kaye, E. *Mansfield College, Oxford: Its Origin, History, and Significance*. Oxford: Oxford University Press, 1996.

Kelly, G. "A New Ecumenical Wave." Public lecture at the National Council of Churches Forum, Canberra, 12 July 2010. Online: http://www.ncca.org.au/files/Forum/7th/Documents/Ecumenical_Address.pdf.

Kent, J. *The End of the Line?: The Development of Christian Theology in the Last Two Centuries*. London: SCM, 1982.

———. "The Shadow of a Grove of Chestnut Trees." In *God's Truth: Essays to Celebrate the Twenty-Fifth Anniversary of Honest to God*, edited by E. James. London: SCM, 1988.

———. *The Unacceptable Face: The Modern Church in the Eyes of the Historian*. London: SCM, 1987.

Kinnamon, M. *Can a Renewal Movement Be Renewed?: Questions for the Future of Ecumenism*. Grand Rapids: Eerdmans, 2014.

———. *The Vision of the Ecumenical Movement and How It Has Been Impoverished by Its Friends*. St. Louis: Chalice, 2003.

Kinnamon, M., and B. Cope. *The Ecumenical Movement: An Anthology of Key Texts and Voices*. Grand Rapids: Eerdmans, 1997.

Korzybski, A. "A Non-Aristotelian System and Its Necessity for Rigour in Mathematics and Physics." In *Science and Sanity: An Introduction to Non-Aristotelian Systems and General Semantics*, by A. Korzybski, 747–61. Lancaster, PA: International Non-Aristotelian Library Pub. Co., 1933.

Kung, H. *Global Responsibility: In Search of a New World Ethic*. London, SCM, 1990.

Lange, E. *And Yet It Moves: Dream and Reality of the Ecumenical Movement*. Grand Rapids: Eerdmans, 1997.

Latourette, K. S. "Ecumenical Bearings of the Missionary Movement and the International Missionary Council." In *A History of the Ecumenical Movement*, edited by R. Rouse and S. Neil, vol. 2, *1517–1948*. 2nd ed. London: SPCK, 1967.

Lings, G., and S. Murray. *Church Planting: Past, Present and Future*. Cambridge: Grove, 2003.

Lloyd, R. *The Ferment in the Church*. London: SCM, 1960.

Lubac, H. de. *The Motherhood of the Church: Followed by Particular Churches in the Universal Churches*. San Francisco: Ignatius, 1982.

Lyon, D. *Jesus in Disneyland: Religion in Post-Modern Times*. Cambridge: Polity, 2000.

Macarthur, A. "The Presbyterian Road to 1972." In *Reformed and Renewed, 1972–1997: Eight Essays*, edited by C. Binfield. Supplement no. 2 to *Journal of the United Reformed History Society* vol. 5. September 1997.

———. *Setting Up Signs: Memories of an Ecumenical Pilgrim*. London: United Reformed Church, 1997.

———. "What Did I as a Presbyterian Expect of the Union." Talk given at Regent Square United Reformed Church, 27 November 1993. Macarthur Papers, Reformed Studies Library, Westminster College.

Macaulay, T. *The Complete Works of Lord Macaulay*. Vol. 7. London: Longmans and Green, 1897.

MacCulloch, D. *Silence: A Christian History*. London, Allen Lane, 2013.

MacMillan, M. *The Uses and Abuses of History*. London: Profile, 2009.

McNaughton, W. "The Principles of Scottish Congregationalism Examined in Their Historical Setting." *Congregational History Society Magazine* 7/1 (Spring 2013) 37–50.

Manning, B. *Essays in Orthodox Dissent*. London: Independent Press, 1939.

Martin, D. *Pentecostalism: The World Their Parish*. Oxford: Blackwell, 2002.

Marx, K. *Manifesto of the Communist Party*. Moscow: Progress, 1952.

Mayor, S. "Congregationalism and the Reformed Tradition." *Reformed World* 33/5 (1975) 196–208.

McLeod, H. *The Religious Crisis of the 1960s*. Oxford: Oxford University Press, 2007.

Micklem, N. *The Box and the Puppets, 1888–1953*. London: Geoffrey Bles, 1957.

———. *The Religion of a Sceptic*. London: Acton Society Trust, 1975.

Micklethwait, J., and A. Wooldridge. *God Is Back: How the Global Rise of Faith Is Changing the World*. London: Allen Lane, 2010.

Milton, J. *Christian Doctrine*. Complete Prose Works of John Milton 6. Translated by John Carey. New Haven, CT: Yale University Press, 1973.

Milton Keynes Intelligence Observatory. "Population Projections." Online: http://www.mkiobservatory.org.uk/page.aspx?id=1914&siteID=1026.

Moltmann, J. *A Broad Place: An Autobiography*. London: SCM, 2007.

Morgan, P. "1972 and Churches of Christ." In *Reformed and Renewed, 1972–1997: Eight Essays*, edited by C. Binfield, 23–29. Supplement no. 2 to *Journal of the United Reformed History Society* vol. 5. September 1997.

Morris, C. *What the Papers Didn't Say: And Other Broadcast Talks*. London: Epworth, 1971.

Morris, J. *The Church in the Modern Age*. London: I. B. Taurus, 2007.

Murray, P. "Hands across the Tiber: Ecumenism in the Wake of Anglicanorum Coetibus." *The Tablet*, 1 January 2011, 14–15.

———, edtior. *Receptive Ecumenism and the Call to Catholic Learning: Exploring a Way for Contemporary Ecumenism*. Oxford: Oxford University Press, 2008.

Newbigin, L. "All in One Place or All of One Sort?" In *Creation, Christ, and Culture: Essays in Honour of T. F. Torrance*, edited by R. W. A. McKinney. Edinburgh: T. & T. Clark, 1976.

———. *Unfinished Agenda: An Autobiography*. London: SPCK, 1985

Norman, E. *The English Catholic Church in the Nineteenth Century*. Oxford: Oxford University Press, 1984.

Novak, M. *The Open Church: Vatican II, Act II*. London: Darton, Longman and Todd, 1964.

Nuttall, G. "Geoffrey Nuttall in Conversation." Edited by Alan Sell. *Journal of the United Reformed History Society*, November 2009, 266–90.

Oldham, J. H. "The Editor's Notes." *International Review of Missions* 1/1 (1912) 1–14.

Olson, R. *The SCM Press A–Z of Evangelical Theology*. London: SCM, 2005.

Paterson, A. "The Origins of the Scottish Congregational Church." Unpublished paper.

Payne, E. A. *Free Churchmen, Unrepentant and Repentant, and Other Papers*. London: Kingsgate, 1963.

Peel, A., and L. H. Carlson. *The Writings of Robert Harrison and Robert Browne*. London: Allen and Unwin, 1951.

Peel, D. *Reforming Theology*. London: United Reformed Church, 2002.

————. *The Story of the Moderators.* London: United Reformed Church, 2012.

Pew Research Center. *The Future of the Global Muslim Population: Projections for 2010–2030.*

Plato. *Plato in Twelve Volumes.* Vol. 1. Translated by Harold North Fowler. Loeb Classical Library. Cambridge, MA: Harvard University Press, 1966.

Podmore, C., editor. *Community, Unity, Communion: Essays in Honour of Mary Tanner.* London: Church House Publishing, 1998.

Porritt, A. *J. D. Jones of Bournemouth.* London: Independent Press, 1942.

Preston, R. *Confusion in Christian Social Ethics: Problems for Geneva and Rome.* London: SCM, 1994.

Purcell, W. *Fisher of Lambeth: A Portrait from Life.* London: Hodder and Stoughton, 1969.

Putnam, R. D. *Bowling Alone: The Collapse and Revival of American Community.* New York: Simon and Schuster, 2000.

Rack, H. D. *Reasonable Enthusiast: John Wesley and the Rise of Methodism* London: Epworth, 1989.

Raiser, K. *Ecumenism in Transition: A Paradigm Shift in the Ecumenical Movement?* Geneva: WCC, 1991.

Reardon, J. *The Council of Churches for Britain and Ireland, 1990–1999.* London: Churches Together in Britain and Ireland, 1999.

Relations between Anglican and Presbyterian Churches. London: SPCK, 1957.

Relations between the Church of England and the Presbyterian Church of England. London: SPCK, 1968.

Robbins, R. *England, Ireland, Scotland, Wales: The Christian Church 1900–2000.* Oxford: Oxford University Press, 2008.

Ricoeur, P. *Freud and Philosophy.* New Haven, CT: Yale University Press, 1970.

Ritson, J. H. Letter to H. Smith, 24 July 2008. Bible Society Archives, F4/3/1 fol. 69, Cambridge University Library, 2008.

Robinson, J. *Honest to God.* London: SCM, 1963.

————. *The New Reformation?* London: SCM, 1965.

Robinson J., and D. Edwards. *The Honest to God Debate.* London: SCM, 1993.

Robinson, W. G. "A Congregational Comment on the Anglican-Methodist Conversations." *The London Quarterly and Holborn Review,* July 1963, 294–96.

Rorty, R. *Philosophy and the Mirror of Nature.* Princeton, NJ: Princeton University Press, 1979.

Routley, E. *Congregationalists and Unity.* London: Mowbray, 1962.

Rosen, A. *The Transformation of British Life, 1950–2000.* Manchester: Manchester University Press, 2003.

Rowntree, B. S., and G. R. Lavers. *English Life and Leisure: A Social Study.* London: Longmans, Green, 1951.

Sandbrook, D. *Seasons in the Sun: The Battle for Britain, 1974–1979.* London: Penguin, 2013.

————. *White Heat: A History of Britain in the Swinging Sixties.* London: Little, Brown, 2007.

Sawkins, J. *Church Affiliation Statistics: Counting Methodist Sheep.* Edinburgh: Heriot-Watt University, School of Management, 1998.

Schleimacher, F. *On Religion: Speeches to Its Cultured Despisers.* Translated by John Oman. London: Kegan Paul, Trench, Trubner, 1893.

Schulz, K. *Being Wrong: Adventures in the Margin or Error.* London: Portobello, 2010.

Selbie, W. B. *Positive Protestantism*. London: Congregational Union of England and Wales, 1926.

―――. *Schleiermacher: A Critical and Historical Study*. London: Chapman and Hall, 1913.

Sell, A. *Nonconformist Theology in the 20th Century*. Bletchley: Paternoster, 2006.

―――. *Testimony and Tradition: Studies in Reformed and Dissenting Thought*. Aldershot: Ashgate, 2005.

Shakespeare, J. H. *The Churches at the Cross-Roads: A Study in Church Unity*. London: William and Norgate, 1918.

Sheppard, D., and D. Worlock. *Better Together: Christian Partnership in a Hurt City*. London: Hodder and Stoughton, 1988.

Sherry, P., editor. *The Riverside Preachers*. New York: Pilgrim, 1978.

Slack, K. *The British Churches Today*. London: SCM, 1969.

―――. "Our Potential Union and the Churches Mission." Unpublished paper, 1964.

Smith, C., and P. Snell. *Souls in Transition: The Religious and Spiritual Lives of Emerging Adults*. Oxford: Oxford University Press, 2009.

Spong, J., and S. Stephens. "An Interview with John Shelby Spong." *Faith and Theology*, 6 September 2007. Online: http://www.faith-theology.com/2007/09/interview-with-john-shelby-spong-i-am.html.

Stacey, N. *Who Cares?* London: Anthony Blond, 1971.

Stanley, B. "The World Missionary Conference, Edinburgh 1910: Sifting History from Myth." In *Walking Humbly with the Lord*, edited by V. Mortensen and A. O. Nielsen. Grand Rapids: Eerdmans, 2010.

Stark, R. *The Triumph of Christianity*. New York: HarperOne, 2012

Steinfels, P. "Praying for Christian Unity, When Diversity Has Been the Answer. *New York Times*, 19 January 2008. Online: http://www.nytimes.com/2008/01/19/us/19beliefs.html.

Temple, W. *The Church Looks Forward*. New York: Macmillan, 1944.

Thompson, D. M. "The Church: God's Call and Our Future." Unpublished paper written for the Faith and Order Reference Group of the URC, 2012.

―――. *The Decline of Congregationalism in the Twentieth Century*. London: Congregational Memorial Hall Trust, 2002.

―――. "The Dissolution of the Association of Churches of Christ, 1979: An Afterword." *Journal of the United Reformed Church History Society* 8:2 (May 2008) 110–12.

―――. "Edinburgh 1910: Myths, Mission and Unity." *Journal of the United Reformed Church History Society* 8/7 (December 2010) 386–99.

―――. *Let Sects and Parties Fall*. Birmingham: Berean, 1980.

―――. "The Motivation of the Ecumenical Movement." In *Religious Motivation: Biographical and Sociological Problems for the Church Historian*, edited by D. Baker, 467–79. Oxford: Blackwell, for the Ecclesiastical History Society, 1978.

―――. "Reformed or United? Twenty-Five Years of the United Reformed Church" *Journal of the United Reformed Church History Society* 6:2 (May 1998) 131–44.

Thompson, P. *The Voice of the Past: Oral History*. 3rd. ed. Oxford: Oxford University Press, 2000.

Thorpe, K. *Daughters of Dissent*. London: United Reformed Church, 2004.

Tovey, A. "An Evangelical Fellowship of Congregational Churches, 1972–1997." In *Reformed and Renewed, 1972–1997: Eight Essays*, edited by C. Binfield. Supplement no. 2 to *Journal of the United Reformed History Society* vol. 5. September 1997.

Travell, J. "The Congregational Federation, 1972–1997." In *Reformed and Renewed, 1972–1997: Eight Essays*, edited by C. Binfield. Supplement no. 2 to *Journal of the United Reformed History Society* vol. 5. September 1997.

———. *Doctor of Souls: A Biography of Dr. Leslie Dixon Weatherhead*. Cambridge: Lutterworth, 1999.

Tucker, T. "Nathaniel Micklem and the Ecumenical Movement." *Journal of the United Reformed History Society* 6/9 (October 2001) 700–709.

———. *Reformed Ministry*. London: United Reformed Church, 2003.

United Reformed Church. *A Book of Services*. Edinburgh: St. Andrew, 1980.

United Reformed Church in Norwich. "The Way Forward." Unpublished paper, 2012.

United Reformed Church, Southern Synod. *Handbook 2010–11*.

United Reformed Church, Zero Intolerance Steering Group. "ZI and the Sexuality Issue." Unpublished paper.

Vercruysse, J. E. "Prospects for Christian Unity." *One in Christ* 26 (1990) 185–200.

Vincent, J. J. *Christ and Methodism*. London: Epworth, 1965.

———, editor. *Faithfulness in the City*. Hawarden: Monad, 2003.

Vischer, L. "The Process of Reception in the Ecumenical Movement." *Midstream* 23 (1984) 221–33.

Visser't Hooft, W. A. *The Evanston Report*. London: SCM, 1955.

———. *The Genesis and Formation of the World Council of Churches*. Geneva: WCC, 1982.

———. *Has the Ecumenical Movement a Future?* Belfast: Christian Journals, 1974.

———. *Memoirs*. Geneva: WCC, 1973.

———. *The New Delhi Report*. London: SCM, 1962.

Wainwright, G. *The Ecumenical Movement: Crisis and Opportunity for the Church*. Grand Rapids: Eerdmans, 1983.

Walker, W. *The Creeds and Platforms of Congregationalism*. Boston: Pilgrim, 1960.

Ward, K. *The Case for Religion*. Oxford: Oneworld, 2004.

Warner, R. *Secularization and Its Discontents*. London: Continuum, 2010.

Watts, M. *The Dissenters*. Vol. 1, *From the Reformation to the French Revolution*. Oxford: Clarendon, 1979.

———. *The Dissenters*. Vol. 2, *The Explosion of Evangelical Nonconformity*. Oxford: Clarendon, 1995.

Webb, E. J., D. T. Campbell, R. D. Schwartz, and L. Sechrest. *Unobtrusive Measures: Nonreactive Measures in the Social Sciences*. Chicago: Rand McNally, 1966.

Wellman, J. K. *The Gold Coast Church and the Ghetto*. Urbana: University of Illinois Press, 1999.

Welch, E., and F. Winfield. *Travelling Together: A Handbook on Local Ecumenical Partnerships*. London: Churches Together in England, 2004.

Whale, J. S. *Christian Reunion*. Cambridge: Lutterworth, 1971.

———. Commemoration sermon. In *Congregationalism through the Centuries*. London: Independent Press, 1937.

Williams, D. D. *God's Grace and Man's Hope*. New York: Harper, 1949.

Willimon, W. *This We Believe: The Core of Wesleyan Faith and Practice*. Nashville: Abingdon, 2010.

Wilson, A. N. *Our Times: The Age of Elizabeth II*. London: Hutchinson, 2008.

Wilson, B. *Religion in Secular Society*. Harmondsworth: Penguin, 1969.

Winslow, E. *Hypocrisie Unmasked: A True Relation of the Proceedings of the Governor and Company of the Massachusetts Against Samuel Gorton of Rhode Island*. London, 1646. Reprint, Club for Colonial Reprints Providence, 1916.

Woodhead, L., and R. Catto, editors. *Religion and Change in Modern Britain*. Abingdon: Routledge, 2012.

Woollcombe, K., and P. Capper. *The Failure of the English Covenant*. London: British Council of Churches, 1982.

Worsley, P. *The Trumpet Shall Sound: A Study of "Cargo" Cults in Melanesia*. London: MacGibbon & Kee, 1957.

Wuthnow, R. *Boundless Faith: The Global Outreach of American Churches*. Berkeley: University of California Press, 2009.

Index